# THE FREIREAN LEGACY

Randall Keithly

June 2008

# Studies in the
# Postmodern Theory of Education

Joe L. Kincheloe and Shirley R. Steinberg
*General Editors*

Vol. 209

PETER LANG
New York • Washington, D.C./Baltimore • Bern
Frankfurt am Main • Berlin • Brussels • Vienna • Oxford

# THE FREIREAN LEGACY

*Educating for Social Justice*

EDITED BY
## Judith J. Slater, Stephen M. Fain, and Cesar A. Rossatto

PETER LANG
New York • Washington, D.C./Baltimore • Bern
Frankfurt am Main • Berlin • Brussels • Vienna • Oxford

2002

Library of Congress Cataloging-in-Publication Data

The Freirean legacy : educating for social justice /
Judith J. Slater, Stephen M. Fain, Cesar A. Rossatto, editors.
p. cm. — (Counterpoints, New York, NY; v. 209)
Includes bibliographical references and index.
1. Freire, Paulo, 1921– 2. Education--Philosophy. 3. Critical
pedagogy. 4. Postmodernism and education. I. Slater, Judith J.
II. Fain, Stephen M. III. Rossatto, César Augusto.
IV. Counterpoints (New York, N.Y.); v. 209.
LB880.F732 F745 370.11'5—dc21 2002001864
ISBN 0-8204-5671-3
ISSN 1058-1634


Die Deutsche Bibliothek-CIP-Einheitsaufnahme

The Freirean legacy: educating for social justice /
ed by: Judith J. Slater, Stephen M. Fain, Cesar A. Rossatto.
−New York; Washington, D.C./Baltimore; Bern;
Frankfurt am Main; Berlin; Brussels; Vienna; Oxford: Lang.
(Counterpoints; Vol. 209)
ISBN 0-8204-5671-3

Cover design by Joni Holst

The paper in this book meets the guidelines for permanence and durability
of the Committee on Production Guidelines for Book Longevity
of the Council of Library Resources.

© 2002 Peter Lang Publishing, Inc., New York

Printed in the United States of America

To the enduring legacy of Paulo Freire
and to Ana Maria Araújo Freire, who continues the struggle


To Edward A. Slater, a man who exemplified the spirit
of liberation, humanity, and freedom
J. J. S. and S. M. F.


To Ana Maria (Nita) Freire, my college mentor and friend,
and to Paulo Freire, my greatest social justice inspiration.
Muito Obrigado (Thank you)
C. A. R.

# CONTENTS

*Michael W. Apple*

# PREFACE: THE FREIRIAN LEGACY

I AM ONE of those people who were fortunate enough to spend time with Paulo Freire, both in the United States and in Brazil. Before he became secretary of education in Sao Paulo, he and I had a number of public dialogues in the United States in front of large audiences. We spent a good deal of time in those dialogues discussing the ways in which power relations in education, culture, and the economy are hidden. We agreed on the utter importance of speaking honestly about both the nature of differential power and about the effects of the politics of exclusion and of the oppressive realities that large numbers of people experience every day. One of the things that was always so impressive about Paulo was his constant struggle to expand his understanding of—and action against—the relations of dominance and subordination that are so deeply cemented into all of our societies.

During these dialogues, it was clear that Paulo was struggling with the realities of gender oppressions. He had been so articulate for so many years about the ways in which class worked, it was fascinating—and compelling—to see him come to grips with the realities of the patriarchal state and the ways in which gender hierarchies worked as forms of exclusion. In response to the criticisms that had been made of his work by some feminists, he set about to incorporate a number of their criticisms. His rethinking of his theoretical, political, and educational positions—without giving up the immense power of his original insights and arguments—provided a model for many of the other critical educators who were struggling to expand the kinds of power relations they dealt with, without forgetting the capitalist materialities that organized and disorganized the societies in which they lived.

During the time when he was secretary of education in Sao Paulo and then later on, Paulo and I had a number of opportunities to continue these dialogues both in public and in private. He and I spent hours discussing the importance not only of theoretical interventions but also of the crucial importance of praxis, of intervening into the daily lives of cultural and pedagogic realities and of letting these interventions speak back to one's political and theoretic work. Unfortunately, all too many "critical theorists" in education have forgotten about the necessity of such action (Apple, 1999, 2001). Theory "rules," with little correction from the realities of real institutions in real communities in real struggles. For all too many of these people, reality had become a "text," a subject for deconstruction, but with little concrete action in solidarity with the oppressed. Paulo, rightly, was worried about this, even though he also, again rightly, was very committed to interrupting the epistemological, political, and ethical underpinnings of our accepted forms of knowing.

One of the issues on which we spent time was race. From Paulo's own experiences in northeastern Brazil, he clearly had the sense that in many ways oppression was "color-coded." When he spoke about the murderous histories of the treatment of indigenous people in Brazil and throughout the world, this sense became even stronger. He and I discussed the "myth of racial democracy" in Brazil and the rapidly growing politics of racial identity that had been taking place among Afro-Brazilian people. For him, this was one of the most important movements in Brazil and elsewhere, and he reflected on its meaning for his own sense of a pedagogy of the oppressed. I can't remember his exact words, but the points were decidedly similar to what he wrote in *Pedagogy of the Oppressed* when he stated "The pedagogy of the oppressed is a pedagogy which must be forged *with,* not *for* the oppressed . . . in the incessant struggle to regain their humanity. This pedagogy makes oppression and its causes objects of reflection by the oppressed, and from that reflection will come liberation" (Freire, 1982, p. 25). The struggles by Afro-Brazilian people against subjugation were not abstractions to him. He saw them as part of the necessary struggles against domination. Class, of course, was a crucial reality to him. But, just as he understood the importance of the gendered realities that organized his and our societies, he also saw the politics of race as a major arena that needed equally serious transformations. While he did not write a large amount on this in his later work—although it is incipient throughout his writing and can be seen in his concern for "re-Africanization" in *Pedagogy in Process: The Letters from Guinea-Bissau* (1978)—once again, his thinking on this issue lent support to others' struggles.

I mention all of this because, as the essays included in this book demonstrate, understanding Paulo Freire is not simple and the implications of his work are extensive. He was constantly growing, his analyses shaped by the emerging politics of progressive social movements. Just as importantly, his life and work were also shaped by the destructive effects of neoliberal policies that have been so damaging throughout the world. The processes of setting the market loose on everything that we hold dear, of disciplining people so that they lose their collective organizations and sensibilities and act as "rational" economic actors (as "possessive individuals"), was truly distressing to him, as it should be to all of us.

It is becoming ever more clear that neoliberal ideological positions and policies have, aggressively, interrupted more progressive critiques of schools and the development of movements aimed at more critical forms of popular education in many nations. It is equally clear that the arrogant policies of what I elsewhere call "conservative modernization"—and most especially the neoliberal attacks that are so central to it—have had a truly major impact on countries throughout the world (Apple, 2000, 2001).

Freire himself clearly saw the dangers associated with the global development and widespread acceptance of neoliberal beliefs and practices. In his book, *Letters to Cristina* (1996), he commented on what he saw happening all around him. He took this statement that he originally had written in his "letters":

> The dominant class, deaf to the need for a critical reading of the world, insists on the purely technical training of the working class, training with which that class should reproduce itself as such. Progressive ideology, however, cannot separate technical training from political preparation, just as it cannot separate the practice of reading the world from reading discourse. (p. 83)

and then added a commentary on it based on what was happening in the 1990s, a situation he called "reactionary postmodernism:"

> Perhaps never before has the dominant class felt so free in exercising their manipulative practice. Reactionary postmodernity has had success in proclaiming the disappearance of ideologies and the emergence of a new history without social classes, therefore without antagonistic interests, without class struggle. They preach that there is no need to continue to speak about dreams, utopia, or social justice . . .[The] postmodern reactionary . . . suggests in his pragmatic discourse that it is now the duty of capitalism to create a special ethics based on the production of equal players or almost equal players. Large questions are no longer political, religious, or ideological. They are ethical in a "healthy" capitalist sense of ethics. (p. 84)

For Freire, then, the equality promised by "we are all consumers," and its accompanying depoliticization and creation of the possessive individual, needs to be rejected. A pedagogy that focuses on production and consumption "without any preoccupation about what we are producing, who it benefits, and who it hurts" is certainly not a critical pedagogy (Freire, 1996, p. 84). But in saying this, once again, he was not an apologist for the past. For him, the task was clear. He knew that we need to recognize the mistakes that progressive forces may have made in the past. By this he meant that such things as dogmatism, mechanistic proposals and analysis, an inflexible and teleological sense of history that removed or ignored historical specificity and human agency, pedagogies that limited "the marginalized classes' universe or their epistemological curiosity about objects that have been depoliticized"—all of this was to be critically and radically examined. Yet, at the same time as we were to question what we have too often taken for granted, we must not let ourselves become enchanted by the present neoliberal ideology, "an ideology of privatization that never speaks about costs, the costs are always absorbed by the working class" (Freire, 1996, pp. 84–85).

Freire's position raises crucial questions about critical pedagogic work. How *do* we interrupt neoliberal common sense? How do we create pedagogies that are deeply connected to the daily realities of people's lives and to struggles to overcome exploitation and domination in a time when the right has already understood how such connections might be creatively (albeit manipulatively) made? Who is this "we" in the first place? How do we avoid the possible arrogance of a position that assumes that "we" know the best and only path to emancipation and we will bring it to "you?"

These of course are difficult questions. And our answers to them may be partial, flawed, contradictory, or temporary. Yet, only by asking the hard questions—as Paulo did—can we continue the never-ending struggle of what Raymond Williams (someone whose theoretical work was independent of but had major parallels to Freire's work) so poetically called "the long revolution" (Williams, 1961). While these questions are difficult, they do have immense theoretical and practical implications. We should not pretend that they can be answered by one person, although Paulo Freire comes as close as anyone in our time to providing the outlines of answers to many of them.

For this very reason, as these essays recognize, the way to honor Paulo Freire is to extend his struggles into the present and the future. We owe it not only to Paulo but also to oppressed people throughout the world. In this way, we can do what the teacher of all of us reading this volume, Paulo Freire, urged us to do: "We can take the role of agents, makers and remakers of our world [in] a permanent critical approach to reality in order to discover the myths that deceive us and help us maintain the oppressing, dehumanizing structures" (quoted in Taylor, 1993, p. 53). He constantly demanded that we educate not for "domestication," but for liberation. From my intense discussions with him, I am certain that had he lived, he would have become an even stronger participant in the struggles over gender and racial subjugation and would have continued to provide a model of how we might act to interrupt multiple forms of dominance inside and outside of education as well. This is one more reason why so many of us miss him.

## References

Apple, M.W. (1999). *Power, meaning, and identity*. New York: Peter Lang.

Apple, M.W. (2000). *Official knowledge* (2nd ed.). New York: Routledge.

Apple, M.W. (2001). *Educating the "right" way: Markets, standards, god, and inequality*. New York: Routledge.

Freire, P. (1978). *Pedagogy in process: The letters from Guinea-Bissau*. London: Writers and Readers Cooperative.

Freire, P. (1982). *Pedagogy of the oppressed*. Hammondsworth: Penguin.

Freire, P. (1996). *Letters to Cristina*. New York: Routledge.

Taylor, P. V. (1993). *The texts of Paulo Freire*. Buckingham, Philadelphia: Open University Press.

Williams, R. (1961). *The long revolution*. London: Chatto and Windus.

# ACKNOWLEDGMENTS

WE WERE INDEED fortunate to have the support of many in the production of this work. First, we gratefully acknowledge the support provided to us from Florida International University. The editors would like to thank our sponsors, Florida International University's College of Education, Division of Academic Affairs, the Latin American and Caribbean Center, the Center for Labor Research & Studies, and the Asian Studies Program, for making the International Conference on Education, Labor and Emancipation possible. Without their help, *The Freirean Legacy: Educating for Social Justice* would not have become a reality. We applaud their commitment to the ideals of Paulo Freire and their commitment to dialogic pedagogy.

We are particularly grateful for the support provided by Florida International University in producing this work. Specifically, we would like to thank the Center for Urban Education and Innovation in the College of Education and Dean Linda P. Blanton. We would be remiss if we did not mention the significant level of support provided to us by Judith A. Bucker, executive vice provost, and Julissa A. Castellanos, assistant director of the Latin American and Caribbean Center, and their staffs for continued assistance and support. Finally, we must acknowledge our appreciation to Shirley R. Steinberg for her efforts in support of this work at Peter Lang.

# INTRODUCTION

PAULO FREIRE WAS opposed to a culture of ideologies that limits possibilities for action. He believed that dialogic pedagogy formed the basis of the content that could provoke social change. Individuals act to create social change because they act on the conscious awareness of their own reality. They recognize that collective knowledge is an opportunity for revision of the self as a productive member of society. Then, through the collective efforts of a literate populace that knows how to "read the world" and "read the word," society begins the process of changing. He advocated empowering the people through active participation rather than submissive, passive acceptance of the current social order. Community is reinvented when oppression is eliminated. Then, the disenfranchised are no longer excluded from the world that controls them. The elimination of oppression reveals opportunities for the ethical participation of individuals in the work of the collective. Without this revelation, they submit unwittingly, unaware of their means of participating. Thus, through an understanding of one's own condition, the dialogic serves to humanize and develop a consciousness of the obligation a free person has to improve the world.

The opening of possibilities does not occur naturally, because there is an ignorance of the system and a fear of participation. As false charity and carrots of complacency abound, the controlled assume that they are being taken care of and that their fate is determined. They can do nothing about it. It is out of their control; they accept what is or blame themselves for their condition. They do not participate in their own freedom unless they are transformed through the dialogic. The dialogic exposes oppression; it exposes privilege, money, property, and life restrictions. Liberation is achieved as critical consciousness is heightened and the world is seen for what it is and what it could be. This practice is never finished. It is always in progress, and the task of the individual is to bring the collective along into an ever-evolving community that is better for all. This knowledge of the individual, this raising of consciousness, or *conscientização,* in concert with others, can alert the social condition and liberate the group.

In October of 2000, a conference was held at Florida International University in Miami, Florida, with the intent to bring together students and scholars interested in extending and perpetuating the legacy of Paulo Freire. Convened as a "Conference on Education, Labor and Emancipation," participants from far and wide gathered to share and hear the dialogue. Rallying around the keynote speaker, Ana Maria Araújo Freire, three areas emerged that speak directly to the legacy of Paulo Freire. The themes form the organizing focus for this book, as selected participants were asked to extend their conversation and share their work in this text. The themes are: The Personal; The Theoretical; and The Practical.

Each section of the text seeks to present different understandings of Freire's work. The first is the personal narrative—how he touched the lives of those he knew and loved. We hear the voice of his wife, his colleagues, and his student. Ana Maria Araújo Freire sets the tone of this volume with "Paulo Freire and the Untested Feasibility" and the promise of the untested feasibility (inédito viável, the possibility of doing something that has not been tried before). This is followed by a personal recollection in dialogue between Joe L. Kincheloe and Shirley R. Steinberg. A former student from Brazil, Veronica Gesser, recalls her teacher in "Paulo Freire: The Man, His Work, and His Character."

The second section contains theoretical applications of his message. It begins with a call for critical educators in "Freire, Marx, and the New Imperialism: Toward a Revolutionary Praxis" by Peter McLaren and Ramin Farahmandpur. Judith J. Slater presents the problems inherent in access and participation in the public forum in "Limitations of the Public Space: Habitus and Worldlessness." Gerard Huiskamp, in "Negotiating Communities of Meaning in Theory and Practice," discusses popular collective action and the revolutionary movements of the 1960s and 1970s, asking if these provide a basis for popular democratic action consistent with Freire's theoretical constructs. Jill L. Haunold, in "Idle Hands are the Devil's Workshop: A History of American Child Labor and Compulsory Education; Emancipation or Reconstituted Oppression?" links Freirean liberation to the child labor movement in the United States. Finally, Ricky Lee Allen presents a theoretical analysis of white identity in the popular culture in "Wake Up, Neo: White Identity, Hegemony, and Consciousness in *The Matrix*."

The third section includes applications of Paulo Freire's oppressor-oppressed contradictions in various disciplines and in diverse locations. Stephen M. Fain offers a dialogue on how to participate titled "The Quest for Authentic Engagement." Wendy Brandon, in "Interrupting Racial Profiling: Moving Pre-Service Teachers from White Identity to Equity Pedagogy," focuses on class and race bias in the pedagogy of one White pre-service teacher to analyze the acts of racial profiling witnessed in her classroom. Three grassroot social projects are presented by Cesar A. Rossatto in "Critical Pedagogy Applied Praxis: A Freirean Interdisciplinary Project and Grassroot Social Movement." Laureen A. Fregeau and Robert D. Leier, in "Praxis and Teacher Visions of Socially Just School Reform," present the view that for critical social reform in schools to occur, teachers must become grass-roots educational activists who recognize their capacity and potential as both intellectuals and leaders in reform that follows a social transformational model. Dawn E. Addy posits, in "Community Dialogue: A Tool for Social Engagement and Class Awareness," that developing awareness about community issues or raising social consciousness is the precursor to social movements. Charles Reitz questions the promise of enhanced opportunity, mobility, personal growth, and advancement versus the screening, tracking, and cooling-out roles of the community college system in "Elements of Education: Critical Pedagogy and the Community College." Finally, Arisve Esquivel, Karla Lewis, Dalia Rodriguez, David Stovall, and Tyrone Williams focus on participation and exclusion of minorities in "We Know What's Best for You: Silencing of People of Color."

The chapters in this text represent Freire's legacy in the struggle for social justice. They remind readers that, through critical dialogical encounters, individuals can move from a state of oppression to one of liberation. This transformation becomes a reality when persons learn how to engage in dialogical encounters with others and how to become agents of their own history rather then passive participants. Liberation is a process where all group members develop consciousness of their historical possibilities and learn to act on them. We hope this text provides a starting point for others to realize the generative themes of Paulo Freire's life work and spurs them to act on their newfound liberation.

# The Personal

*What something is, as it is, we call its essence or nature. The origin of something is the source of its nature. The question concerning the origin of the work of art asks about the source of its nature. On the usual view, the work arises out of and by means of the activity of the artist. But by what and whence is the artist what he is? By the work: for to say that the work does credit to the master means that it is the work that first lets the artist emerge as a master of his art. The artist is the origin of the work. The work is the origin of the artist. Neither is without the other.* — MARTIN HEIDEGGER (1971)

 WHAT FOLLOWS ARE three essays that tell us much about Paulo Freire. Each, in a different way, reveals facets of a man who is clearly a scholar but who, because of his style, is perceived first as a teacher. Grounded in personal experience, the authors provide the reader with more than accounts of personal experiences; they illuminate the character of their teacher as a compassionate and caring person. Each essay demonstrates the greatness of a man who is humble and who, in his humility, gives meaning to his life. Here, we encounter an exemplar of Arthur Jersild's observation that "the humble person can tolerate himself not only as one whose knowledge is imperfect but also as one who himself is imperfect. Here, humility interweaves with compassion and provides a person with the beginning of wisdom" (1955, p. 99).

It is clear from these accounts that Paulo Freire understood his role as teacher in a truly classical way. He was more than compassionate and understanding; he was a disciplined man with a mission who made each moment come alive with ideas and suggestions for actions. He naturally understood the point made by Alfred North Whitehead that "an education which does not begin by evoking initiative and end by encouraging it must be wrong. For its whole aim is the production of active wisdom" (1929/57, p. 37). Clearly, Paulo Freire's work is who he is—for all of us, a great teacher.

*References*

Heidegger, M. (1971). *Poetry, language, thought* (Albert Hofstadter, Trans.). New York: Harper & Row.

Jersild, A. J. (1955). *When teachers face themselves*. New York: Teachers College Press.

Whitehead, A. N. (1929/57). *The aims of education and other essays*. New York: The Free Press.

*Ana Maria Araújo Freire*

# PAULO FREIRE AND THE
# UNTESTED FEASIBILITY

TO SAY I shouldn't be the one to speak is—as my husband Paulo Freire would say—false modesty. Were this hypothesis true, I shouldn't have been writing this at all; I am quite sure that I wouldn't even have been invited to take part in a pedagogical dialogue of such magnitude.

To say, however, that I am the only one who has something to tell about Paulo's legacy for educating for social justice would be not only blatant personalism, thus sterile and unethical, but also an epistemological and political mistake. Unethical, since it would not correspond to the truth. Political, since it would mean denying the possibility of establishing a relationship of understanding with those reading this dialogue. Epistemological, since it would mean denying the very essence of Paulo's liberation theory—the dialogue. It would mean turning my back on him, whereas my struggle has been precisely the opposite—to face him, with love and seriousness—so as to help keep his presence alive, not only in me, but first and foremost in the world.

Bearing these principles in mind, I reflected and realized that I could do something else other than speaking. I could talk and listen[1] to what you have to say about my message: To listen to what you have to say with your own expression, the fruit of your thoughts and lived experiences, talking and thinking about bearing witness to the possible education of human beings with a view toward social justice, based on Paulo's understanding of education. This possibility was raised a few years ago when Paulo realized and explained the political aspect alongside the ethical, cognitive, affective and pedagogical character of the act of educating. This possibility is based on the formulation of his dialogical and liberating theory, which is also ethical, political, educational, and of his truly ontological praxis.

Thus, I kept thinking and reflecting, I could turn this moment into one of dialogical exchange—rather than of enclosure—with respect to Paulo's legacy. I could talk, wholeheartedly, about the subject matter herein addressed and about what circumscribes it. I realized more than that in these moments of reflection. I noticed that what often happens to us, intellectuals and activists, is to fear daring, to be afraid of remaking or re-creating Paulo on our own without denying his principles, but, by keeping ourselves abreast and updated, revisiting him from a historical standpoint. I moved a little further and came to the conclusion that we cannot embalm and plaster what we have once thought and said in the realm of eternity and truth. Every single moment, every single context, demands from us to think and to express in a new approach. I observed that, upon crystallizing positions, values, concepts, or texts—that is, when we deliver them untouchable, sacred, and fully completed—not only do we reveal our emotional, cognitive, and epistemological immovability, but we also—out of fear to take risks or being certain that the truth we and others claim shall not be revised—take them as eternal. Even if our statements have once been said properly and correctly, they tend to stratify into inert, sterile matter if they don't keep up with the present moment. They cease to be truths.

Hence, I must speak. And speak grounded on a strong wish not to have a speech delivered unilaterally, with no feedback, crudely poured over an "eyeless" and "earless" audience who would award me the narcissistic satisfaction that I know everything about hope in Paulo's liberating pedagogy. Not that I know everything about how to act for social justice. Such an attitude would annihilate this very hopeful utopia of an "untested feasibility" (*inédito viável*, the possibility of doing something that has not been tried before), and this, idealistically speaking, would suffice for me. It would make peace with "my knowledge." I then decided, with some daring and the fear mentioned above, to openly participate in an international meeting of renowned intellectuals who, I should remark, are committed to these dreams as well. I undertook this task, holding a belief that this moment is one of development to all of us. That communication, co-participation, mutual cooperation, and understanding, whether reaching a consensus or not, can say no to the "banking system" (*bancarismo*) adopted in education as well as in the broader social and political context. That these dreams can set us free from the shackles of what is "deposited" and "poured into" people. From what has been done, said and experienced as an absolute whole, and consequently undermined by nonhistoricity.

Paulo's work and life teach us about his constant, implied search for hope as an untested feasibility, which encompasses better times for everybody. By contextualizing himself, he would seek in his self, in his relationship with reality, the "Being More" or "To be/become more human" (Ser Mais) who each of us can become. By thoroughly reflecting on Paulo's attitude, on the manner whereby he improved his epistemology and his self, I decided to propose the following:

"Paulo Freire and the untested feasibility: the category which, having incarnated his way of being before the world, portrays all ontological, epistemological and historical beauty and plenitude of hope in his pedagogy of freedom," revisiting[2] myself, so as to more accurately establish the necessary relationship between this category and our subject matter: educating for social justice.

The untested feasibility is not a mere combination of letters, or a meaningless idiom. It is a word, within the strictest Freirean terminology: a "word-action" (*palavra-ação*), and therefore, praxis. It is a word epistemologically constructed to express—with a great deal of emotional, cognitive, political, ethical, aesthetic, and ontological meaning—the dreams we are able to fight for in view of the human possibility to project whatever s/he wants and thinks; a word that carries the embryo of possible changes steered at a more humane future; a word that consequently entails beliefs, values, dreams, aspirations, fear, anxiousness, will, and the possibility to be and to know, as well as human frailty and greatness and that bears healthy restlessness and the beauty underlying the condition of being a woman or a man. A word that inherently carries the duty and the pleasure—as Paulo liked to say—of changing ourselves, dialectically changing the world, and being changed by it, is essentially what carries our collective feelings and wishes. It is also what we fight for and dream about, or, on the other hand, it is also what bothers us, what makes us feel uneasy and sad before the weaknesses of human beings led by naiveté or by the deformation of possible antiethics.

The untested feasibility is a word that entails the understanding of time and space. Time and space in which we, in an impatiently patient manner, nurture the epistemological curiosity that ought to take us to philosophical and scientific knowledge, which in turn would materialize the ontological and historical hope through the transformative ingenuity underlying human dreams. The science and philosophy that are not put into service of such possible dreams of incorporating the untested feasibility materialized into changing actions[3] are unworthy of respect and consideration; rather than science, it becomes *scientificism,* and rather than philosophy, it becomes *philosophism.*

A word for Paulo, carrying in its very essence the acts of denouncing and announcing, creates a new epistemology based on a new, hopeful, and substantively political, ethical, and ontological reading of the world. It urges us to create a new woman and a new man for a new society—a fair, less ugly, and more democratic one—while refreshing our memories as to what Paulo has so much insisted on telling us because he thought in this manner and acted for it. It gives us all (when the problem is already a perceived and a detached situation, "percebido destacado," the necessary unity of the present moment of lucidity, joy, and transparency of the dream, in an ontologically human process, which arises as a possibility amid a background of injustice, distress, and suffering, which was inflicted on us to such an extent that we clearly realize it as a problem awaiting solution. Having a future of mildly disquieting sheltering and peace of mind is a result of rescuing the notion of ethics and the feeling and certainty that everything keeps going and has to undergo a seamless change process in order for us to materialize the ever-changing "Being More" of us all, which inexorably pervades social justice.

The untested feasibility makes clear to us that the realm of what is definite, ready, and finished, of the nirvana of certainty and perfect quietness, does not exist. Once the untested feasibility we dream of and fight for is achieved, other untested feasibilities—as many as our feelings and our reason, dictated by our most human needs can hold—sprout from its very existence, since it is no longer a dream that could possibly come true, but a dream that eventually came true, an attained utopia. This takes place considering the dynamics that this category implies, in that as word/praxis, it is radically and intrinsically related to what is mostly ontologically human inside us: the hope for our own improvement and for our moves toward improvement and for the social-historical framework we construct for peace and social justice. The more untested feasibilities we dream of and materialize, the more they evolve and proliferate in the context of our praxis, in our political wishes, and in our destiny to affirm our most genuine humanity, our ingenious ability to excel when we jump into the fertile and unlimited world of possibilities. Untested feasibility can teach us a wise utopia, into a world of hope that corresponds to plenitude, a seeking of the ontological essentiality of women and men.

The richness of the untested feasibility, a category that Paulo devised in *Pedagogy of the Oppressed* and reworked in *Pedagogy of Hope,* is indeed of such importance and depth that it "imbrues," as he would say, all his work. It translates his way of being in coherence with his reading of the world. For it is, as mentioned earlier, a "category which, having incorporated his way of being before the world, portrays all ontological, epistemological, and historical beauty and plenitude of hope in his pedagogy of freedom." He combines the term purposively, not to tie us to its linguistic beauty, but so that its semantic vibrancy could open a truly human world before us. That is, a world of possibility of ethics and liberation, embraced by the untested feasibility and flagged by the category's critical analysis: to meet multiple, legitimate wishes, yearnings, needs, will, reason, creation, renovation and, notably, an equity, harmony, and justice of spirit.

These are qualities and feelings that characterize us—or not, since we are in part, or sometimes in full, antiethical or unethical—and have to be collectively engendered. If they come, materializing step by step, steadily constituting a tactical action, we will certainly attain the untested feasibility's strategy or its ultimate goal, the most radical instance, utopia. Paradoxically, however, to preserve its very own characteristic, that of the possible dreams in view of our human incompleteness, utopia has no end, no definite finish line, since it is our incompleteness that brings about and nourishes hope, with its ceaseless searching movement. Utopia shall always entail surpassing what is no longer left unattended, which will thus be temporary on the ethical path toward materializing human beings' ontological vocation to become more human, and consequently toward social, ethnical, gender, sexual, racial, and religious justice, and ultimately democracy, ceaselessly remaking itself in search of improvement. I'm positive that this is our hope.[4] By means of our lucid, serious, and conscious acts, collectively constructed, we render ourselves to the untested feasibility.

Such dreams and hopes, which are pervasive in Paulo's entire work and being, would not make him a romantic idealist, as some people maliciously—or naively—claim he is. He understood human subjectivity in a revolutionary way, though he was far from being a subjectivist. He showed to us how not to stop at or limit ourselves to the dichotomous subject-object dialectics so as to act and transform, to know, or to adjust to, certain necessary conditions pertaining to the given world. This is to say, Paulo came to grips with this relation by radicalizing our subjectivities in such a way that, out of subjects who relate to each other mediated by the object-world, we could construct, with love, not only knowing acts, but also conditions and relations of knowing, of being in the world and of aspiring to changing the future. He did understand that we are not mere spectators of history, which passes in front of us arbitrarily, without our intervention. That history is possibility contingent upon what we do today in and with the object world, with pretensions to change. Like many other thinkers, he understood that we neither reflect reality nor we part of it merely based on our own constructions. That reality is constructed from the relationship between our consciousness and the daily routine of observing, creating, making, remaking, intuiting, understanding, feeling, making intelligible, systematizing what the well-established natural and cultural worlds have to offer us or impose on us. Within this view of reality construction, possible dreams—untested feasibility, ultimately—are the cultural products that full intersubjectivity can construct in its relationship with the real world. They are agents and products that constitute and mobilize re-creation, thus potentially constituting and mobilizing sociopolitical change. Should any one of us think about changing the world alone, merely via one's lonely relationship with the given world, it would not take so much time for him or her to find out that this is not a possible dream; it is rather a schizophrenic daydream, without any possibilities. For hope as a political and ontological category that moves the untested feasibility forward is meaningful and constructible solely by means of collective human praxis.

In addition to collective dreams, untested feasibility should also be dialectically put into service of the collectivity, inasmuch as it does not have an end in itself. Therefore the untested feasibility is basically a democratic dream put into service of what is most human in us, as human beings: the fulfillment of our ontological vocation of being and offering the conditions to other women and men for "Being More." Intentionally put forth by Paulo in his comprehension of education and society to make us feel indignation, fair anger, and repudiation, this serves to mobilize ourselves in denying unjust and inhuman conditions. It also provides us with a more accurate dimension of our political ability and ethical and aesthetic need to consciously educate ourselves, our students, and friends and workmates, for concreteness of peace and social justice. This was intentionally put by Paulo so that we would ceaselessly reflect on the possibility to become more woman and more man when we act guided by ethics and political will toward possible dreams filled with our hopes.

We must rethink this category in order to realize how much the world is "impregnated" with utopias awaiting our hopeful, wholehearted, and decided actions. Our genuine humanity makes us more than alert; it sets us in motion, in ingenuous, nearly unlimited dynamism, starting from the imaginary set of what is beautiful, ethical, poetical, and political from a world of possibilities. It renders itself feasible everyday in the educators' effective praxis as progressive political activists, when these subjects—who shall assume a critical attitude toward the world—perform actions of true citizenship.

If, today, we have not yet reached the ultimate dream, democracy—the true enforcement of which entails social justice at all levels and degrees—we have come to understand that we can fight for it, since it is, in Freirean terms, a possible dream. This is despite the fact that we are currently under severe threats represented by political neoliberalism and its aftermath, the globalization of the economy.

In sum, I believe that Paulo's apprehension of the world and of education is absolutely necessary and sufficient for us to construct social justice as a democratic virtue that we should be concerned over and fight for since it is an untested feasibility. We know that Paulo's anthropological and philosophical, ethical and aesthetic, social-historical, cultural, and psychosocial epistemology provides the tactical elements—by means of truly Freirean pedagogic-political praxis and in communion and solidarity with our peers and the oppressed—for us to attain the possible education, as well as to materialize the long-pursued strategy: true democracy, which conveys social justice.

It is also important to emphasize that, if Paulo's work was and still is definitely impregnated with the untested feasibility, we need to and must materialize it, thus re-creating him. This is not only due to his scientific discourse and his personally coherent posture. I believe that he was an untested feasibility himself incarnated: a thinker, credulously believing in men and women. Actively loving the world upon creating and displaying his understanding of liberating education, he filled the history of pedagogic ideas conceived all over the world, in all times, with ethical and political—in short, hopeful—contents.

I want to say that, for having captured, out of intuition, sensibility, and reason, the limiting situations of Brazilian society—the way we have been socially organized up to the present—and considering his reading of the oppressive conditions prevailing for centuries in Brazil,[5] Paulo was an untested feasibility himself. It was he, and not another man or woman, who told us everything he said, who clearly understood, as no man or woman had ever done before, the dialectic relationship between education, ethics, hope, and politics. He gave voice and was able to denounce and act through his limited acts, among which I should further emphasize his own theoretical creation and the untested feasibility therein apprehended, precisely because he could grab what the world was uttering and crying out, in a blatantly evident manner, but that so many others could not hear. He was humble and wise to consciously assume himself, within his historical boundaries, and he could propose to us overcoming the narrow limits imposed by the denial of human beings' ontological vocation of "Being More," through the hope embedded in the untested feasibility, announcing through it, having the hopefully feasible announcement embedded in it. Denouncing what he strongly repudiated, such as the unhumanized and antiethical, that the untested feasibility itself announces what is a feasibility never tested before, what is a utopian dream. This he announced with strong generosity, humanitarianism, and hope for a future, peculiar to such an announcement. He personally announced and denounced because he was able to position himself under a collective perspective.

Paulo was an untested feasibility himself, precisely because he saw with emotion, observed with tolerance, felt compassionately, apprehended intuitively, listened patiently, analyzed affectionately, and systematized generously[6] everything that was there to be seen and reflected upon in the obviousness of daily life. Furthermore, thanks to the power of untested feasibility, he gave obviousness and daily life the magnitude of a problem of philosophical-ontological nature, gave them a gnosiologic-social status at the moment when the problems arising therefrom became a perceived and detached situation to his intelligent and sensitive consciousness, to his conscious body (in Paulo's words), and therefore demanded a primarily humanist explanation and resolution.

In conclusion, I wish that these thoughts, which give room to pedagogical and primarily political debate, and are aimed at letting us know more than we already know—hoping that we may contribute to academic discussions but, more importantly, to transformative praxis—be, ultimately, in space and time, made into untested feasibility, so as to fulfill the democratic dream of social justice. This dream is undoubtedly made possible by means of an education for citizenship, that which educates collectively, in a Freirean manner, for this utopia.

## Notes

1. From what I learned by listening and observing, together with Paulo, I started making a distinction between hearing and listening. The latter goes beyond and overcomes the act of hearing, since it entails not only hearing, but also feeling what is listened to, getting involved with what is listened to, and being actually engaged with the speaker–and then, reflecting on all this, systematizing what has been listened to first.

2. Please refer to my Note 1 in *Pedagogy of Hope* (1994) on the untested feasibility, pp. 205–207.

3. Paulo was able to create in the political-educational-philosophical fields not only because he read philosophers, educators, sociologists, and listened to the people and reflected on what they were saying, or because he observed and calmly apprehended reality as "given data," but also because he worked on and intentionally improved his personal virtues, originating from his Christian education. Far from being fettered to the virtues of primitive Christianity, which had expressly geared him toward the oppressed, his theoretical work was built on them, and they were given emphasis in it as political-ethical-epistemological categories. For instance, generosity, faith, belief, hope, duty, etc. were central to Paulo's beliefs.

4. "Hope is part of human nature. It would be a contradiction if we who are aware of our incompleteness were not involved in a movement of constant search (p. 57). . .[if]. . . we were not disposed to participate in a constant movement of search (p. 69). Hope is a natural, possible, and necessary impetus. . . . Hope is an indispensable seasoning in our human, historical experience. Without it, instead of history we would have pure determinism. History exists only where time is problematized and not simply a given. . . . A future that is inexorable is a denial of history (p. 69). . . . a mechanistic comprehension of history." (Freire, 1998, p. 91)

5. I refer to the slavery regime that remained effective in Brazil during the colonial and imperial periods, whose strength imprinted, in effect, in Brazilian society as to its outlook toward the world. In this regard, I should highlight, among others, the danger of our education, that adopts elitist and authoritarian practices and, theoretically speaking, is deficient and retrograde, therefore constituting the "banking system" Paulo denounced.

6. The following describes the generosity and hope in Paulo Freire: Paulo's generosity displayed in his feelings, contained in the very anthropological generosity in his reading of the world as a time-space of hope, gives us a dimension of his unquestionable epistemological generosity in view of the myriad of studies, works and practices based on his theory and praxis. Anyone who shared his/her life moments with Paulo, even if just a few, felt and enjoyed his generosity. It is the presence of Paulo's existential-epistemological generosity that he offered in multiple scientific-political possibilities; his hope an existential-epistemological category, offered in multiple philosophical-historical possibilities of his life-work. Both of them give a sense of Truth to his humanist-utopian-liberating proposals. Paulo's hopeful generosity, deeply rooted in concreteness, is oriented to the possibility of the materialization of societies in which the highest values are placed on respecting and dignifying women and men, regardless of their color, religion, gender and social class.

## References

Freire, P. (1998). *Pedagogy of freedom*. Lanham, Maryland: Rowman & Littlefield.
Freire, P. & Freire, A. M. A. (1994). *Pedagogy of hope: Reliving "Pedagogy of the Oppressed."* New York: Continuum.

*Joe L. Kincheloe and Shirley R. Steinberg*

---

# A LEGACY OF PAULO FREIRE:
# A CONVERSATION

 STEINBERG: HOW DID Nita Freire meet Paulo? "We met when I was four and he was sixteen, and I remember him perfectly well when he was still very much a child, thin, angular, and energetic—earning for this the reason the nickname of 'Mr. Kilowatt'—walking around the hallways of the Oswaldo Cruz School in Recife, owned by my parents, Genove and Aluizio Pessoa de Araújo, who strongly influenced him in his development as a humanist. I remember him when suffering from tuberculosis, at the age of nineteen, and myself, how I cried upon learning that, since back in those days the disease spared no one who contracted it. He returned to the Oswaldo Cruz School, finished high school, and was accepted into the traditional Recife School of Law. He abandoned law and became a Portuguese teacher at the same Oswaldo Cruz School, where he was also my teacher; I was eleven and in the first year of high school" (Freire, 2000, p. 5).

I just think that idea of historicizing the paths that Nita and Paulo followed for many years is important for understanding them.

"Our lives ran parallel, touching each other from time to time ever since my childhood and his adolescence. The military coup of '64 took Paulo to Bolivia, Chile, and the United States and finally Switzerland. There in Geneva we met in July 1977 for lunch" (p. 6).

And then time moves on, and in 1985 Nita had become a widow and Paulo had become a widower, and he had stopped working. They entered into a pact together to push each other in their writing and to live up to it. And as Nita says, at the time she didn't realize, but it was a path for a return to life.

"One morning in June 1987, he interrupted my reading of a segment of my dissertation and said, looking at me with a strong gaze, "Nita you look so beautiful!" I was startled. We were silent for a few minutes. What does that mean? I asked myself. I continued to read, then, suddenly, a new statement from him on what he judged to be the truth—my beautifulness—a word he loved to use for people and things that aesthetically touched him. With his second statement, I understood that with the strength of his gaze, more than the words softly spoken, he was opening a path to get to me, "changing the nature of our relationship," as he liked so much to say later" (p. 6).

With this concept in mind, Joe and I would like to change the nature of our relationships to Paulo Freire and to bring in this new millennium—a time that Paulo knew he wouldn't live to see. He so very much wanted to see the new millennium. So, seeing that new millennium with Paulo is how we can redefine the concept of what a legacy is.

Kincheloe:

Our theme is social justice and the legacy of Paulo Freire—a compelling concept. One of the things that is so important to Shirley and me is this constant reconceptualization of what it is that Paulo stood for in light of changing times. In our own conversations with Paulo, I was always struck by the way he argued vociferously that he was not a text to be looked at in its finality. That he was not the one who should not be changed as the times continue to change. In that context it seems to be so important, as we look at what Peter McLaren describes so wonderfully and in such a frightening way, the vivid picture that he is able to paint of desperate times. For those of us concerned with the Freirean legacy, with those of us who feel passionate about issues of social justice, these are desperate times. These are times where there is an erasure of the concept of social justice. There is an erasure also of the notion of bringing the issues of social justice to the table throughout society and in education in particular. That is terrifically disturbing. And so, in that context, I think that we have to take what Paulo has left us. We have to rethink what it might mean to pursue social justice and new ways of being human within this particular social context and that it is a terrifically difficult—horrible in many ways—task to try to inject these issues of social justice into this contemporary conversation.

Steinberg:

If we retrace the steps and look at the concept of critical pedagogy and the Freirean legacy, I first want to talk about what the word "legacy" means, because what I have seen and I think, what many of us have seen, is when we have a legacy, we tend to want to replicate it, perpetuate it, and not change it. And it is very important that we understand that the work of Paulo Freire is ever-changing. It is tentative and it is elastic—it flows. It is not a stagnant text. And that is very important to understand. We are so used to learning canons and text, and I would like to offer the idea of taking the Freirean legacy and making it more than just an inherited testament; making it someth.ng that lives and breathes and changes as the times do. The very first time I heard Paulo speak was in Chicago. He was very conscious of the critiques, especially by feminists, that his language was exclusive. Well, of course it was. He had written it in 1970. Naturally it would be for any male, especially a person in a

Latin country where the Latin language lends itself only to using male definitions and male endings of words. Of course, this gave his work the appearance of exclusivity, although it was inclusive at the time. By 1990 we saw it, or feminists saw it, as possibly exclusive. I think it is ridiculous to start engaging ourselves in a concept that needs to move on. I have had people say, "I have read *Pedagogy of the Oppressed*. What does that say to me as a teacher? How does that apply to me? I am not in Recife. I am not in northern Brazil. People are not agrarian workers." Let's just divest ourselves of the past and the present ways of viewing Paulo, and let's advance into the future to keep the legacy moving on. Legacy is important only for the fact that it can be changed. It should not be stagnant. Very much using a method that Paulo used especially with Ira Shor, Joe and I are going to work on developing this conversation in dialogue.

Joe, can you encapsulate in one or two words what the essence of *Pedagogy of the Oppressed* means to you?

Kincheloe:
    It seems to me that I was drawn to Paulo early in my life as an undergraduate student from Tennessee, so geographically and culturally far away from who Paulo was. But, as Paulo wrote in *Pedagogy of the Oppressed,* there is no resonation that came from my own experience growing up in the mountains of Tennessee, growing up among very poor people. I knew nobody that was middle class, and I had these intuitive feelings of myself as a school student of opposition. I didn't have the language or the conceptual framework to express it. But very much I understood, given the nature of my personal relationships with many of the students I grew up with, that there were particular kids who came from homes where there was no reading; there were illiterate parents or parents who didn't have words and newspapers and books and magazines in their homes. It became quite obvious that these were kids who were not going to do very well in school. In my immature mind and the way I tried to characterize it, I felt that there was a snobbishness at the school. That there were particular kids who didn't fit within that school and that they would never succeed. I was fascinated by that process. I saw it so consistently work itself out in the schools of the mountains of Tennessee, and I felt terrifically angry about that. I felt very depressed about it because I had a sense of resignation that there was really nothing I could do about it. When I first ran into Paulo's work, I was fascinated with liberation theology. I was looking in particular at some of the liberation theology coming out of Brazil. I was taking some religion classes, and this was not making me particularly popular in the little Methodist College of Religion class. I ran into Paulo's work via that route about 1970 when *Pedagogy of the Oppressed* had first come out. I think it was one of those moments in one's life that, you know, there was an epiphanal aspect to it, and at the same time it was more than that for me. It was not only conceptually and intellectually eye-opening, but there was a particular personal validation

that came about that there was somebody else in the world who had noticed this unfairness that I'd seen that was developing around class lines, certainly racial lines, and, as I would come to understand, gender lines.

I am taking the long way around to answer your question, but to me it was a validation that there are other people in the world who are disturbed, who are perplexed, and who are angry about these types of injustices. Not only are there particular words for these problems, but there are particular strategies that we can pursue to correct them. There are particular ways of thinking about education. There are particular ways of reconceptualizing the purpose of schooling. There are particular ways of thinking about the pedagogical act that we can understand and engage in and actually begin to address this type of unfairness that seems to permeate the educational systems that we are a part of. There was an understanding that other people recognized oppression, that there were names for it. There were methods for analyzing it, making sense of it, and in the process of making sense of it, that something could be done about it. That oppression is real; it exists. There are particular structures within the larger social order that support it and perpetuate it, and we have to understand as scholars those particular structures and be able to act upon our understanding.

Steinberg:

What you're saying is you developed a sense of purpose from Paulo's work.

Kincheloe:

Absolutely. There was a sense of purpose that education could be conceptualized as far more than some simplistic reductionist transmission of truth from teacher to student. There was always an element of the problem that the process of curriculum development and what was to be taught, what was always taught, never had a sense of a final set of ideas and a set of facts that were validated in such a way that they could be passed along unproblematically to a group of students anywhere. That curriculum was a cultural politics. And we were engaged in a constant, universal, worldwide, long-term, never-ending fight about the nature of what we perceive to be the knowledge of most worth within the culture. Those were terrifically liberating understandings for me, and they are central to why I wanted to be a teacher and why I wanted to write.

Steinberg:

What about the concept that people would actually claim victim status because they wanted to be the victim?

Kincheloe:

One of the things that is so liberating in Paulo's notion of oppression is the idea that we don't just simply play on the oppression status, and we don't seek to point out to people that they are oppressed. That's not the end of what we're attempting to accomplish in this context. I was teaching in Tennessee, or teaching whatever it is that I taught on the Rosebud Sioux Reservation, and one of the things that I was attempting to do was to point out to people who had to work and live in particularly oppressive structures, that, often, their lack of success, or even failure certainly, within the educational system was not a product of their own personal inadequacy or deficiency as they had come to believe. I think the schools did a wonderful job of impressing on many people, whether it be from the mountains of Tennessee, or from reservations in South Dakota, or African Americans in all areas of the United States, that the reasons for their failures within schools was a product of their own deficiency. I think that one of the most powerful lessons that schools teach is that lesson. I have talked to so many people who express it in such sad and depressed ways, and I understand the sadness and the depression that they feel about that. I'm lucky. I was told myself in Tennessee that I could never go to college, and that I didn't have the intellectual capacity. I was told that I should be a piano tuner by my graduate counselor in the twelfth grade. I'm very thankful in the sense that he gave me the determination not to be one! One of the great messages of *Pedagogy of the Oppressed* is that we are able to name those social structures that inhibit people from reaching higher goals and succeeding within their own definition of an educational system. We point out those social structures not for the purpose of simply naming victimizations but for the purpose of empowering ourselves and helping others empower themselves to move beyond and to challenge those social structures that have actually held them down so much in the particular circumstances in which they find themselves.

Steinberg:

It sounds to me that we are constructing this flexible "taxonomy." We need to understand and identify the oppression by dealing with the concept of oppression and in a very large sense we need to understand it and we need to recognize it. We need to name the condition. It seems to me that, many times, a lot of people who try to adopt the concept of a pedagogy of the oppressed find themselves the "Johnny Appleseeds" of oppression. They scatter their seeds of oppression to let people pick up the seed, but no one seems to know what to do with it. And then we get into the concept of an anger that is unchanneled, that is not understood. It seems to me also that the idea of going to the Gramscian notion of hegemony is essential to understand the subtlety of oppression. It is easy to understand Franco's guards standing in front of buildings. It is easy to understand guards walking around Kosovo shooting young women and children. We can understand that kind of oppression. We can also go to New Delhi and see the oppression of starving people with bloated bellies, lice, and disease lying on the ground. Those are oppressions that are horrendous and evil. But they are understandable. What is difficult to understand is oppression that is hidden and made consensual by a population that is being oppressed. That becomes a very difficult understanding. Whenever I teach the concept of hegemony, what is so ironic to me is that the majority of people who understand hegemony first are the people that are less privileged. It is harder for me to teach hegemony to privileged people than it is to those that would fall into what I would consider an oppressed status or oppressed unstatus. What we need to do is guide people to the discovery of those insidious concepts of hegemony that may be hard to discover. It is amazing how many we are surrounded by. That idea takes me as a human to the concept that would take me from the main to the next taxonomic step, which would be the anger that I would feel once I realized the oppression.

Kincheloe:

In my own interaction with Paulo himself, this idea of anger, of the productive power of anger, to me is so important. I loved Paulo's anger. I truly loved being around and feeling the anger that he had, and in my own personal context of that feeling of unfairness, the feeling of recognizing those forms of oppression I saw around me. I think of it as a battery in a car. I can draw upon that anger to spark the work that I do and to spark the writing, to spark the teaching, to spark a kind of political work. Of course there is a dialectic to that anger at the same time. What is terrifically difficult for me, and I think for my friends who love the work of Paulo Freire around the world and in the United States, I don't see how it is possible to love Paulo and to love his work and not be terrifically depressed at this particular kind of human misery. It is something I have struggled with on a daily basis. It is something that I see scores and scores of people having to deal with, but we are, in many ways, a politically depressed group of people right now at this particular point in human history. With Peter McLaren's analysis of the globalization process and the victory in capital that we have seen over the last decade, as well as the inability to even talk about issues of social justice that I was referring to earlier, we are depressed. I am depressed. One of the things that I have to deal with is that we have to be able to have the social vision out in front of us, we have to be able to rearticulate it in light of changing circumstances, and we have to keep ourselves sane. How is it that we can see the victories of so many things that undermine the vision that Paulo held? And yet at the same time continue to go on? I fought it off on a daily basis, and I think that one of the things that will help us fight it even better is to name it and to realize that, as people who love Paulo and his work, part of our mission and part of our requirement in that love is to help one another cope in these particularly desperate times.

Steinberg:

When one is depressed, as many of us are aware, sometimes the realization of depression is a good place to get lost, and we get into a paradigm of wallowing, if you will. I think there are two types of wallowers. There is the Sean Connery wallower who is the helpful wallower. Then, of course, there is the Blair Underwood wallower who stays in the victim status and doesn't move. Peter, in his book on Che and Paulo, talks about the hellions of the seminar rooms who are involved in postmodernism at the toxic intensity of bohemian knights where the miserable and the wretched of the earth simply get in the way of their fun. And so it is that concept of Sean Connery sitting in the boardroom talking about what we will do, and the Blair Underwood characterization saying "I am a victim. I am mad. And that is where we stop."

Kincheloe:

I think one of the things that happens in this context that is very much characteristic of a depressed people is that we become pathological in our own behavior, and then we take out this depression on others, often those with similar ideologies as ourselves. One of the things that is so hurtful to me, and I am so depressed about this, is to watch this. I guess this has always been true to a large extent on the left, looking at it historically, looking at the pettiness and the fighting and the backbiting of people who operate in the name of Paulo Freire and in the name of *Pedagogy of the Oppressed*. I see that in many ways, not to be psychoanalytical, there is a displacement of depression and anger that we feel, given our marginalized role in this particular historical time and place. I find that to be one of the most pathological and disturbing trends of this last year. In this context I think that we have to pursue a form of social, psychological help where we come to understand and name our depression. Then in very much the spirit of Paulo, just move into the ontological realm that Nita talked about so beautifully, by rethinking the notion of being. One of the things that absolutely amazes me in looking at the educational conversation of the last few years is that, embedded in that conversation, is absolutely no sense of what we could become. The idea of imminence, the idea of what we could be, of the relationship between what is and what could be is the Freirean school the scholars talk about so often. That there is just simply no notion of that. To me one of the most exciting aspects of my relationship with Paulo is just reading him and knowing he was implicit in everything he said and everything he did and his teaching and his writing was this notion of new forms of human being. That we can go to another level. We can be better. And as I look at the last 250 or 300 years of scholarship within western culture, one of the things that I think we have begun to see in the last few years—I hope we see it much more—we have begun to see that we consistently underestimate the possibility of human beings. That in every area that we look at, whether it be a cognition, whether it be a physicality in sports, or whatever area, we said we could never do this. We could never jump this high. We could never run this fast. We could never play the game in this way. And we continue to break those expectations. The same thing is true in cognition. What developmental psychologists said just a few years ago and continue to say is the nature of formal thinking and the expression of the highest forms of understanding of human beings, we surpass without impunity. I mean we just go beyond; we transcend them, as we have more experiences and begin to understand in a multicultural sense more forms of genius and brilliance among people. We study peoples from Africa or indigenous people from aboriginal Australia or Native Americans or whoever, the types of abilities and the cognitive abilities that people have. We keep finding new levels of expression that go far beyond what we thought was the norm before. As a result, I want to infuse as a part of Paulo's legacy and a part of a critical pedagogy, a critical ontological dimension that says we place no limits on human possibility and human ability. That regardless of what the psychometricians may say or regardless of what the educators and standard setters may say, human beings are always capable of much more than what they have been traditionally allowed to be.

Steinberg:

So, what in a sense we are doing is we take the boundaries, and we refuse to acknowledge that they exist, and we push the boundaries and push the boundaries. Through this concept of creating and looking at the essence of human beings, the essence of being human, which is all ontology is—the study of being, the study of being human—what we do is we start to understand that we have only potential. We start to look for different ways of cognition, a critical cognition, and critical consciousness where we start to survey and grab different ways of thinking. It has taken Howard Gardner a few years to figure out that there are more than six, more than seven, intelligences. It seems to me that the idea of limiting cognition is absurd and dehumanizing. The one thing we need to do is not number and not count, but constantly be on an exploration of different ways of seeing the world and of understanding the world through every single lens.

Kincheloe:

Yes. Just in the context of Paulo's work on critical consciousness. In my study of critical consciousness, and going back and looking at the work in the early 1970s and looking at critical consciousness itself, and the number of times the concept has resurfaced from the late 1960s all the way through into the 1990s, what could be a more sophisticated view of cognitive ability than the notion of Freirean critical consciousness? I really don't know. If we think in the most simple way what critical consciousness is, what we are talking about here is the ability, the cognitive ability, to understand the world, understand the structures that shape it, how the structures interact with everyday life, and shape the nature of how the world works. I know that is terrifically simple, but nevertheless I think it is a tremendously sophisticated notion, that we can understand how the world works. Then, in the process of understanding the nature of how this social world works, we can begin to see it in such detail and understand it in such detail that we can come up with interventions within it where we can address issues of inequality and the way that the issues are subtly and insidiously structured into the social order and into the educational order. We can increase one's consciousness, one's ability to name those dynamics that are at work. Then, in the process, we may actually be able to come up with pragmatic actions that address those forms of inequality. Now as I look at it, I have been fascinated with the standards; we have been terrified and fascinated at the same time. I look at this instrumentally rational, top-down imposition of a particular body of ideological knowledge that is to be rote-memorized, measured numerically, and then used to determine the quality of educational work in the United States. I look at that and study it and try to make sense of it. Shirley and I have done a couple of books on this, taking the notion of standards and re-conceptualizing the notion of rigor within the context of a Freirean notion of crit-ical consciousness and many other aspects of understanding and making meaning of the world. As we begin to reconceptualize and to rethink those notions of criti-cal consciousness and begin to understand them in some specificity and in some detail, what we are able to do is say, "Here is an alternative rationale. Here is a form of rigor that allows us to penetrate everyday life and to be able to make sense of it, to make meaning of it, and to act upon it." I want to be able to articulate that vision of this new rigor, grounded in a Freirean notion, to counter the types of ideological malformations that try to represent this as some form of an undermin-ing of academic standards. To attempt to make the argument that acting on im-pulses of egalitarianism and acting with an understanding of the way the learners of the social work works and to have some form of social justice as a goal for the educational process is, by definition in the year 2000, to undermine standards. I will make just the diametrically opposed arguments: that to be able to do those things and to be able to understand the world in the way that Paulo asked us to understand it, is one of the most rigorous and one of the most profound forms of scholarship. It is our responsibility—those who love Paulo and his work—in these desperate times, to be able to articulate that vision within colleges of education, within universities, within school districts, and to the public at large. We have to be able to make the argument that we are the ones who are provoking a form of rigor that goes far beyond what is typically provided as rigor and is really a very productionistic form of rote learning and ideological diatribe. We are the ones who are provoking this type of rigor and no longer should we be positioned as people who are calling for some form of watered-down education. That is absurd! It is absurd that we have allowed ourselves to be put into that circumstance.

Steinberg:

This idea of the critical consciousness demands that there be a tremendous sense, a pervasive sense, of the political; it cannot exist without the political. I think one of the biggest issues involved is for those who have read Freire's work as it has been taught by people who assume the mantle of critical pedagogy. It be-comes this terribly difficult context of the critical pedagogy professor of theory and the practitioner. There is a tremendous inability, it seems to me, in many col-leges of education to combine the practical with the theoretical. Unfortunately, it began in the movement by a man who did exactly that. Paulo Freire was a practi-tioner, and he was a theoretician, a philosopher. He managed to do this. I don't believe many others have succeeded. I think that is very unfortunate. It seems to me that we are moving as we identify and understand and name what is going on. Then we have our anger and our resolve and our understanding of the hegemony and dominance of oppression. Then we start to move on, and we start to look at this legacy. Unfortunately, this is where we tend to part paths. We get the concept of the type of scholar who is going to talk about her love and her warm fuzzies of Paulo, or McClaren, or Giroux. The idea of taking critical pedagogy to the warm and fuzzy level, to the giving of straight A's, to the lack of rigor, to the inability of being able to challenge a student to say "no"—now wait. Let's review this; let's talk; let's look at the theoretical. The journaling, the eternal conflict of journaling and posters and sharing and cooperative learning groups—that is one side. The second side is the side that Peter refers to, that of the pedagogical seminar room, usually white men speaking pontifical statements about what they can do to help the little people. And, of course, nothing is working. We are sending teachers out into the field who are able to know when pedagogy was written, who wrote it, but have no concept of understanding how to combine the theory and knowledge of Freirean philosophy with the practitionerization of working and school. Now, practice does not mean lack of rigor. Holding a chalk and eraser does not mean we cannot be rigorous in our expectations. It also does not mean a concept of democratic pedagogy that reduces itself to some head-scratching professor with a beard and a submarine sandwich sitting there saying, "Just talk. I want to feel what you feel. I want to know what you know. I am not going to be pontifical, I am not going to be authoritarian in this class. I just want to share and be democratic."

Kincheloe:

Yes. When we were visiting Paulo and Nita in Sao Paulo, the last conversation I had with him was about this very subject, and I found his emotion and his anger about this to be fascinating. We commiserated in our frustration about this. Paulo said, "I am so upset at people who call themselves Freireans going into a classroom and not having anything to teach. That is an imposition on students who have knowledge." I have been around so many people who will walk into a class and sit and say, "It would be violent of me to bring up a body of knowledge here—I want you (the class) to generate it." But, Paulo said, "Any teacher that is worth his or her salt has a body of knowledge to bring to a group of students. Any teacher that evokes my name and says that it is an act of violence to bring knowledge into a classroom is missing the entire point of what we are talking about." Of course, this is said by a man who talked about banking education, and he certainly understood the danger of a problematized body of knowledge being brought in and simply transferred unproblematically to a group of students. Nobody understood that better than Paulo Freire. But at the same time, he said that we have to have knowledge, we have to have content, we have to bring that to the table, and then how we deal with that is a very different idea. We don't just sit and transfer it, but we engage with it, we problematize it, we understand its entomology. We see competing bodies of knowledge. They are produced by other people in other times, and you compare them and you worry over them. We fret with it; we just sweat as we attempt to make sense of the nature of these knowledges, their productions, and their relationships to the world and to us in this larger struggle. That seems to be such an important idea. I have been fascinated along this same line with many of the ways that Paulo has been appropriated and then kind of preprocessed for the late twentieth century United States. Shirley and I were writing a book a few years ago, *Contextualized Teaching*. We signed a contract for that book in 1994, wrote it in a couple of years, and had it finished. For about three or four years, it sat at the publisher. The publisher was very upset with the book. So we kept trying to figure out what exactly they wanted us to do, and we kept having meetings and negotiations. Basically, what they were saying to us was that it was too political and that a foundation's textbook cannot be that political.

Steinberg:
   What does education have to do with the political?

Kincheloe:
   Yes, right. "We don't understand the relationship, and, in addition, and maybe even more importantly, it won't sell." So we argued and talked and negotiated and on and on and on. I really came to the conclusion that, after a couple of years of doing this, it would never be published. So finally in desperation, the editor from the publishing company brought me a manuscript. She said, "Joe, I want you to read this manuscript, and I want you to rewrite the book in light of this particular manuscript. I think this is the way your book ought to look." This wasn't very pleasant to hear. So I read the manuscript, and it was a book about a Freirean critical pedagogy. In the entire manuscript of about 350 typed double-spaced pages, there was not one mention of the political. There was not one mention of looking at how schools reflect particular ideological viewpoints and shape what we do. So I went back and said, "I can't do this. I just simply can't do it." Luckily, that editor was replaced by a new editor, and our book was published immediately. Just the idea that there was a distastefulness and a lack of marketability confuses this issue of a kind of humanistic pedagogy where everybody feels good. An unfortunate tendency within the last decade or so has also been a reaffirmation of Freirean ideas within the classroom in a way that confuses what Paulo was talking about.

Steinberg:
   There is an attitude of "cocktail Marxism" I think. Cocktail revolutionarism where one sits in one's upper-middle-class home and "tsks, tsks" at all that happens but never engages in the concept of the political. I think that is real unfortunate. Let me try to conclude this dialogue. If you can envision Edvard Munch's painting "The Cry" (which everyone always calls "The Scream") the man has his hands over his face, and he is screaming or crying, and there are those circles going around the painting. It seems to me that, so many times, one looks at the painting or the concept of the painting, or in different ways one stops at the open mouth and at the cry. But it seems to me that there is a different reading of this. We can start to focus in on a concept of the circles and the irony of the circular and the critical consciousness that surrounds "The Cry." Then that circle becomes where we involve ourselves as teachers and professors and students of Freirean pedagogy. So my last thought and my last words to you would be something along the line of urging you to take the legacy of Paulo Freire, take from the social desperation that

Joe so aptly feels and so well describes, take the social depression and transform them into a way of socially inventing and reinventing the concept of pedagogy and critical consciousness. Take the concepts of rigor, the concepts of anger, the concepts of understanding oppression, and hegemony into helping us become social activists in the classroom and to help allow an empowerment to take place. And to never cite Paulo in vain as so many times he is cited. Rather cite him in the light or in the angry, but better within the contextual. This is a person, a philosopher, and a teacher, who is always within the contextual. His greatest argument, I believe, was to always consider the contextual. I think where we fail as teachers, professors, and students of education many times is because we divorce the contextual from the issues that are at hand, and I believe that becomes very, very important. With that we close.

*References*

Freire, Ana Maria Araújo. (2000). A bit of my life with Paulo Freire. *Taboo: The Journal of Culture and Education,* 4 (1), 5–18.

*Veronica Gesser*

# PAULO FREIRE: THE MAN, HIS WORK, AND HIS CHARACTER

IT WAS 1994, and I was a new graduate student at Pontific Catholic University in São Paulo, Brazil. I had a bachelor's degree in pedagogy, and I had taught third and fourth grade for about five years. Now I was entering graduate school to fulfill one of my dreams as an educator and as a citizen. I was eager and I was excited. I understood that this was a special opportunity. I would not only have a chance to develop my teaching and learning skills, sharpen my thinking, and acquire new knowledge; I also knew that I would meet exciting people who could have a profound influence on my life. After all, I was about to begin a graduate program, which was (and still is) considered to be one of the top graduate programs in curriculum in my country.

This program was unique. Rather than being organized around the traditional disciplines, it was structured around a series of *núcleos* (themes). This concept served to shape a curriculum made up of learning experiences designed around cognitive structures focused on process functions that served as themes around which course experiences were organized. These *núcleos* focused on curriculum, instruction, teacher education, and *Educação para os Excluídos da Escola* (literally translated from the Portuguese as "the education of those excluded from schools" or interpreted as "education for the urban and rural poor"). The responsibility for the organization and delivery of each fell to the two or three professors who led each team by facilitating discussions and coordinating all of the class activities as a team. This was a unique structure that challenged students and required a special kind of leadership. It was essential that faculty be driven by the cause and not by their egos. Paulo Freire was an integral part of both the program and one of these *núcleos*. He was a strong influence in shaping the program, his thinking greatly influenced the thinking of his program colleagues and students, and his presence served to energize all participants and to add to the reputation of the program.

## AULA INAUGURAL: FIRST MEETING

In Brazil the first class is called *aula inaugural* (the inaugural class). When my entire class came together for this first meeting, there was excitement in the air. The topic for the meeting was the relationship between a graduate student and his or her major professor (advisor) and advisory committee. The class was convened by Paulo Freire. The students were looking forward to hearing him because, although most of us had never been in his presence before, we had all read his work. When Paulo Freire stepped into the classroom, the silence was absolute and awesome. Not a single sound could be heard, not a voice or even a breath; the room was perfectly still; there was no movement, not the scraping of a chair sliding on the floor, not a shrug, a twitch or even a blink. Everyone was absolutely and completely focused on him. Mouths hung open in the air as students sat in astonishment and admiration. We knew we were in the presence of greatness.

When he started to speak with his calm firm voice, all of the students were staring at him, trying to absorb, understand, and reflect on every single word. He began by sharing his philosophy of life, which he had honed in his most renowned book, *Pedagogy of the Oppressed* (1970). He called for us, the students, to accept the challenge of creating "dialogical" relationships between teachers and students based on authentic dialogue. He was clear: Graduate students and their professors do not necessarily need to agree with each other but they needed to deeply respect each other. He made the point that it would be fine for a graduate student and his or her major professor to hold different points of view. The student needs to be willing to support his or her argument with evidence and logic. As Stephen Fain, one of my Florida International University professors would say, "You had better be grounded when you advocate a point of view." Freire's message on that particular day was that there could only be authentic dialogue if the student and his or her major professor were able to make clear what they stood for and why. To those of us at this first class meeting, it was apparent that authenticity and dialogue were the cornerstones of Freire's philosophy. We came to understand that they were also the integral principles upon which he based his life as a man and as an educator. He tried to live what he preached, and that is what made him special as a man who, in the exercise of his life's activities, honored his character.

## LESSONS

Although I was pleased to be in this special program I wanted to be in the group that Paulo Freire led. I understood that each group would study each *núcleo* with its major professor. But I wanted the opportunity to engage in a closer conversation with Freire, with the hope getting a clearer understanding of his work and ideas. After all, having the opportunity to read his books was one thing, but having the opportunity to ask him questions about his work and ideas was something quite different and special. Knowing the person who is behind the ideas in a book helps make much more sense of what he or she is proposing. One is able to get details and explanations that a reader cannot. I convinced my advisor to include me in Freire's class from the beginning. Then, there I was, face-to-face with the incredible wisdom of Paulo Freire.

My sense of pride and astonishment were a constant while in his class. I was the newcomer in the group, and my career as a graduate student was just starting. Really, all I wanted to do was to listen to Freire and ask him questions in order develop a better grasp of what he was proposing in his books about general issues in education. As I sat in his class, I sometimes felt intimidated by the power of his thoughts. The wisdom he so naturally shared with his students during class was always clear, but sometimes it was so powerful that we had to stop and reflect on his words in order to understand the full meaning of his observation. The theme of this *núcleo* was *Educação para os Excluídos da Escola*. Paulo Freire invited the class to engage in dialogue with him from our very first meeting, by either raising issues to be discussed or by proposing alternatives that could help those who were excluded from the schooling process. Sometimes, we felt that we were not prepared enough for the discussion, especially at the beginning. The students always respected Paulo Freire, but it was obvious that he also always respected the students. His power of engagement gave meaning to the principles of authenticity and dialogue; the relationships he established within the class gave meaning to our collective lives. Actually, this is what Freire (1998) would define as moral education. Although he never explicitly defined moral education in our class, he made it clear that we do not teach moral education by telling; we teach moral education and ethics to our children by living what we preach. This experience also exemplifies what Freire (1974) means when he writes that, as a teacher, one can be rigorous without being "oppressive" and how a teacher can give voice to the students without being "permissive."

I remember once, when we left our classroom for a coffee break, I started to discuss my paper for his class with him. I was writing about an adult education program in my school district, and I explained that I was having difficulty getting specific information about the program from the administration. This was important information for my study as it related to specific details related to the rationale for this particular program. He listened carefully, and then he asked me which institution was funding that program. I explained to him that it was a partnership initiative funded by the public school district and some very strong local industries. Based on this initial discussion, he began to explain to me the relationship between the oppressor and the oppressed. He explained that the factory owners were interested in maintaining control over the education of their employees, not because they wanted to assist them in achieving a more decent life or in becoming better citizens, but because they wanted to keep them in their oppressed state so that they would be better workers for their production system. The purpose, he explained, was not to liberate the workers as a group or as individuals. The purpose was to alienate them into the belief that the factory owners were so good to them that they were funding even their education. Then, he said to me, "This is oppressive." He explained that, even though there are exceptions, I should try to understand that this oppression is easily transferred to the school setting where, in the final instance, the teacher becomes the oppressor and the student the oppressed. This quiet, yet important, conversation is the kind of experience that we do not often have. It is what Freire (1993) defines as formal commitment in an informal setting. He was a simple man, but he was not simplistic; he was accessible, but he was not easy; and he was effective, but he was not driven by efficiency. One thing that made Paulo Freire special was his constant pursuit of dialogue and authenticity in formal and informal settings.

Our classes often took the form of informal discussions between the students and professors, including Paulo Freire. Together, we came up with the idea of having a special session in a subsequent semester to study and discuss some of Freire's books. We saw our moment as opportune, since he had recently published *Pedagogy of the City* (1993), where he explained his visions and the reality of his time as secretary of education in São Paulo. This was the most interesting experience I ever had as a student. We were able to read his books, go to his classes, and ask him for specific details and further explanations about educational concepts and examples included in his work. For instance, we were able to discuss his conception of curriculum, evaluation, the teacher's role, the school's role, and political issues related to these concepts. More importantly, we were able to ask him how he would describe his theories and actions in this practical setting. We asked him to discuss how he actually implemented his ideas while secretary of education, and we continued to ask him, and he continued to explain and invite us into the discussion.

Since we were enrolled in more than one course at a time, it is not really surprising that concepts and knowledge gleaned from one experience connected with questions asked in another. As it happened, while taking a course with Paulo Freire I was also enrolled in a class called "Educational Supervision." In this class, we were supposed to develop a project in which each work team proposed an ideal model for a school system, including specific approaches for administration and pedagogy. This was an exciting challenge for a team composed of students who were simultaneously enrolled in the special course with Freire. Since all members of my work team were taking that special session with Freire, he was an inspiration for our work, and we decided to propose an approach for a school system based on Freirean principles.

I remember that, after reviewing his writings, we felt the need to speak with him directly. We arranged an interview with him in order to get precise information about a critical issue because of what we had learned from him already. We wanted to devise a plan for getting the entire school community involved in developing a collective project in order to exercise and teach the highest level of democracy. Our ideas for this project had to do with the concept Freire (1993) called "to change the face of school" (*mudar a cara da escola*). His conception was based on the conviction that we do not transform the school face by decree or veto or by replacing names and titles. He said that we change the system by changing concepts and by reeducating people. During our interview, he made this clearer to us by explaining that there are different levels of participation and collaboration and accessibility that make one school system more oppressive or more democratic than the other.

Participation, he explained, can be understood at three different levels. The first and second levels exist in the schools as they are. The first level is the "ordinary," where parents, students, and teachers are given one or two predetermined choices; the second level, which I will call "opinions," is where the school's actors (parents, students, and teachers) are called to express their opinions or propose alternatives. In each case, the actors are not given the opportunity to participate in the decision-making process. The third level, effective participation, in which the whole school community is included, can only be achieved if we change the system (Freire, 1993). Here the school's actors (specialists, parents, students, teachers, and administrators) are called on to bring alternatives forward that will be the basis for the final decision-making process. Freire (1998) says that, in this process, the teachers are seen as "cultural workers" who will mediate the relationship between the students and their schooling. In our model, we strove to achieve the third level by changing the role of the teacher in the planning process.

During this experience, I became a college professor for preservice teachers in elementary education. In my class I taught about Paulo Freire, Ralph Tyler, Michael Apple, Antonio Flavio Moreira, and others. Teaching about Freire was exciting for me because, as I told my students stories about the man and his work, I also relived my own exciting times. I wanted to provide my students and other teachers with an opportunity to know Freire personally or, at least, to give them a chance to hear what he had to say. I approached the president of my university and suggested that we convene a conference open to as many teachers and students as we could accommodate. She agreed, and then I had the difficult task of finding an open date in the calendar of our special guest. In October 1995 he came to my university, and the conference became a reality. For the first half of the day, he spoke to 2500 teachers who came from all over my area. His message for them was about hope, dreams, educational ideals, possibilities, and democracy (Freire, 1994, 1998). For me, this conference was a special event. From the moment Paulo Freire entered the auditorium, the silence and the attention were complete and contagious. It was for the audience as it had been for me on my first day in class. He immediately established a connection with the audience and, as he spoke, the bond between teacher and student grew stronger. Some of my students were crying while he was speaking for, as he touched upon issues of hope and hopelessness, many who believed in the goodness of teaching and the power of learning understood that he was sharing a passion for people that touched them deeply. For the second part of the day, he addressed the university faculty. He expressed his ideas about the relationship between research and instruction and asserted that it was important to understand the relationship between the two. He eloquently argued that, at the university level, those who conceive of research and instruction as two distinctive activities are not fully capable of doing one or another. Freire (1995) advanced the notion that these activities are always interrelated. He explained that no university professor can be effective if he or she is teaching without doing research and noted that no university professor can be professionally respected if doing research without teaching. It would not be authentic to keep these two activities separate. His coming to my city and my university gave me a sense of a great accomplishment as an educator, as I knew that I had brought a great teacher into our lives (authenticity). His presence and his ideas refocused the conversation and stimulated a new and different political debate at the university (dialogue).

## REFLECTIONS ON THE LEGACY OF PAULO FREIRE

To conclude my story, I believe that the legacy of Paulo Freire has had a great impact in many fields. His work has primarily been directed to education, through which he worked to achieve his ideal, his dream, and his hope. But his impact has gone beyond the schoolroom and the teachers. He has influenced all who are serious about social justice, no matter what their discipline. Freire's most important goal, through his struggle as a man and educator, has been his commitment to the construction of a public school where everyone could be included. His vision is of a place where there are equal rights and equal access, as well as equal responsibility and equal opportunity. The world he sees is one in which people matter—not race, social class, nor religion. As a man and educator, his claim has been a struggle for social justice, for critical awareness, and for the liberation of the individual (Freire, 1985). Honan (1997) respects him as one of the thirteen innovators who have changed education.

Paulo Freire is a special man. Not only because he is a recognized educator in his homeland, from which he was sent away for almost 16 years, but because he has earned the respect of scholars and peasants the world over. Not simply because he was a great teacher, but because he has created a legacy of students who are now teachers who share his vision, respect his principles, and choose to work diligently to advance the principles for which he lived. I hope I am worthy of joining the group of teachers and scholars who will carry the legacy of Paulo Freire into the 21st century.

## References

Freire, P. (1974). *Pedagogia do oprimido (Pedagogy of the oppressed)*. São Paulo: Paz e Terra.
Freire, P. (1985). *The Politics of education: Culture, power, and liberation* (D. Macedo, Trans.). South Hadley, MA: Bergin & Garvey.
Freire, P. (1993). *Pedagogy of the city* (D. Macedo, Trans.). New York: Continuum.
Freire, P. (1992/1994). *Pedagogy of hope: Reliving pedagogy of the oppressed* (R. R. Barr, Trans.). New York: Continuum.
Freire, P. (1994/1998). *Teachers as cultural workers: Letters to those who dare teach* (D. Macedo, D. Koike, & A. Oliveira, Trans.). Boulder, CO: Westview Press.

Freire, P. (1996/1998). *Pedagogy of freedom: Ethics, democracy, and civic courage* (P. Clarke, Trans.). Lanham, MD: Rowman & Littlefield.

Freire, P. & Macedo, D. (1995). A Dialogue: Culture, language, and race. *Harvard Educational Review, 65* (3), 377–388.

Honan, W. H. (1997, November, 2). Looking back at forward thinkers. *New York Times,* 24–29.

# The Theoretical

*The simple fact is that all the deliberately liberal and progressive movements of modern times have based themselves on the idea that action is determined by ideas, up to the time when Hume said that reason was and will be the "slave of passions"; or, in contemporary language, of the emotions and desires.*

—JOHN DEWEY (1989)

 PAULO FREIRE OFFERS each one of us a theory of action grounded in the passionately held belief that liberation cannot be achieved without dialogue and that "true dialogue can not exist unless the dialoguers engage in critical thinking—thinking which discerns an indivisible solidarity between the world and the people . . ." (1968/73). What follows are scholarly efforts at crafting theoretical positions grounded in the challenges raised by Freire. These essays stand as evidence of the force he has had on the thinking of others and the power his ideas have had on drawing the conversation towards questions of social justice and the emancipation of the individual and society.

At the heart of the theories that buttress the work of Paulo Freire are the principles of authenticity and engagement. In many ways, he provides a paradigm that ultimately seeks the emancipation first of the individual and secondarily of the society by raising questions of conduct and attitude. We learn from Jacob Bronowski (1956/65, p. 55) that "if we are to study conduct, we must follow it in [two] directions: into the duties of men, which alone hold a society together, and also into the freedom to act personally which the society must still allow its men. The problem of values arises only when men try to fit together their need to be social animals with their need to be free men. There are no values and there are no problems until men want to do both." And we learn from Freire how to move beyond the social animal state and to bring humanity into the equation.

*References*

Bronowski, J. (1956/1965). *Science and human values* (Rev. ed.). New York: Harper & Row.
Dewey, J. (1989). *Freedom and culture*. Buffalo, NY: Prometheus Books.
Freire, P. (1968/1973). *Pedagogy of the oppressed* (Myra Bergman Ramos, Trans.). New York: The Seabury Press.

*Peter McLaren and Ramin Farahmandpur*

# FREIRE, MARX, AND THE NEW
# IMPERIALISM: TOWARD A
# REVOLUTIONARY PRAXIS

## THE TRIUMPH OF CAPITALISM

THE DEFEAT OF socialist regimes in Eastern Europe and the former Soviet Union, followed by the blue wave of pinstriped warriors from Wall Street, armed with laptops, and taking up positions in Red Square where steely-eyed statues of Lenin once stood, leaves little doubt as to who won the major ideological battle of the twentieth century.

The capitalist world is gloating, and free marketeers from the advanced capitalist nations are vastly expanding capitalism's role, disrupting the capacity of nation-states to manage the interface between transnational corporatism and the politics of everyday life. Neoliberal reformers and regional integrationists have launched a frontal, no-holds-barred attack on social justice, accelerating the incapacity of individuals to recognize capital's internal logic of accumulation and diminishing the power of individuals to counter the pressure of vested corporate interests and the politics of the capitalist class, while at the same time mystifying the entire process by linking democracy to the so-called natural pulsations of the market. Deliberately occluded in this process are the market's internal relations of production, exploitation, alienation, and politics (Ollman, 1998a).

The methods used by corporations have, to a large extent, devolved beyond legal boundaries and government control. Corporate power and state repression have become an intertwined dynamic, as corporations and governments collude in ways that overwhelmingly serve the interests of the ruling class. The outcome is a community of mutual interests—a countervailing and mutually reinforcing coalition that legitimizes itself through an appeal to geopolitical correctness. Geopolitical correctness, as we have defined it, is a process of paying lip service to the internationalization of profit making in the interest of stabilizing national and domestic markets while willfully overlooking the benefits of uneven resources that favor the global ruling class.

## THE NEW IMPERIALISM

Under the Dixiecrat leadership of Dick Cheney and his understudy, George W. Bush, the new Right has been busy orchestrating a full-fledged return to the pre-Civil Rights era. They have steeled their efforts toward privatizing social security, abolishing affirmative action, instituting voucher programs in public schools, reviving the "Star Wars" strategic missile program, eliminating abortion rights, and paving the way for appointing the next two conservative supreme court justices.

The global aristocracy's New World Order has obscured the distinction between the sacred and profane. By imposing the law of the market, it has been engaging in dismantling the welfare state, expanding global production, elevating the tide of export in the manufacturing sector, intensifying competition among transnational corporations, increasing part-time and contingent work, reducing the pool of full-time jobs, and accelerating immigration from Third World and developing countries to industrial nations (Bonacich & Applebaum, 2000).

To this list we could add the following: support by the global aristocracy of imperialist military intervention primarily disguised as humanitarian aid; the submission of international institutions such as the United Nations to the social and economic demands of United States' imperialist conquest; and the instigation of ethnic and nationalistic conflicts to weaken nations refusing to submit to the rule of the market (Azad, 2000).

Neoliberal social and economic policies carried out under the banner of "democracy" have facilitated the privatization of the public sector, helped to lower corporate taxes, and vehemently attacked labor unions. In developing countries, these policies have been carried out largely through international banking institutions, such as the International Monetary Fund and the World Bank, which have been responsible for transferring surplus value from developing countries to Western industrial nations (Azad, 2000).

John McMurtry notes that on 12 December 1991, the chief economist of the World Bank wrote in a leaked memorandum that his colleagues in the least developed countries should strive to achieve a "welfare environment" by increasing the migration of "dirty industries" and "toxic waste" to their societies. McMurtry is devastatingly accurate in summarizing the logic of the World Bank's top ideological warlord. He writes that it posed a comparative advantage to Third World countries to pollute their environment by storing toxic wastes; and that, because the "demand for a clean environment" has "very high income elasticity"—meaning that cost demand for clean air varies with people's income—the rational thing to do where the consumption of clean air is non-tradable, was to import polluted air by means of dirty industries and wastes. Such a move would vastly increase their financial revenues on their "welfare environment." When the chief economist concluded that the "economic logic" of dumping toxic wastes into the developing countries was "impeccable, " McMurtry notes that it was exactly in accordance with the money-sequence chain of life-destructive, annihilative, and morally grotesque logic. And, of course, McMurtry is correct. McMurtry writes:

> Life itself in this calculus is conceived as being of worth only to the extent of its price, and with no price received it is counted as being worthless. Disease and death are of no concern except as they cost money. Pollution and toxic wastes are not to be prevented, but assigned a money value to increase the output of the money-sequence. The poor are to be poisoned by the richer for their own welfare of more revenue, which they now lack. Health and life themselves are to be sacrificed to a higher good, an advanced place in the money order of worth. (1998, p. 323)

However, even with the retreat of socialism, capitalism's post-Cold War II victory has created a number of fundamental structural challenges to its global domination. For example, it has caused new interimperialist competition among various capitalist camps (i.e., the United States, Germany, and Japan), in addition to growing social and economic disparities between the rich and the poor in Western industrial countries, in particular the United States. As an article in *The Economist* reports:

> Never in the history of human wealth-creation has so much been pocketed so quickly by so many. The United States now boasts 300 billionaires and 5m [million] millionaires, with Silicon Valley adding 64 new millionaires every day. Nine million Americans have household incomes above $100,000 a year, up from just 2m [million] in 1982. If Great Britain was the first country to produce a mass middle class, the United States is the first country to produce a mass of upper class. (2000, p. 42)

During the 1970s, capitalism successfully averted a deepening economic crisis primarily caused by the falling rate of profit. It achieved this feat by taking advantage of the technological revolution (i.e. computer technology and automation) to cheapen labor. Marx (1977) recognized that technology in the service of capital has a disposition towards both "cheapening" commodities and labor while simultaneously raising productivity and profitability. Similarly, current employment patterns in the United States have shifted towards a service-based economy, caused, in part, by the transferring of the skills and knowledge of workers to computerized and automated machinery (Bello, 1999). Thus, an army of low-skill, low-wage, "key-punch" laborers has emerged.

Western Industrial countries have also benefited from economic structural adjustments including the exporting of manufacturing jobs to developing countries and expanding the service and retail sector of the economy. Since the late 1960s, part-time employment in the United States has increased threefold. Declining full-time employment has followed in the wake of a widespread corporate trend of reducing wages and benefits and abolishing overtime pay. In the service-related industries of the New Economy, full-time employment is no longer acknowledged as forty hours per week. In Wal-Mart, for instance, full time employment is twenty-eight hours a week, while at the GAP clothing company, full time employment is limited to thirty hours per week (Klein, 1999).

The global economy is increasingly relying on low-wage, part-time jobs comprised of an army of "contingent," "disposable," "temporary," and "footloose" laborers. The current expansion of the service and retail sector represents 75 percent of the overall work force in the United States (Klein, 1999). More importantly, education in the "new economy" is no longer heeded as a significant factor in securing higher wages for high school and college graduates. For instance, the average real hourly wages for men declined from $14.60 in 1989 to $13.65 in 1996, while for women, it decreased from $13.17 to $12.20.

According to Persuad and Lusane (2000), the new methods employed in capital accumulation are part of the "dual regime of accumulation." On the one hand, capital depends on the "absolute surplus value exploitation" of a growing class of unskilled and semi-skilled laborers in the service sector of the economy. On the other hand, capital relies on the "relative surplus value extraction" of a new class of educated professionals in the knowledge industry. Persuad and Lusane (2000) also suggest that the two regimes of accumulation enjoy a symbiotic relationship. While relative surplus value depends on the intensification of the rate of exploitation, absolute surplus value rests upon the breadth of the rate of exploitation.

These social and economic readjustments have been followed by persistent attacks on labor unions and a reduction of workers' wages and benefits, mainly by employing innovative methods in production, including flexiblization and informalization. Flexiblization permits corporations to tap into cheap, contingent, and temporary labor markets. In addition, it allows transnational corporations to move to cheaper labor markets. Informalization of the workforce operates by the expansion of sweatshops in garages where workers are paid by piece-rates in slave-like conditions (Wichterich, 2000). Although these structural changes have temporarily suspended the arrival of an economic crisis, they have nevertheless failed to offer long-term solutions to capitalism's structural contradictions. In fact, capitalism relies on the exploitation of labor more than ever.

We believe that the primary antagonism in capitalist economies exists between labor and capital, between the owners of the means of production and workers who are forced to sell their labor in exchange for wages. These contradictions are further visible in the growing disparities between the wealthy and the poor. Consequently, the failure to find long-term solutions to the existing contradictions within capitalist mode of production has shifted the political terrain to the Right. As Bahman Azad remarks,

> The global contradiction between labor and capital; the contradiction between a handful of imperialist states and the rest of humanity; the ever-widening gap between wealth and poverty in the world, which increasingly manifests itself in the gap between over-production by transnational monopolies, on one hand, and lack of purchasing power for these same products among the great majority of the world population, on the other; the economic bankruptcy of a great majority of the "third

world" countries and their inability to repay their heavy international debts—all these are increasingly causing great problems for the financial and banking systems of the imperialist countries. The loss of credibility and the ever-increasing economic and political bankruptcy of "social democratic" policies aimed at "resolving" the problems and contradictions of the capitalist system from within the system itself has led to a continuous shift of the social democracies to the right, the ascendancy of various right-wing bourgeois parties to power, revocation of most social protection plans, and the widening gap between the rich and the poor in all of the advanced capitalist countries. (2000, pp. 27–28)

## THE (UN)RESPONSE OF THE EDUCATIONAL LEFT

In recent years, a large body of literature has been written on the growing convergence of corporate interests and public education in the United States. Yet, very little work has been advanced by critical educators that attempts to develop a concerted and programmatic counteroffensive to the corporate takeover of our educational institutions. The field of critical pedagogy has been moderately successful in providing symptomatic readings of the current privatization and commercialization of public education. Educators in the field of critical pedagogy have not attempted to situate the current crisis of education within the historically persistent struggle between capital and labor, particularly in relation to the expanding low-skill, low-wage service economy.

A certain complacency has grown up around matters of capitalist exploitation and class struggle. Much of the work being done in critical pedagogy has focused on corporate-sponsored curricula, and the exchange of free technological equipment. Considerable attention has been given to uncovering the relationship between the commercialization of public education and the growing erosion of a civil society, presently excluding working-class and minority participation in the social and political sphere (Boggs, 2000), as well as exploring the connection between the persistent right-wing attacks on public education by conservatives who excoriate schools for their bureaucratization, inefficiency, low academic performance of students attending urban schools, and their ideological alignment with neoliberal social and economic policies that support aspects of the current corporate anorexia: downsizing, outsourcing, and flexible arrangements of labor markets. In fact, many of these efforts evidence support for an antistatist capitalism, an antiegalitarian relativism, or else unconsciously reposition themselves within a liberal, capitalist-inclined discourse of social justice, all under the banner of critical pedagogy. Paulo Freire foresaw these developments as domesticating and vulgarizing radical efforts at educational reform.

Today, even among some of the most progressive accounts by critical educationalists, class struggle has remained an ambiguous, indistinct, and undigested place. The twilight existence suffered by Marxist educational reformers can be traced to the fact that class struggle has been perceived as anodyne, or has been banished as a primordial category in critical pedagogy following the collapse of the Soviet Union and the Eastern European bloc regimes. The disappearance of class politics from the ramparts of history has coincided with the growing interest in identity politics, which has assumed a prominent place in the agenda of the postmodern educational left. Surfing hybrid identities within spaces opened up by furious clashes in the fight clubs of culture, has been a primary pursuit of post-modern educationalists (see McLaren & Farahmandpur, 1999, 2000). Yet, such a pursuit has consistently ignored the role played by the forces and relations of pro-duction. While attention is given to controlling capital in the interests of a demo-cratic redistribution of wealth, postmodern educationalists have so far failed to recognize the importance of labor as the source of all value and the substance of all value (abstract labor); thus, they have failed to argue for the uprooting of the basis of value production, which is the abolition of capitalist social relations and capital itself.

## THE PRIVATIZATION AND COMMERCIALIZATION OF PUBLIC EDUCATION

Examining education policies within the context of economic globalization and neoliberalism raises a number of critical questions that include the following: What are some of the effects of globalization on public schools and public educa-tion? To what extent is the content of teaching and curriculum under the perilous influence of the shifting social, economic, and political relations within global cap-italism? Spring (1998) identifies a key paradox that frames education and economic policies pursued in the United States as well as in a number of European countries. First, education under globalization is viewed as a vehicle that assists the growing market economy. For many developing countries, an educated and skilled work force ostensibly would mean higher levels of productivity and economic develop-ment. Second, education is viewed as a tool in solving problems associated with economic globalization, such as unemployment and poverty. If, however, the mar-ket economy is itself the cause of social and economic inequality, then it would ap-pear a contradiction in terms to argue that the goal of education should be to assist in the expansion of the market economy (Spring, 1998). Economic globalization has not only failed to provide political stability and social and economic equality for many nations around the world, it has also led to deepening social and eco-nomic polarization. Willie Thompson notes:

> Marx's insights into the nature of capital's reproduction and accumulation have never been bettered or displaced: his prevision of its future was extraordinarily per-cipient and impressively fulfilled. He was never a better prophet than when he in-sisted that capitalism was hastening towards its unavoidable destruction, that its internal forces carried it in a certain identifiable direction, which (*contra* Keynes) can-not be reversed or evaded. What capital produces above all is its own gravediggers. Marx meant the working class, and he was mistaken. What looks more likely to be

capitalism's executioner is capitalism itself—the problem is that everything else is practically certain to be entombed with it. (1997, p. 224)

As the logic of capital accumulation is shifting towards knowledge-based economies and as new forms of computer technology and biotechnology are being integrated into today's high-tech economy, information itself is fast becoming a high-priced new commodity. Transnational corporations are laboring vigorously to privatize the socially produced knowledge associated with the educational system. Decreased government funding of public education has forced an unholy partnership with private corporations who are seeking to create "high-tech knowledge industries" (Witheford, 1997). Transnational corporations are sponsoring research centers in universities across the United States by donating millions of dollars for the research, development, and production of for-profit technologies. This has resulted in the "high-tech colonization of education," transforming public universities into corporate operated "techopolises" that have little interest in coexistence with the poor (Witheford, 1997).

Under the command of the market economy, not even universities, colleges, and vocational schools are immune from the economic policies favoring capital accumulation. Niemark (1999) reports that the increasing social policies which support for-profit universities have made higher education an extension of the market economy. She writes that social policies that support privatization have moved in the direction of

> establishing for-profit degree-granting institutions (such as the University of Phoenix); outsourcing curriculum, instruction, counseling, operations, and administration (in such areas as bookstores, food services, libraries, computer operations, plant maintenance, security, printing, and payroll); signing campus-corporate research and development partnership and licensing agreements; and selling exclusive on-campus marketing rights to companies that sell products as varied as soft drinks, fast food, computers, and credit and telephone calling cards. The campus is becoming virtually indistinguishable from the marketplace, and both universities and their faculties are becoming entrepreneurs. (1999, p. 24)

The restructuring of higher education can clearly be seen as reinforcing class inequality and exposing public higher education to social and economic policies governed by the laws of the market economy (i.e., commodification, proletarianization, and capital accumulation). It also visibly functions as an impediment to the education and active participation of citizens in a democratic decision-making process dedicated to coexistence (Niemark, 1999).

The shift towards the privatization and corporatization of public education is best exemplified by the corporate raider Michael Milken, the Wall Street wizard and junk bond king of the mid-1980s, who deceptively swindled millions of dollars by luring investors into high-risk investment schemes. Milken has returned to the business world, this time by focusing on the lucrative $800 billion education business and has decided to create for-profit education enterprises with the help of his powerful—yet comparatively obscure—$500 million company known as

Knowledge Universe. Milken has invested heavily in several companies producing educational materials. Knowledge Universe owns such companies as Children's Discovery Centers, Bookman Testing Services, Pyramid Imaging Inc., Nobel Education Dynamics, and Leapfrog, that produce educational tools used at learning centers of the Riordan Foundation (Vrana, 1998). In a recent interview with the *Los Angeles Times,* Milken calculated that if the net worth of the United States is placed at $120 trillion, three-quarters or roughly $75 trillion, consists of human capital. This means that every American is worth $400,000 to $500,000 (Vrana, 1998). In short, Milken has discovered that the knowledge business is a profitable commodity.

Recent attempts by corporations to influence policy and curriculum decisions in urban schools abound. According to Kalle Lasn,

> Corporate advertising (or is it the commercial media?) is the largest psychological project ever undertaken by the human race. Yet for all of that, its impact on us remains unknown and largely ignored. When I think of the media's influence over years, over decades, I think of those brainwashing experiments conducted by Dr. Ewen Cameron in a Montreal psychiatric hospital in the 1950s. The idea of the CIA-sponsored "depatterning" experiments was to outfit conscious, unconscious or semi-conscious subjects with headphones, and flood their brain with thousands of repetitive "driving" messages that would alter their behavior over time. Sound familiar? Advertising aims to do the same thing. Dr. Cameron's guinea pigs emerged from the Montreal trials with serious psychological damage. It was a great scandal. But no one is saying boo about the ongoing experiment of mass media advertising. In fact, new guinea pigs voluntarily come on board every day. (1999, p. 19)

It is not unusual these days to see school buses in certain states covered with advertisements for Burger King and Wendy's fast-food chain restaurants. It has become fashionable for elementary schoolchildren to carry books wrapped in free book covers plastered with ads for Kellogg's Pop-Tarts and Fox TV personalities. School districts have gleefully granted Coca-Cola and Pepsi exclusive contracts to sell their products in schools. In health education classes, students are taught nutrition by the Hershey Corporation in a scheme that includes a discussion of the important place of chocolate in a balanced diet. A classroom business course teaches students to value work by exploring how McDonald's restaurants are operated and what skills are needed to become a successful McDonald's manager, and provides instructions on how to apply for a job at McDonald's. Ecological and environmental education now involves students learning ecology from a "Life of an Ant" poster sponsored by Skittles candy and an environmental curriculum video produced by Shell Oil that concentrates on the virtues of the external combustion engine. Finally, a new company called Zap Me! lures schools into accepting thousands of dollars worth of computer equipment, including a satellite dish, fifteen top-level personal computers, a furnished computer lab and high-speed Internet access in return for a constant display of on-screen advertisements in the lower left-hand corner of the screen (see Fischman & McLaren, 2000). Kalle Lasn writes:

Your kids watch Pepsi and Snickers ads in the classroom (The school has made the devil's bargain of accepting free audiovisual equipment in exchange for airing these ads on "Channel One"). . . .Administrators in a Texas school district announce plans to boost revenues by selling ad space on the roofs of the district's seventeen schools— arresting the attention of the fifty-eight million commercial jet passengers who fly into Dallas each year. Kids tattoo their calves with swooshes. Other kids, at raves, begin wearing actual bar codes that other kids can scan, revealing messages such as "I'd like to sleep with you.". . . A few years ago, marketers began installing ad boards in men's washrooms on college campuses, at eye level above the urinals. From their perspective, it was a brilliant coup: Where else is a guy going to look? But when I first heard this was being done, I was incensed. One of the last private acts was being co-opted. (1999, pp. 19–21)

A math book published by McGraw-Hill is spiked with references to Nike, Gatorade, Disney, McDonald's, Nabisco, Mattel's Barbie dolls, Sony play stations, Cocoa Frosted Flakes, Spalding basketballs and Topps baseball cards (Collins & Yeskel, 2000, p. 78). This list goes on.

John Borowski (1999), a public school teacher, has recently noted in the *New York Times:*

At least 234 corporations are now flooding the public schools with films, textbooks and computer software under the guise of "instructional material." A lesson in self-esteem sponsored by Revlon includes an investigation of "good and bad hair days." In a history lesson, Tootsie Rolls are touted as a part of soldiers' diets during World War II. Exxon provides a video on the Valdez spill playing down its ecological impact. And Chevron, in a lesson for use in civics science classes, reminds students that they will soon be able to vote and make "important decisions" about global warming, which the company then rebuts as incomplete science. (A23)

Another example of corporatism in schools is Channel One, a commercially produced news station that now operates in many American schools. As part of a contractual agreement, teachers agree to broadcast Channel One programs in class for ten minutes a day in return for a satellite dish, video cassette recorders, and as many television sets as they want. A study of its effects revealed that the students were no better informed than their contemporaries, but that the advertisements broadcast on the Channel had a significant effect on their consumer tastes (Aitkenhead, cited in Cole, 1998, p. 327).

On the one hand, schools, in a limited sense, do contribute to the ideals of democratic organizations (in terms of trying to provide access to knowledge relevant to surviving within in a capitalist society). At the same time, schools operate in sustaining and reinforcing the logic of capitalism, functioning as a reproductive force that offers different and unequal kinds of knowledge and rewards based on the social class, gender, and racial characteristics of the learners (McLaren, 1997). Here we see inequality as having to do with the place that individuals and groups occupy in the historically determined system of social production, their relation to the means of production, their role in the social organization of labor, and the means at their disposal of acquiring social wealth (Lenin, 1965). This, in turn, relates to how capitalist society regulates the distribution of different types of capital. Perrucci and Wysong (1999) describe these as: *consumption capital* (having to do with wages or salary); *investment capital* (having to do with a surplus of consumption capital that you can invest and on which you can earn interest); *skills capital* (having to do with specialized knowledge that people accumulate through their work experience, training, or education); and *social capital* (having to do with the network of social ties that people have to family, friends, and acquaintances as well as the collectively owned economic and cultural capital of a group). Educators have long made the case that schools traffic in cultural capital (values, attitudes, dress, mannerisms, personal style, etc.) (McLaren, 1998), but they have rarely linked the production of cultural capital to various "capitals" described above or to the international division of labor brought about by uneven development.[1]

## BEYOND CAPITALIST SCHOOLING

Capitalist schooling participates in the production, distribution, and circulation of the knowledge and social skills necessary for reproducing the social division of labor, and hence, capitalist relations of exploitation. As consumers of school knowledge, students as citizens-in-the-making are largely beholden to the physics of capitalist accumulation.

Capital is a force that colonizes the entire social universe. Within this social universe, the workers and capitalists are in objective conflict with each other. The workers are exploited by the capitalists whether the workers subjectively know it or not, or whether they like it or not (Hill, 2001). The capitalist class owns the means of production. This reality obtains today in much the same way as it did during capitalism's infancy. While it is possible to identify a transition from a mass production (Fordist) to a specialized (post-Fordist) economy, such changes are limited to certain areas of the world; furthermore, these changes are relatively superficial. The relationship of workers to the means of production is essentially the same. To argue that there has been a shift from relations of production to an emphasis on consumption patterns works to obscure the relations of exploitation of the capitalist class who own the means of distribution and exchange. From the standpoint of capital, education is considered a commodity with quantifiable and measurable outcomes that help to increase the efficiency and the productivity of workers. Working-class students partake of particular knowledges, skills, and social capital that prepare them as workers to produce surplus value for capital accumulation.

Recognizing the "class character" of education in capitalist schooling and advocating a "socialist reorganization of capitalist society" (Krupskaya, 1985) are two fundamental principles of a socialist pedagogy. Following Marx (1973), we argue that it is imperative that teachers recognize the contradictions of "free" and "universal" education in bourgeois society and question how education can be "equal" for all social classes. Education can never be "free" or "equal" as long as there exist social classes. We believe that the education and instruction of working-class students must be linked to productive labor and also to social production. Thus, we envision a working-class pedagogy that pivots around a number of key linkages: the production of critical knowledge and productive work; the organization and management of critical knowledge and the organization and management of production; and the utilization of critical knowledge for productive consumption (Krupskaya, 1985).

Furthermore, the severing of workers from the products of their labor under the capitalist mode of production mirrors in a number of basic instances the separation of the production and consumption of knowledge among students. For instance, in public schools today, theoretical knowledge is seldom linked to labor practices. Our vision of a socialist schooling, on the other hand, consists of teaching students how knowledge is related historically, culturally, and institutionally to the process of production and consumption.

According to Marx, capitalist production and consumption constitute a totality of inter-connected social relations which can be divided into productive and unproductive consumption. While productive consumption satisfies the physical, spiritual, and social needs of individuals, unproductive consumption (its antithesis) appropriates and transforms the surplus-value of labor into capital. Thus, it is imperative that teachers and students question how knowledge is produced and ask the following: Who produces it? How it is appropriated? Who consumes it? How is it consumed? Working-class pedagogy gives priority to the struggle between labor and capital, to the relationship between the forces of production and the means of production, and to the relationship between nature and society.

In the space that follows, we attempt to sketch out in broad strokes the key characteristics of a socialist working-class pedagogy that attempts to move beyond current liberal and left-liberal efforts at making capitalist schooling less barbaric and more democratic. The democratic working-class pedagogy that we envision here agitates on behalf of pedagogical practice connected to a larger socialist political project. This struggle not only includes the struggle against the globalization of capital, but also against capital itself (Mészáros, 1995).

RESPONSES TO THE RULE OF CAPITAL: FREIRIAN PEDAGOGY

Paulo Freire's critique of capitalism, in particular his critique of class exploitation, has largely been ignored by critical educationalists operating within the precincts of postmodern theory and cultural studies. In his early work especially, Freire (1978) positioned education as an ideological and political activity that is intimately linked to social production. Critical education, he argued, empowers students and workers to organize and classify knowledge by differentiating between bourgeois ideology and working-class ideology, bourgeois culture and working-class culture, and ruling-class interests and working-class interests.

As an offspring of Freirian pedagogy, critical pedagogy seeks to reclaim these distinctions identified by Freire as well as to transcend the existing antagonisms between manual and mental labor, theory and practice, teaching and learning, and what is known and what can be known. In this respect, Freire raised important questions regarding the relationship between education and social production, such as: "Why is anything produced? What should be produced? How should it be produced?" (1978, p. 107). We join Freire in arguing that, as part of a larger concerted effort of educating workers and students, critical pedagogy must also address the following questions: "What to know? How to know? In benefit of what and of whom to know? Moreover, against what and whom to know?" (1978, p. 100).

Following Freire's (1978) lead, critical pedagogy not only supports the practice of students and workers reflecting critically upon their location *in* the world, but also on their relationship *with* the world. Freire maintained that productive labor is the basis for critical knowledge and vice versa. Subsequently, a critical analysis of schooling begins by examining the relationship between productive labor and critical knowledge. That is, critical education is associated with productive labor, with labor that privileges use value over exchange value.

While capitalist schooling provides students with basic knowledge and skills that increases their productivity and efficiency as future workers and subsequently reproduces class relations, critical pedagogy works towards the revolutionary empowerment of students and workers by offering them opportunities to develop critical social skills that will assist them in gaining an awareness of the exploitative nature of capitalist social and economic relations of production.

Worker and student empowerment requires teachers in urban schools to acknowledge and exploit critically the dialectical unity between theory and practice and action and reflection (Freire, 1978). Reflection on one's own social practice means being attentive to the concrete social and economic issues in the workplace and in schools. It further stipulates that workers and students gain a critical purchase on their social location. Freire referred to this as achieving a "radical form of being," which he associated with "beings that not only know, but know that they know" (Freire, 1978, p. 24).

The revolutionary character of Freire's approach is lucidly reflected in Bertell Ollman's recent description of what constitutes a "dialectical understanding" of everyday life. Ollman argues that a dialectical understanding of social life is "more indispensable now than ever before" (1998b, p. 342) because he believes that the current stage of capitalism is characterized by far greater complexity and much faster change and interaction than at any time in human history. In tracing the social, economic, and political antagonisms under capitalism, Marxist dialectics understands capitalism as constituted by

> intersecting and overlapping contradictions. . . . Among the more important of these are the contradictions between use-value and exchange-value, between capital and labor in the production process (and between capitalists and workers in the class

struggle), between capitalist forces and capitalist relations of production, between competition and cooperation, between science and ideology, between political democracy and economic servitude, and—perhaps most decisively—between social production and private appropriation (or what some have recast as the "logic of production vs. the logic of consumption"). (Ollman, 1998b, p. 350)

Bertell Ollman captures the essence of the Marxian dialectical process when he writes, "Marx's dialectics views reality as an internally related whole with temporal as well as spatial dimensions. Things that are separate and independent . . . cannot be in contradiction, since contradiction implies that an important change in any part will produce changes of a comparable magnitude throughout the system" (1998a, p. 349).

In exposing the underlying contradictions inherent in the capitalist mode of production, socialist pedagogy encourages critical educators to employ a dialectical understanding of the social world in their classroom by creating conditions for students to explore how class exploitation, racism, and sexism constitute a set of complex social, cultural, political, and economic relationships in which every individual is implicated (Ollman, 1978). In underscoring the significance of the concept of "relations," Ollman remarks:

> The relations that people ordinarily assume to exist between things are viewed here as existing within (as a necessary part of) each thing in turn, now conceived of as a relation likewise, the changes which any "thing" undergoes. The peculiar notion of relation is the key to understanding the entire dialectic, and is used to unlock the otherwise mysterious notions of totality, abstraction, identity, law, and contradiction. (1978, pp. 227–228)

Ollman articulates a dialectical method that he breaks down into six successive moments. The *ontological moment* has to do with the infinite number of mutually dependent processes that make up the totality or structured whole of social life. The *epistemological moment* deals with how to organize thinking in order to understand such a world. The *moment of inquiry* appropriates the patterns of these internal relationships in order to further the project of investigation. The *moment of intellectual* reconstruction or *self-clarification* puts together the results of such an investigation for oneself. The *moment of exposition* entails describing to a particular audience the dialectical grasp of the facts by taking into account how others think. Finally, the *moment of praxis* uses the clarification of the facts of social life to act consciously in and on the world, changing it while simultaneously deepening one's understanding of it. These acts, versed repeatedly over time, bear a striking similarity to the pedagogy of Paulo Freire.

Ollman (1993) maintains that a dialectical understanding of the social world is both critical and revolutionary. It is revolutionary because it makes connections among past, present, and future histories. This allows educators to examine past social revolutions and, by using the present as a point of departure, to explore the possibilities for the future revolutionary transformation of society. Dialectical understanding of the social world is also critical, because it allows educators to recognize their common class interests with the working class and, in effect, act as revolutionary agents of class struggle. Consequently, by linking theory to practice, a dialectical understanding of the social world illuminates both the limitations and the possibilities for the revolutionary transformation of society. Finally, a dialectical understanding of the social world shows class struggle to be an amalgamation of the existing sociohistorical contradictions between capital and labor. For educators, this translates into being active participants or passive spectators in revolutionary struggle. Therefore, educators need to address the pressing question: Where do we wish to stand? On the side of the oppressed or the oppressors?

We agree with radical educationalist Paula Allman (2001) that teaching practices grounded in a theoretical synthesis of the ideas of Freire, Gramsci, and Marx can indeed work in formal contexts in public educational institutions. Allman's discussion and analysis of her own teaching is highly illuminating. Her perspicacious grasp of Freire is especially welcome, given the often grave misperceptions about Freire's pedagogy that have proliferated over the last several decades, following in the wake of what has been a steady domestication and embourgeoisement of his work.

Following in the footsteps of Freire, Allman successfully activated in her classroom a pedagogical site that facilitated the development of critical consciousness, a mode of dialectical engagement with everyday life that disposed her students to reflect upon their own historical experiences. They achieved this through the act of decoding everyday life and, in the process, were liberated to deal critically with their own reality in order to transform it. Students learned that they do not freely choose their lives, and that their identities and their objects of consumption were adaptive responses to the way that the capitalist system manipulates the realm of necessity. With a perceptive understanding that Freirean pedagogy is decidedly prescriptive and that Freirean educators are unwaveringly directive, she created the context for her students to name their world and, through dialogue, come to creatively reshape their historical reality. She carefully delineates Freirean pedagogy from its imitators who would turn the teacher into a passive facilitator. She does this by asking the following questions: Is it not prescriptive that we should ask students to "read the world" critically in order to transform it in a way that will foster humanization? Is it not also prescriptive to demand that the world needs transforming and that education should play a critical role in this effort? Furthermore, shouldn't educators use their authority that comes from their own critical reading of the world and their understanding of Freire's philosophy of education? Isn't the most facilitative, nonprescriptive and nondirective form of progressive teaching doubly prescriptive in the sense that it is a prescription for nonprescription as well as for political domestication and adapting successfully to the social universe of capital and the law of value? Of course, Freirean educators direct and prescribe, but in a way redolent of humility and in a spirit of mutuality, dialogical reciprocity, and self-respect.

## TOWARD A SOCIALIST PEDAGOGY

One of the fundamental principles of socialist pedagogy is the revolutionary empowerment of working-class students. Empowering working-class students means having them explore the complex linkage among sexism, racism, and the exploitation of labor. This requires a decidedly dialectical grasp of everyday social relations.

Challenging the causes of racism, class oppression, and sexism, and their association with the exploitation of labor demands that critical teachers and cultural workers reexamine capitalist schooling in the contextual specificity of global capitalist relations. Critical educators recognize that schools as social sites are linked to wider social and political struggles in society and that such struggles have a global reach. Here the development of a critical consciousness enables students to theorize and critically reflect upon their social experiences, and also to translate critical knowledge into political activism.

A socialist pedagogy actively involves students in the construction of working-class social movements. Because we acknowledge that building cross-ethnic/racial alliances among the working class has not been an easy task to undertake in recent years, we encourage the practice of community activism and grassroots organization among students, teachers, and workers. Yet, we believe that the task of overcoming existing social antagonisms can only be accomplished through class struggle—the road map out of the messy gridlock of historical amnesia.

## REMAINING SKEPTICAL

We are not altogether convinced that we have entered into a postindustrial economy where production can be moved easily from advanced capitalist countries in the North to developing countries in the South. As Kim Moody (1997) has noted, most production still occurs in the North and most foreign direct investment is still controlled by the North. In fact, 80 percent of this investment is invested in the North itself. While it is true that northern industries are being transplanted to the South to take advantage of the cheaper labor markets, the North merely modernizes its economic base while making it more technologically sophisticated. We don't believe that the state has withered away under the onslaught of an information economy or information-based capital. In fact, we have not seen a qualitative rupture in capitalist relations of production. We still live within monopoly capitalism or late capitalism, and, internationally, the struggle between capital and labor as part of the practice of imperialism has not seen a qualitative change or shift in direction. For this reason, we still regard the working class as the privileged agent for fundamental social change with the state still serving as the central target of the revolutionary struggle of the masses. This is because the state is still the main agent of globalization, in that it continues to maintain the conditions of accumulation, undertakes a rigid disciplining of the labor force, flexibly enhances the mobility of capital while ruthlessly suppressing the mobility of labor, and serves as a vehicle for viciously repressing social movements through the state apparatuses of the police, the military, the judicial system, etc. That the state is still the major target of working-class struggle should be made clear in the recent mass political strikes in France, South Korea, Italy, Belgium, Canada, Panama, South Africa, Brasil, Argentina, Paraguay, Bolivia, Greece, Spain, Venezuela, Haiti, Columbia, Ecuador, Britain, Germany, Taiwan, Indonesia, Nigeria, and elsewhere (Holst, in press).

We remain skeptical of the new social movements dedicated to democratizing civil society but leaving the state apparatuses largely untouched. We are not interested in ways to democratize civil society if that means (and it usually does) that capitalism will be strengthened in the process. The new social movements mistakenly believe that industrial production has declined in relevance, engage in a self-limiting radicalization of the public sphere, largely struggle on behalf of bourgeois rights for the petite bourgeoisie, fail to consider the state as a unitary agent of intervention and action in promoting structural reform, and eschew the goal of revolutionary Marxists of taking over the state and the economy. In fact, John Holst (in press) notes that, at a time when segments of the left have embraced a politics of discursive struggle and fragmentation, capitalism as a world economic system has become more universal and unified.

Finally, we support a socialist pedagogy that follows Marx's life-long struggle of liberating labor from its commodity-form within relations of exchange and working towards its valorization as a use-value for workers' self-development and self-realization (Eagleton, 1999).

TEACHERS' WORK AND THE VALUE FORM OF LABOR

We believe it is important to engage the issue of educational reform from the perspective of Marx's value theory of labor. Marx's value theory of labor does not attempt to reduce labor to an economic category alone but is illustrative of how labor as value form constitutes our very social universe, one that has been underwritten by the logic of capital. Value is not some hollow formality, neutral precinct, or barren hinterland emptied of power and politics but the very matter and anti-matter of Marx's social universe. It is important to keep in mind that the production of value is not the same as the production of wealth. The production of value is historically specific and emerges whenever labor assumes its dual character. This is most clearly explicated in Marx's discussion of the contradictory nature of the commodity form and the expansive capacity of the commodity known as labor-power. For Marx, the commodity is highly unstable, and nonidentical. Its concrete particularity (use value) is subsumed by its existence as value-in-motion or by what we have come to know as "capital" (value is always in motion because of the increase in capital's productivity that is required to maintain expansion). The issue here is not simply that workers are exploited for their surplus value but that all forms of human sociability are constituted by the logic of capitalist work. Labor, therefore, cannot be seen as the negation of capital or the antithesis of capital but the human form through and against which capitalist work exists (Rikowski, 2000). Capitalist relations of production become hegemonic precisely when the process of the production of abstraction conquers the concrete processes of production, resulting in the expansion of the logic of capitalist work. Class struggle has now been displaced to the realm of the totality of human relations, as abstract social structures such as labor now exist as the trans-substantiation of human life as capital (Neary, 2000). So, when we look at the issue of educational reform, it is important to address the issue of teachers' work within capitalist society as a form of alienated labor, that is, as the specific production of the value form of labor.

This becomes clearer when we begin to understand that one of the fundamental functions of schooling is to traffic in labor power, in the engineering and enhancement of the capacity to labor so that such labor power can be harnessed in the interests of capital. Glenn Rikowski's premise is provocative, yet compelling and perhaps deceptively simple: Education is involved in the direct production of the one commodity that generates the entire social universe of capital in all of its dynamic and multiform existence: labor-power. Within the social universe of capital, individuals sell their capacity to labor—their labor power—for a wage. Because we are included in this social universe on a differential and unequal basis, people can get paid above or below the value of their labor power. Because labor-power is implicated in human will or agency, and because it is impossible for capital to exist without it, education can be redesigned within a social justice agenda that will reclaim labor power for socialist alternatives to human capital formation. Helen Raduntz (1999) has made a convincing argument that teachers' work—work implicated in the trafficking of labor power—is fraught with contradictions and is situated in both sides of the labor-capital divide. More specifically, teachers' work is located both on the side of capital and that of wage-labor. It is also an important process of mediation in the class struggle between capital and wage labor, especially as both sides attempt to maximize their margins of surplus value. Raduntz argues that the major source of contraction in teachers' work arises from the social relations of production. Teachers' work is a productive activity—both structurally and developmentally—and it is constitutive of the reproduction of capitalist social relations. Yet teachers' work is integral to class struggle. This is because education is fundamental in the process of human development, but such a process becomes dehumanizing when it attempts to regulate education to coincide with and support the interests of capital. Raduntz calls for informed human development by teachers into this process of dehumanization.

The struggle entails understanding that teachers' work is productive both for capital and for wage-labor. It is productive for capital in that teachers' work constitutes value transferred to wage laborers' labor power in the acquisition of knowledge and skills; the value of teachers' work is also embedded as a component of the capital earned from surplus value as well as the wage paid to workers. In producing the use value of labor power for capital, teachers' work is productive for capital. But teachers' work is also productive for workers because it adds to the value of workers' labor power and their ability to attract a wage that will enable them to sustain a livelihood. What is needed is an approach to educational reform that can help teachers understand their relationship both to capital and to labor and thus challenge education's embeddedness in the value form of labor via corporatization and privatization and push towards reclaiming labor power for the fulfillment of human needs. Then it may be possible to develop a model of education outside of the current neoliberal agenda that can enable educators and their students to navigate and survive—and eventually flourish—outside the social universe of capital. Of course, to offer an alternative to capitalist social relations is a daunting struggle, and one that has untiringly exercised socialists for generations. Once, such struggles occupied the efforts of labor unions, but especially since the demise of the Soviet Union and the Eastern Bloc countries, unions have been all too happy to co-exist with the value form of labor under capitalism.

## CONCLUSION

In a provocative discussion, David Harvey (2000) suggests that Marx did not openly support the concept of social justice because he believed that the struggle for social justice was limited to the redistributive characteristics of capitalist mode of production. For Marx, a redistribution of wealth and income merely addresses one of the several "moments," or dimensions, of the mode of production that includes production, exchange, distribution, and consumption, all of which constitute the elements of an "organic totality." Emphasizing one "moment" while ignoring other moments does little to advance the elimination of exploitation. However, this does not mean that Marxists should abandon the *idea* of social justice. Far from it. Critical educators must work towards liberating the concept of social justice from its liberal and left-liberal roots, which has, for the most part, operated from within the boundaries drawn by capitalist social relations of production.

In an insightful passage in *Capital* (1997), Marx remarks: "A spider conducts operations which resemble those of a weaver, and a bee would put many a human architect to shame by the construction of its honeycomb cells. But what distinguishes the worst architect from the best of bees is that the architect builds the cell in his mind before he constructs it in wax" (1977, p. 284). In other words, the fundamental distinction between humans and other species is that humans are endowed with a social imagination, which operates as a tool for transforming their social conditions. Marx believed that while consciousness is conditioned by social and economic structures, it continues to remain a powerful mediating force in transforming the existing social and economic structures that constrain it. Thus, it is imperative that critical educators transform themselves into an army of skilled architects of socialism by imagining a socialist alternative, and by engaging in a critical analysis of existing social and economic conditions and the degree to which forces of production and relations of production have developed. In short, critical educators are called to grasp the dynamic movement of history and to help set its course towards the horizon of liberation.

*Notes*

1. "Cultural capital," a term made popular by French sociologist Pierre Bourdieu, refers to "ways of talking, acting, and socializing, as well as language practices, values, and styles of dress and behavior" (McLaren, 1997, p. 193). According to McLaren,

> Schools systematically devalue the cultural capital of students who occupy subordinate class positions. Cultural capital is reflective of material capital and replaces it as a form of symbolic currency that enters into the exchange system of the school. Cultural capital is therefore symbolic of the social structure's economic force and becomes itself a productive force in the reproduction of social relations under capitalism. (1997, p. 193)

*References*

Allman, P. (2001). *Critical education against global capital: Karl Marx and revolutionary critical education*. Westport, CT: Bergin & Garvey.

Azad, B. (2000). *Heroic struggle!—bitter defeat: Factors contributing to the dismantling of the socialist state in the USSR*. New York: International Publishers.

Bello, V. (1999). *Dark victory: The United States and global poverty* (2nd ed.). London: Pluto Press.

Boggs, C. (2000). *The end of politics: Corporate power and the decline of the public sphere*. New York: The Guilford Press.

Bonacich, E. & Appelbaum, R. P. (2000). *Behind the label: Inequality in the Los Angeles apparel industry*. Berkeley: University of California Press.

Borowski, J. F. (1999, August 21). Schools with a slant. *New York Times*, A23.

Cole, M. (1998). Globalization, modernisation and competitiveness: A critique of the New Labour Project in Education. *International Studies in Sociology of Education, 8* (3), 315–332.

Collins, C. & Yeskel, F. (2000). *Economic apartheid in America: A primer on economic inequality and security*. New York: The New Press.

"The Country-club Vote." (2000, May). *The Economist*, 42.

Eagleton, T. (1999). *Marx*. New York: Routledge.

Fischman, G. & McLaren, P. (2000). Schooling for democracy: Towards a critical utopianism. *Contemporary Society, 29* (1), 168–179.

Freire, P. (1978). *Pedagogy as process: The letters to Guinea-Bissau* (C. St. John Hunter, Trans.). New York: The Seabury Press.

Harvey, D. (2000). Reinventing geography. *New Left Review* (4) (2nd series), 75–97.

Hill, D. (2001). State theory and the neoliberal reconstruction of schooling and teacher education: A structuralist neo–Marxist critique of postmodernist, quasi-postmodernist, and culturalist neo–Marxist theory, forthcoming in *British Journal of Sociology of Education*.

Holst. J. (in press). *Social movements, civil society, and radical adult education*. Westport, CT: Bergin & Garvey.

Klein, N. (1999). *No logo: Taking aim at the brand bullies*. New York: Picador.

Krupskaya, N. (1985). *On labour-oriented education and instruction*. Moscow: Progressive Publishers.

Lasn, K. (1999). *Culture jam: The uncooling of America*. New York: Eagle Brook.

Lenin, V. I. (1965). A great beginning. In *Collected works* (Vol. 29). Moscow: Progressive Publishers.

Marx, K. (1973). *Critique of the Gotha program*. New York: International Publishers.

Marx, K. (1977). *Capital: A critique of political economy* (Vol. 1) (B. Fowkes, Trans.). New York: Vintage Books.

McLaren, P. (1997). *Revolutionary multiculturalism: Pedagogies of dissent for the new millennium*. Boulder, CO: Westview Press.

McLaren, P. (1998). *Life in schools: An introduction to critical pedagogy in the foundations of education* (3rd ed.). New York: Longman.

McLaren, P. & Farahmandpur, R. (1999a). Critical pedagogy, postmodernism, and the retreat from Class: towards a contraband pedagogy. *Theoria* (93), 83–115.

McLaren, P. & Farahmandpur, R. (1999b). Critical multiculturalism and globalization. Some Implications for a Politics of Resistance. *Journal of Curriculum Theorizing, 15* (3), 27–46.

McLaren, P. & Farahmandpur, R. (2000). Reconsidering Marx in post–Marxist times: A requiem for postmodernism? *Educational Researcher, 29* (3), 25–33.

McMurtry, J. (1998). *Unequal freedoms: The global market as an ethical system*. West Hartford, CT: Kumarian Press.

Mészáros, I. (1995). *Beyond capital*. New York: Monthly Review Press.

Moody, K. (1997). *Workers in a lean world: Unions in the international economy*. London: Verso.

Neary, M. (2000). Travels in Moishe Postone's social universe: A contribution to a critique of political cosmology. Unpublished paper.

Niemark, M. K. (1999). If it's so important, why won't they pay for it?: Public higher education at the turn of the century. *Monthly Review, 51* (5), 20–31.

Ollman, B. (1978). On teaching Marxism. In T. M. Norton & B. Ollman (Eds.), *Studies in socialist pedagogy* (pp. 215–253). New York: New York Press.

Ollman, B. (1993). *Dialectical investigations*. New York: Routledge.

Ollman, B. (1998a). Market mystification in capitalist and market socialist societies. In B. Ollman (Ed.), *Market Socialism: The debate among socialists* (pp. 81–121). New York: Routledge.

Ollman, B. (1998b). Why dialectics? Why now? *Science and Society, 62* (3), 338–357.

Perrucci, R. & Wysong, E. (1999). *The new class society*. Boulder, CO: Rowman & Littlefield.

Persuad, R., B. & Lusane, C. (2000). The new economy, globalisation, and the impact on African Americans. *Race & Class, 42* (1), 21–34.

Raduntz, H. (1999). A Marxian critique of teachers' work in an era of capitalist globalization. A paper presented at the AARE-NZARE Conference. Melbourne, Victoria, November–December, 1999.

Rikowski, G. (2000). Messing with the explosive commodity: School improvement, educational research and labor-power in the era of global capitalism. A paper prepared for the Symposium on "If We Aren't Pursuing Improvement, What Are We Doing?" British Educational Research Association Conference 2000, Cardiff University, Wales. 7 September, Session 3.4.

Spring, J. (1998). *Education and the rise of the global economy*. Mahwah, NJ: Erlbaum.

Thompson. W. (1997). *The Left in history: Revolution and reform in twentieth-century politics*. London: Pluto Press.

Vrana, D. (1998, September 7). Education's pied piper with a dark past. *Los Angeles Times,* A1.

Wichterich, C. (2000). *The globalized woman: Reports from a future of inequality* (P. Camiller, Trans.). London: Zed Books.

Witheford, N. (1997). Cycles of circuits and struggles in high-technology capitalism. In J. Davis, T. Hirschil, & M. Stack (Eds.), *Cutting edge: Technology, information, capitalism and social revolution* (pp. 195–242). London: Verso.

*Judith J. Slater*

# LIMITATIONS OF THE PUBLIC SPACE: HABITUS AND WORLDLESSNESS

## CONSTRUCTION OF THE PUBLIC SPACE

THE PUBLIC SPACE is a faith-like capitalistic construct (Lefebvre, 1997), created in people's minds and consecrated through their participation, actions, and obedience to the form and practice of the theory of social life prescribed by the constructs that define it. The social space is created as a social product, a political positioning of the players who dominate the arena as observers watch and wait, hoping that they will be taken care of and be heard. It has turned into a public space of domination and control. Producers of space act in ways consistent with the representation, while users passively experience what is provided for them. They have had no part in the making, only in the using or observing, but they think they have contributed. This is manipulation, and it occurs when the observer is lost in the speech of the actor on the stage and when the user is taught to follow and obey the *habitus* (Bourdieu, 1993) blindly. Users don't protest since they are not enlightened as to their manipulation. They exist in what Greene (1995) calls the opaqueness of life that does not let them see clearly how they are separate from the stage actors. Taking the stage are the vocal, political, perpetuators of the acceptable speech, the spokespersons for the bureaucratic structures of limitation and control.

Space emerges from its creation consecrated (Bourdieu, 1993). The space grows and develops, becomes more complex as it sustains itself with surrounding structures. Different social spaces penetrate each other and support each other's existence. School bureaucracies help ignorance perpetuate all sorts of structures that occupy spaces around it; thus the stronger the surrounding structures, the more difficult it is to change practices within. There are supporting visible boundaries of spaces in education, such as the diploma, titles, structure, order, etc., which create restrictions and imbedded social relationships that solidify the public space of schools.

Each space has status, and the subjects within have status. That status is conveyed by those who hold the space and those who aspire to enter. The public space has more status than the private space. This creates great class distinctions. The established culture of the public space has a specific reference point since it supports its own brand of truth, exploits those events which are congruent, and suppresses ideas, actions, and people who are outside. What occurs is a "banal consensus" to the space by the public. The onus is on the holders of the public space to make the audience believe. They can do this truthfully, building up structures that support the common good, or they can do this by advancing their own hidden agendas of power and position. The public supports those who offer quick solutions to problems that do not address their underlying causes. They believe they are being taken care of. Public speech about poverty does not ameliorate the fact of living. Public speech about literacy does little to teach the adult and child how to sound out the words. Public speech about equity and vouchers does not deliver competitive programs that level playing fields with elite schools.

The public space protects itself from intrusion. Violence is used to keep people away from the stage, a violence to the minds of the public, the unschooled, which keeps them from thinking independently. The enactment of correct, compliant knowledge tries to reverse the private space ideas of the audience, defragmentizing and integrating them through the power of privileged knowledge.

Schools transmit the social space; they consecrate certain actions over others as part of the transmission of the *habitus* of the culture that prepares students for adulthood. What schools also consecrate is obedience to authority, the scientific proof of test scores and standards, and legally imposed attempts at equality. The public, the audience for these consecrations, accepts them without question. They have faith in the predictions of success and failure, and they bend to the explanations given by the speakers on the public stage that the solution to the crises lie in this voucher, that charter, this or that new program, or a return to the tried and true solutions of the past. The *habitus* is cemented by the fear and doubt in their own private ability to solve the problems of a more just, democratic community of caring through means other than those that are publicly preached. Unfortunately, the behaviors of educators are conforming to that which is promulgated by the stage actors. They, too, have been taught to believe.

## NORMS OF BEHAVIOR AND EXPECTATIONS

Societies are governed and operate under a consensual norm, a set of habitual consecrated daily routines and taken-for-granted rules of law and codes of behavior that everyone follows as a given. It is a part of the rationale for community, and the rules are followed blindlessly, tweaked by elections and implemented in varied forms of compliance. Basically, the governing factors remain the same. Their goals are the orderly operation of the society designed for the protection and maintenance of the system of compliance that has been designed to preserve and protect the union of people.

In education, the parallel is the structure of bureaucratic schools—the rule-driven, culture-laden, role- determined and-followed teacher, student, and community understanding and cultural assumptions about schooling. This structure resists change as the *habitus* of the operations and expectations duplicate themselves and stop innovation from occurring. We are lulled into acceptance that the system of bureaucratic schooling works well and has for the past 150 years. This vision of schooling is accepted by a public that has little influence and limited choices and opportunity to intervene in policy-making and institutional practices.

Why is this so? Arendt (1958) describes the construct of worldlessness, a position people take that is a passive response to an idea, like charity, devised to "keep a community of people together who had lost their interest in the common world and felt themselves no longer related and separated by it" (p. 53). The public space is a created forum of ideas that Arendt argues becomes stronger over time and sets the standard for the way people are supposed to act who are a part of it. They consecrate the norms and become worldless in obeisance. Criticism is considered to be not playing the game. Outsiders who are critical are restricted from achieving a voice or gaining access to the public space forum. There are certain rights that come with obeisance. Using Baudrillard's (1998) example of the right to clean air, protection by the police, or free and appropriate education for all, each of these signifies that there is a loss—a loss of clean air, of safety, of good schooling opportunities—and that these givens become a commodity that is not egalitarian in its distribution. Some people become more protected than others. Some people have to fight for adequate classrooms, books and materials, and safe and clean places for children to learn. Equality is the sought-after goal, but happiness is assumed to be measurable, tied to social standing, college affiliation, job status, money, etc. (p. 49).

Fear of not having order and rules to follow, fear of chaos, makes worldlessness "a political phenomenon . . . possible only on the assumption that the world will not last . . .(which) begin(s) to dominate the political scene"(Arendt, 1958, p. 54). This idea of submission to the rules is transformed "into a potential earthly immortality," which makes possible politics, and a "common world" and a "public realm." It is the active loss of the individual's voice that collectively politicizes the process. People then establish preconceived notions of others and their practices without understanding any but their own point of view, basing expectations of behavior on those perceptions. In education, this pessimistic view defeats any change effort. It limits perspective by relying on what was, on what is acceptable, rather than what could be improved. It looks at new ideas as waste (Baudrillard, 1998, p. 42), throwaway notions that could innovate, but are overused and applied indiscriminately, then tossed aside as they dwindle in value and disappear. The more common they become, the less they are valued. Many examples of such innovations exist. When brain research revealed a dominant left-brain, right-brain proclivity, immediately simplified versions were delivered en masse to teachers who were urged to teach to the whole brain without understanding that every person is a unique cognitive processor. Another example is Gardner's multiple intelligence theory. The cognitive construct that broadens the idea of intelligence was molded into practice that, it was assumed, would raise achievement scores; this renders the construct valueless when the results do not appear to be foolproof and immediate.

In education, the socializing preferences of the peer group, the competition, the evaluations that are comparative and create class-based distinctions based on performance, are all filtered through a code of appropriateness that is devoid of individuals but represents an abstraction of competition that starts out unfairly traversed. The cycling of innovations is arbitrary and often politically motivated. They are culturally imbedded with the new thing, the innovation that is touted as the cure-all for not only educational problems, but those of society at large.

## BREAKING THE BOUNDARIES OF THE PUBLIC SPACE

The outside forces influencing the practice of local districts and schools, and those who are frontline workers in education are clear—they are business, world comparisons reports, a manufactured crisis (Berliner & Biddle, 1995) of low scores and low expectations. The response has been for the organizing structure of government, influenced by outside forces, to create new rules of play—new names, such as accountability, standards, and local control. The workers—the teachers—and their schools and districts are under the scrutiny of those who have laid the foundation but left the workers to fend for themselves as long as they are contained and meet the overriding criteria of standards, accountability, and local control. An example of this is tying teacher-rating systems into their students' test performance and the rejection of current systems of teacher evaluation that do not comply. In fact, some districts have been mandated by government to base teacher and administrator salaries on student performance (Ferrechio, 2000). School workers are structured to comply, but it is unclear how they should achieve what is demanded. How can the new initiatives benefit the students without punishing the system that delivers it and the teacher workers who are on the front lines?

The breakdown of the possibility of a social order of community leads to reflection on the pervasiveness of difference in access and in equity. The basic commodities of schooling form the basis of inequality. Reading has been commodified as a consumer product. There are companies that track what is read by a student (Accelerated Reader) but also restrict what can be read by the budgetary ability of the school to purchase materials from the company that computerizes the pace and content. You cannot read a book for which you don't have a CD-Rom, and, since the tracking and grading is done for you, the wealth of the library is limited to that which is bought and paid for. Reading is a business commodity that is not equally accessible to those less well off.

Max Frankel wrote (2000) in the *New York Times Magazine,* that the walls of sovereignty are falling around us and, therefore, it is important to collect the artifacts before they disappear. We need to take the core cultural conventions that we take for granted and give them another, closer look, before we exchange all the old for the "new, new thing" (Lewis, 2000). Preserve the one-on-one interactions of teachers and students; preserve the one-room schoolhouse concern for each and every student who was an individual within a connected family, full of fears and uncertainties, skills and abilities. Shared beliefs in right and wrong, Frankel (2000) writes, are replacing common law as we globalize and realize that people everywhere are after the same thing, not just economic and financial security and success, trade and communication, global politics, but personal sameness in transnational action. Autonomous individuals who share a new social consciousness, human rights and wrongs, all exhibit subjective preferences that are consciously made. That is the key to connectiveness. But, who is making the decisions in education? Not individuals, but rather an impersonalized system beyond that has transformed what was an interactive process into mandated policies that have little regard for the individual's needs. Just comply and you will succeed. Policies are established that are no longer about the person, but are national and international; not about national or local sovereignty, but about global comparisons. There are sanctions for noncompetition and condemnation for teachers on the front lines of educational practice. There is a collapsing of local pride and spirit into a statistical representation of where a child exists in relation to others on standard-driven, accountability-created, locally administered relational scales that seal the fate of teachers who are made accountable for factors that are beyond their control.

The result is that there is a squelching of ideas and a squelching of opposition. That must be overcome, or reach a crisis of what Brin (1998) describes as Richard Dawkin's idea of *memes,* self-replicating ideas, that can stop new ideas from fermenting and emerging. These *memes* are concepts that invade host organisms and reproduce in their minds, causing hosts to react prejudicially against competing ideas. Exclusionary practices in education are guarding teachers and children against opposing doctrines. A tendency prevails for everything to be either right or wrong. Little is merely gray, until, of course, a crisis arises at the core of convention. It is not, of course, that simple. People reject the *memes* on moral, ethical, empirical, educated grounds, but it is hard for them to make others see the possibilities of difference and to convince others to take a risk and act out of their own convictions. It takes a whole lot of discomfort with the status quo, or an internal conflict, to reject the norms and rules of behavior in school environments. It takes a belief change that the rules are no longer functioning coupled with an environmental change so dramatic that the conflict is brought to a head. A dichotomy is created where freedom is at odds with government function, where liberty and efficiency become polarized, and a whole set of behaviors and expectations are connected to each. We want education to be accountable and liberating, structured and innovative, diverse and tolerant, public and private; we want high scores to flourish and to be sensitive to individuals and their needs, and we want this for everyone.

Popper (cited in Eco, 1998, p. 25) referred to social conspiracy theories to explain this phenomenon: the blame falls on outside forces for things that go wrong or on powerful men and sinister group plots and conspiracies as the way people explain the failure of their own actions or reasons that events did not turn out the way they were expected. In education, innovations follow the same pattern. The conspiracy of the larger group tries to explain away the poor performance of students and hide the real causes. Group acceptance of the solution and fear of not doing what they are told, all based on false premises, are confirmed by the actions of the people who follow the edicts. In California, voters ended bilingual education, forcing a million Spanish speaking students into immersion classes. After years of special programs, the lack of program has been deemed more successful, with students showing greater gains over the past two years than they had in the specially funded programs (Steinberg, 2000). Similar concerns have been raised about charter schools across the country and their lack of academic success (Wyatt, 2000). And yet, we persist and continue to add on the new, in the search for the cure, the magic bullet to make everyone literate. It remains elusive and perhaps will never be found while the search is based on false assumptions that a final solution exists.

## EXPLOITATION AND POWER WIELDING

When there is a breakdown of the cultural norms of the normal world, an outright rejection and inability to maintain the rules of society, people follow the powerful out of fear. Thoughtlessly, our society accepts something that has not been shown to be effective, just because the new is different. In education, the question is what happens to the old methods and practices in teaching when an innovation is implemented such as those related to accountability, standards, and local control? What is the particular effect on teachers who must invent new ways of compliance with the new criteria, on parents who are sold on the buzz words, thinking that the new produces better learning, that somehow higher standards affects their child's performance and that this makes all children learn better, be more competitive, and more motivated to learn? What is the effect on students who have had the bar raised? Who wins in this new race? The good student wins again. Who fails and continues to be left behind? The poor and disenfranchised. What is different than reforms of the past is that now the blame is on the school, on the teacher, and the sanctions concern jobs, money, and careers. Everyone complies. But, are the teachers and administrators symbolically buying in when they really do not believe in the innovations that include charter schools, vouchers, grading of schools from "A" to "F", sanctions of money, time, and the perception that somehow managing more efficiently leads to student success and perceptions of quality?

Arendt (1958) questions who controls the praxis. Is it the individual who must make a choice of obeisance to the rules for survival, or is it the public-space conformists in education who accept the rules and make do, subverting in little ways what the collective praxis could change systemically? The power of participation and action in the public space must be worked on and enacted (Arendt, 1958, p. 200); it must constantly be in the face of participants. In education, we have the news media, the hype, the power wielders of the Florida Comprehensive Assessment Test in Florida who are being pushed by the business community to sell their positions of influence to the public. We are lulled into thinking one or two points on a standardized test are significant. Small and well-organized groups, backed by business and politicians, take control of the information and disseminate it to the public who become of like mind. They believe what they read and hear, and what they read and hear is influenced by political gain. How is this possible? Arendt (1958 p. 204) notes that "Power preserves the public realm and the space of appearance." In education we have seen theories and practices return again and again to test the waters, repackaged to look like something new. It is thirty years since vouchers and charters made the scene in California, only to return after being rejected and supported for the very same reasons today as in the past.

What are the limitations to praxis for the rejection of the old restrictions and rules and for new structures to be established? Baudrillard (1998, p. 10) suggests that time is a restriction. Because of Taylor and the efficiency movement, time, a product of culture and our economic system, has become a commodity that is scarce and more precious in a consumer society since it can be exchanged for other commodities such as money. Time is of the essence, we believe, in a crisis of education where solutions that benefit some are at the expense of others. Who benefits from such a crisis? Book companies, business, political electees, power brokers, and those who are seeking to limit those who succeed to those who are acceptable and part of the establishment. The artifacts of such a system are managed, policed, signs of success that are not real, or are pseudoobjects and trophies of success: "A" schools whose criteria of accomplishment is tied to pseudo representations of literacy for all and equal opportunities of success. One innovation in education is copied from another, transferred in content, and adapted in delivery, taking the symbols, the name, the illusions of accomplishment as a rationale for adoption. Schools are a type of consumption that is structured externally to and coercive over individuals. It takes the form of a structural organization, creates a collective phenomenon, a morality, a coded system of signs that individuals are coerced into using as a consumption, and it provides the means through which people communicate with each other. The ideology associated with the system leads to false beliefs: people are affluent, fulfilled, happy, liberated, educated or have the opportunity to be educated. Education is a consumption that is a structure, a process in the guise of a morality, or as Baudrillard (1998, p. 15) calls it, a "panoply of objects," and liberation can only occur when the body of objects are rejected for others that are not merely manipulated signs and symbols that are exchanged one for the other, but in fact are acted-on convictions. Differences of effect and differences of structure and function must be made ideologically viable, value-driven, and part of a kinship that has a function to make society better, more equal and egalitarian in nature.

Where does this chaos lead? It results in what Lyotard (cited in Baudrillard, 1998, p. 21) calls the loss of spontaneous human relations, the substitution of practices for a culture of possibilities, the loss of authentic responses and actions, such as those called for by Freire (1970, 1998a, 1998b). What is needed is a new means of consumption, new rules, rather than the profusion and accumulation of innovations that not only do not go together, but create an unclear vision of how they are related to long-term goals and achievable success. When the old no longer serves the purpose for which it was intended, it is time to seek new options. Eco (1998) states that false beliefs and discoveries that are not creditable can lead to the discovery of something true later on. There is a serendipity in the accumulation of the efforts to make change that provides the rationale for persisting and trying. Even if you don't have the right answer, something good may come out of the trying later on. So, for the conundrum we find ourselves in with regard to accountability, standards, and local control, we must press on with the search for alternatives and not be content with those that are given to us and mandated by others.

## BOUNDARY BREAKING OF THE PUBLIC SPACE

Schutz (1999) describes the conditions that would begin to open spaces that provide opportunity to engage in collective action and public dialogue. This space requires active engagement from each person, the unique voice potential that is an embodiment of our social world. This commodification, as Greene (1995) describes it, is not a conscious representation in either student or teacher, but it exists outside of the awareness of the ritualistic behaviors that compel everyday actions. The freedom created from the erosion of the rigidity of the public space comes from collaboration with others in a responsive community where freedom of action is possible. There is risk involved, and there must be a feel for the game, a conscious awareness of how the rules are played and how to work them for the benefit of the community. Action requires the interpretation of the public space as a potential. When the individual enters the stage, when she participates in a common project with others, she becomes herself rather than someone defined by the system. Greene suggests that the public space actualizes the person through the struggle of discovering that the person has both the ability to act and the choice to comply or to invent for himself and with others that which could be. This requires the identification of the public space obstacles and boundaries that limit freedom of participation and the identification of opportunities for action. The boundaries must be exposed through the coming together of diverse forces of alienated groups who share their bits of knowledge with each other and put together a whole picture of the public space as it is enacted to facilitate a vision of a public space as it could be (Sibley, 1995). Then comes positioning of people in the public space in roles that are not circumscribed by class and status but by common ends and common goals.

Euchner (1996) describes the underlying dynamics that generate transformational change, the civic ethos that precipitates activist reform movements that are

SLATER | *Limitations of the Public Space*     65

part of the evolutionary history in this country. Local public spaces can provide such a forum where audiences can come together over issues and experience a shared participation and shared effort toward action. But the public space also engenders unpredictability with respect to the assertion of a new voice or an attempt to enter the stage. Is this due to the freedom itself, or the fear of freedom associated with the participation of the audience? Community building must come first, because the human condition that Arendt (1958) talks about needs to trust others.

## CREATION OF A NEW PUBLIC SPACE

How can a new humanely fabricated public space be created? Arendt (Schutz, 1999) suggests that public spaces be small enough to allow the individual to contribute and be recognized by others in the space. Therefore, school reform of the public space should focus on individual schools or communities of feeder patterns of schools that can form their own identity and methods of problem posing and solution finding. These groups should also attend to what Greene (Schutz, 1999) describes as the unplanned and contingent details of production to make them their own so that they can be interpreted in accordance with participants' own perceptions of space and time. Individuals can then be schooled to make decisions for themselves about their own choices and the way to live and interact in their lives. Public action must mediate between individual voice and the public mission (p. 78). The public mission is the creation of a common-good cultural core that synthesizes society so that it can influence whatever public space it chooses to be audience of. This is the choice we exercise privately in clubs or in religious affiliations that are culturally unified and represent a coherent position that forms the collective consciousness of participation. True participation is the goal for schools—participation of the teachers, parents, students, and community.

Students represent an opportunity as they acculturate into the social space. They are a potential for democratic participation (Schutz, 1999); therefore, they threaten the stability of the public space and its agenda. Restriction of student participation is the norm in schools. They learn the rules, and the rules restrict their opportunity to participate in the day-to-day operations of the school, especially in their opportunity to affect that structure in any meaningful way. They suffer a school curriculum with subject matter insulated from each other, delivered in closed, ritualistic, boundaried environments with limited input from students and teachers (Sibley, 1995). The system is not tolerant of new ideas, and knowledge is suppressed or ignored when it does not fit into the organizational goals. Teachers are isolated from each other and do not participate in the curricular decision making. Information generation from the university is alienated and isolated from the public space of school reform and policy making. Parents are told what knowledge is most valued, and this perpetuates the public space and the control of those in power. Dewey's vision of embryonic community life is long past, since egalitarian opportunities are severely limited. Teachers can play a role in changing this. They can instruct children about the potential of the stage so that they are future-oriented. Children learn the assumptions about culture, positions of truth, and appropriate acceptable behavior in the public space. But, there is power in the moment for children who are taught to recognize that choice is the freedom of participation in the community. Above all groups, students are subservient to the dominant discourse unless teachers present them with possibilities.

Traditions for students can be open to new ideas and new spaces. These spaces would celebrate participation, blur the boundaries of curriculum content, and provide opportunities for self-government (Sibley, 1995). *Habitus* can be overcome for students by giving them the skills for communal action and public praxis. Greene (Schutz, 1999) suggests that civic learning can provide the skills and desire to form public spaces. Civic learning includes health issues, social awareness issues, drugs, alcohol, political awareness, and technology issues. The teacher must collaborate in the process of liberation from the forces that deny an open public arena by providing students with the necessary abilities, capabilities, beliefs, and values to reflect on who they are in relationship to the collective group. The boundaries between the public stage and the roles and relationships that are tolerated can be made ready for action when the teacher engenders in students situationally appropriate opportunities for problem solving and action on issues that concern their current and future participation in the community.

There are at least four elements needed to create responsive public spaces; these are leadership, discourse, nurturance of the public, and imagination. There needs to be leadership that represents not just the best interests of the public, but morally understands the elixir of leadership and how easily the vision of those in power strays from that of the followers. Leadership must be inclusive of the private space position.

Second, a new discourse must be created, one that is participatory and future-oriented. That future is one where the public discourse is at the heart of participatory decision making. Then the problems that are most relevant to the people can be mediated through authentic clarification of the issues. Public questions must be raised as to the morality of the greater group vs. the individual voice. Voice needs an audience, and the public space should be recreated so that it engenders authentic dialogue concerning relevant issues. It must raise the issues in public forums concerning the amelioration of the objectiveness of the world and the consumerism of desires that suppress the voice of the individual.

Third, the community must be nurtured actively by the public space actors. It must nurture what Arendt calls the "in between," the renewal of the common world. The community of voices must replace the inbreeding of ideas and paternalism of opportunities. It must end the dominion and supremacy over the weak, the children, the disempowered, and the disengaged so that there is opportunity for them to participate. Creation of voice is not merely the empowerment of words. An unspoken general sensitivity to needs is required; an outlet and a platform for an exchange of ideas and the reformation of ideals must exist.

Fourth, there must be a restoration of imagination of possibilities, of "social imagination: the capacity to invent visions of what should be and what might be in our deficient society, on the streets where we live, in our schools" (Greene, 1995, p. 5). This rebirth of community includes a rebirth of images and actions that re-create individual worldviews and understandings. These, in turn, form the basis for action-oriented beliefs that are communicated to others. It requires an icono-clasm of the consecrated tokens of behavior that are followed mindlessly (Bour-dieu, 1993; Langer, 1997). It requires that the public understand the meaning of emerging discourse that is new and future-oriented. It requires soul, vision, and actions that are, as Freire (1970) would say, authentic. It requires spectacles that merge actor and audience and provide the skills to perform in the public space. Di-alogue needs to be opened so that authentic public discourse becomes part of the arena and there is opportunity to recreate the public space. This discourse should be ongoing about ways to create ways of seeing that are authentic and not ready-made by others.

What is the way out of the conundrum we find ourselves in today? How do we authentically evaluate the results of accountability in our schools, of standard-driven curricula, and of local control that even extends to the dismantling of the State University Board of Regents in my state? Who is the voice of reason who will see us through so that reasoned changes can be made in schools, and so that teachers and students are no longer blamed for lack of funds, poor working con-ditions, and low test scores for children who have not been given all the advan-tages of those who are born into environments that assure educational success. Freedom is related to those who hold the power, the decision makers and the pol-icy makers. The espoused truths are created sometimes falsely, but it is the relegat-ing of freedom, of choice, of informed action which renders them powerful. What can be done? Arendt (1958, p. 247) says that what saves the world from ruin is "natality . . . the birth of new men and the new beginning, the action they are ca-pable of by virtue of being born." Arendt (1958) suggests that there is no more pri-vate space when the individual or student is judged by his or her products in com-petition or in comparison to others. When the personal becomes public knowledge (such as the disclosure of test scores in the newspaper so that schools are pitted against each other in a ratings race to be on top), "society mass-produces would-be social critics and individualists as if from an assembly line" (Brin, 1998, p. 45). It does not advance the agenda when everyone spouts the same resolutions.

The answer is to try to see through the opacity; to take the core values of educa-tion and recognize that there may not be only one way, that you cannot legislate and demand high standards, that accountability does not equate to quality but in-stead promotes sameness and stifles creativity and imagination in teachers and stu-dents alike, and that the elimination of resistance and commentary and criticism is the elimination of actions.

I suggest that in order for reason to persist and a balance restored, we take a critical look at the major innovations of accountability, high standards, and local control. The process requires that we look at each in light of what we know of the circumstances surrounding them, their history as curricular innovations, and question their ability to succeed by asking: Does each form a conspiracy of power, political repression, return to the past, fear of the consequences, fear of failure, fear of action, freezing of progress, or public criticism?

The first innovation is accountability. Clearly there is a conspiracy of power wherein there is great business influence that risks exposure to the public who are fearful of private involvement; there is always the risk of exposure for undue business influence, as in the historic backfire of the National Association of Manufacturing investigation of texts so many years ago. There is also political repression as changes in partisan influence in government are reflected in positioning and control of money and power with regard to educational policy making and spending. Accountability is a return to the past where local school initiatives and local control of schools become more responsive to specific family and community needs rather than basing reform on national and international comparisons; there is also the possibility that trust could be restored to the effectiveness of local initiatives for local concerns. On the other hand, there is an abiding fear of the consequences of accountability with the loss of local control when those initiatives come from top down; there is also fear of teacher resistance to increasing documentation and restrictive prescriptive teaching that comes with top-down reform. The real test of accountability will be its ability to raise the scores of students in the poorest schools. Up to now, there is a great fear of failure as most of the reform measures have not shown great strides in ameliorating the problems of the lowest-scoring students. In fact, there is great resistance to change from the traditional teaching practices to those being supported by the reform movement, causing, possibly, a fear of action and lack of faith in the mandated solutions. If accountability measures do not produce quick sustainable change in student achievement, then there is a freezing of progress as time is wasted in documentation, ineffective practice dissemination, testing, and alternative schooling configurations such as charters and vouchers. Lastly, there is the possibility of overwhelming public criticism by individual schools, teachers, parents, and communities that may resist the raising of standards by mandate rather than meaningful supportive measures that are more relevant to individual students and their needs.

The second innovation is high standards. For this innovation, there is the possibility of a disruption through exposure of a conspiracy of power concerning the sources of the imposed standards and the motivation for them to be operationalized: Who benefits from these standards as opposed to others, and are they in the best interests of the public or in the best interests of those in power? Do they provide equality of opportunity or further limit chances for success? Is there political repression and a dollar consequence for lack of compliance for those who are asked to implement the standards? Higher standards have engendered fear of the consequences of noncompliance: the threat of the closing of schools, the firing of teachers, teacher salaries tied to progress in test scores, and privatization. There is an abiding sense, in those places that have not met the higher standards, of a fear of failure that pervades the climate of schools. Resistance to any change is also prevalent in any bureaucratic climate, and fear of action is seen in the reliance on past practices and teacher resistance to innovate. There is the possibility that the implementation and reinforcement of higher standards will not be found to be a means to raise the levels of performance of students, thereby causing a freezing of progress as goals are not achieved quickly, and time is lost that could have been spent on other more authentic programs. Lastly, public criticism could occur due to failure to achieve the promised quick fix that raises scores and makes schools more competitive.

The third innovation is local control. Possible disruptions include the exposure of a conspiracy of power as control of school board decisions represents the agenda of the powerful public brokers through mandated compliance. Political repression would be evident through state and national restrictions in the form of monetary and legal consequences for noncompliance with national and state partisan initiatives. This is always accompanied by fear of the consequences: fear of the government, fear of the loss of personal position, and fear of the loss of power by local school board members who represent single member districts. Fear of failure portends the possibility of more restrictions, while fear of action refers to funding and union issues that easily can interfere with innovations. By far the most potent source of disruption is the freezing of progress by the adoption of simple solutions that appear to appease but do not ameliorate the underlying problems of poverty, loss of community involvement, and concern for education. This can lead to public criticism, as representatives from poor schools demand, through affiliation, what affluent schools have to offer.

This analysis is not definitive. For example, Baudrillard (1998, p. 37) notes a disparity between private consumption and collective expenditure. He suggests that we ask whether the state expenditures make for an objective equalization of social chances when they support initiatives such as accountability, high standards, and local control. We know that redistribution does not achieve social equality and that the education disputes concerning heredity and environment are incurable. Redistribution of funds and resources just reinforces the mechanisms of cultural inertia. Baudrillard cites data that confirms that more children of the upper-middle class stay in education, even higher education, no matter what amount of funds are directed to equity programs. Perhaps only cultural expectations and pressures of society influence these innovations. They lull us into thinking they are purposefully organized when they are merely purposefully implemented. The organizing factors are in the guise of balance. Balance does not exist because the solutions came before the analysis and the predictions. It all is in flux and requires constant interpretation and reinterpretation. That is why innovations like accountability, standards, and local control cannot just be put into practice and left alone. Instead, they must be worked and reworked, and made relevant to circumstances; there must be courage to toss them away if they do not achieve the outcomes that they promise. Changes in point of view make balance and reason hard work. Deborah Meier (2000) suggests that standards-based reform efforts threaten democratic principles by using parents and teachers as instruments of externally imposed policies and practices. These externals impose standards, impose implementation practices, impose accountability criteria, and establish the consequences of failure to achieve. Children are subjected to unprecedented standardized testing at the expense of meaningful forms of teaching and learning.

## RESOLUTION

In a world where laws, policies, and technology make it more and more difficult to keep our affairs from others, we succumb to letting those far removed from our daily personal and public lives dictate policy, and this also applies to schools (Rosen, 2000). In education, it is public knowledge how a school does in comparison to others, but not how much growth each individual student makes. What fears do we succumb to through the bullying of others who take over and control and devise and reinforce rules? Why is there no resistance or critical commentary leading to action, and why do people acquiesce their rights and responsibilities to others?

Alan Wolfe (2000) in a *New York Times Magazine* poll called "The Way We Live Now," found that Americans were cynical about institutions and politicians, and were civically disengaged. It is less a matter of what the issue is, but rather whether it is viewed as a personal or public matter. The public issues are what you have to attend to; the private is what you choose to attend to, and when the personal becomes political, autonomy is sacrificed—the refuge of American life. When the public and private merge, they become "mirror images" of each other (p. 56). For education, this raises an autonomy question of who succeeds, who rises to the top? Are those who do rise more moral than the others, or are we still faced with success based on race and class? Wolfe found that the wealthy and educated find less fault than the least educated with policies and practices that distribute unequal income and support. The wealthy succeed no matter what the policy and no matter what the measure of success. Few oppose opinions shaped by media and television. What is truth is sold and advertised as a commodity. Autonomy is also freedom, not anarchy; to make meaningful change is not to set out to destroy institutions and practices that allow for living together in peace and prosperity. But a rethinking is in order. We need to question what it means to live with others and hold concern for them and to question how it makes the collective better.

According to Wolfe (2000), the disseminators of educational thought to the public need to be concerned that they are persuaders; they need to be less hidden in their biases and responsive to public needs and tastes and desires. We need critics who make us care about the common good, become aware of what is valuable about a way of life and the education system, and make civil society better. If not, the institutions produced will themselves become the driving force, ingrained static constructions, not responsive to the needs of education. Rather, we want to goad our institutions and be dissatisfied so that we can effect change in them, so that we can escape the freedom they purport to establish, and make them better as our displeasure rises.

Those who can should participate in the dialogue and in the action about the blind acceptance of a new idea, program, and policy as it applies to issues in educational practice. There will always be those who think one innovation is better than another. It is the lessons we learn through the work of the arts that gives us the courage to imagine the unimaginable, to dream, to be original, to change, be vague, be vigorous in interpretation, and wander outside the boundaries of what is acceptable (Eco, 1997, pp. 47–48). It is through exercising this imagination that teachers, students, and parents can approach the state where the inactive, unformed idea, or what Kant calls *qualia,* is conceptualized from pure possibility and made into a predictor. If some one, some force, innovates, we then take the innovation and assess it for what it is, seeking its sources and its underlying meaning, so that it can be transformed into action that is purposeful and meaningful for the school rather than for the public space which is anonymous and ineffective to meet real needs and purposes. If we are to address real needs of literacy, high-stakes testing, and fair practices, we must not be blind to the pitfalls and promises that accountability, standards, and local control purport to solve.

*References*

Arendt, H. (1958). *The human condition*. Chicago: University of Chicago Press.

Baudrillard, J. (1998). *The consumer society: Myths and structures*. London: Sage.

Bourdieu, P. (1993). *The field of cultural production*. New York: Columbia University Press.

Berliner, D. C. & Biddle, B. J. (1995). *The manufactured crisis: Myths, fraud, and the attack on America's public schools*. Reading, MA: Addison-Wesley.

Brin, D. (1998). *The transparent society: Will technology force us to choose between privacy and freedom?* Reading, MA: Perseus Books.

Eco, U. (1998). *Serendipities: Language and lunacy*. London: Orion.

Eco, U. (1997). *Kant and the platypus: Essays on language and cognition*. New York: Harcourt Brace.

Euchner, C. C. (1996). *Extraordinary politics: How protest and dissent are changing American democracy*. Boulder, CO: Westview.

Ferrechio, S. (2000, August 23). Broward teacher rating system flunks. *Miami Herald,* p. 3B.

Frankel, M. (2000, March 19). Heresy on 81st Street. *New York Times Magazine,* pp. 28–30.

Freire, P. (1970). *Pedagogy of the oppressed*. New York: Seabury.

Freire, P. (1998a). *Pedagogy of freedom: Ethics, democracy, and civic courage*. Lanham, MD: Rowman & Littlefield.

Freire, P. (1998b). *Teachers as cultural workers: Letters to those who dare to teach*. Boulder, CO: Westview.

Greene, M. (1995). *Releasing the imagination: Essays on education, the arts, and social change*. San Francisco: Jossey-Bass.

Langer, E. J. (1997). *The power of mindful learning*. Reading, MA: Addison Wesley.

Lefebvre, H. (1997). *The production of space*. Oxford, UK: Blackwell.

Lewis, M. (2000). *The new new thing*. New York: W. W. Norton.

Meier, D. (2000). *Will standards save public education?* Boston: Beacon Press.

Rosen, J. (2000). *The destruction of privacy in America*. New York: Random House.

Ross, A. (1999). *The celebration chronicles: Life, liberty, and the pursuit of property value in Disney's new town*. New York: Ballantine.

Schutz, A. (1999). Creating local "Public Spaces" in schools: Insights from Hannah Arendt and Maxine Greene. *Curriculum Inquiry, 29* (1), 77–98.

Sibley, D. (1995). *Geographies of exclusion*. London: Routledge.

Steinberg, J. (2000, August 20). Test scores rise, surprising critics of bilingual plan. *New York Times,* pp. 1Y, 16Y.

Wolfe, A. (2000, May 7). The pursuit of autonomy. *New York Times Magazine,* pp. 53–59.

Wong, E. (2000, August 13). Poorest schools lack teachers and computers. *New York Times,* p. 14.

Wyatt, E. (2000, August 18). Charter school's problems yield cautionary tale. *New York Times,* [On-line], *http://www.nytimes.com/library/national/regional/081800ny-charter-edu.html*

*Gerard Huiskamp*

# NEGOTIATING COMMUNITIES OF
# MEANING IN THEORY AND PRACTICE:
# REREADING *PEDAGOGY OF*
# *THE OPPRESSED* AS DIRECT
# DIALOGIC ENCOUNTER

IN *PEDAGOGY OF THE OPPRESSED* (PO) and other theoretical writings, Paulo Freire sought to critically reexamine what a commitment to the "authentic liberation" of the poor entails, both theoretically and practically. From his adult literacy and rural organizational work in Brazil and Chile respectively, Freire set out in *PO* to develop and employ a pedagogy that would enable intellectuals, in partnership with the urban and rural poor, to transform the conditions of oppression to which they were subjugated. Predicated upon the "liberation" of the "colonized mentalities" of the oppressed, such a transformation of society is to come in the first instance through the cognitive self-actualization of the poor. Freire's use of *conscientização,* or consciousness-raising, was thus intended to awaken people to their collective capacity to analyze and critique a larger social context for the injustice in their lives. And, in this, Freire affirmed the existence of a recursive link between the attainment of new self-awareness, and a resultant proactive commitment and capacity to act upon the world.

Implicit in Freire's work, then, is a tripartite relationship between the act of pedagogical theorizing; the employment of empowerment methodologies by intellectual-activists in Latin America and elsewhere; and the self-defined goals and practices of popular class communities and organizations to be energized by dialogic encounters. While Freire in no way denied the structural manifestations or material bases of oppression, he insisted that powerlessness is also a function of unequal control over the means of knowledge production, or what Anisur Rahman describes as "the social power to determine what is valid or useful knowledge"

(1985, p. 119). Thus for Freirian theory and kindred analyses, such as "participatory action-research" or liberation theology, it is less important in this moment in history to theoretically resolve the ancient Marxian "base-superstructure" debate, since both forms of control reinforce each other in maintaining and perpetuating the fundamental condition of inequality. Radical pedagogues understand their work as a practical means to promote a "dual transformation," that is, both cognitive and macrostructural (Rahman, 1985, p. 120).

*PO* reflects the overlapping layers of dialogue and exchange embedded in this triadic conjunction by presenting Freire's empowerment methodology on two planes simultaneously. Most obvious is the surface text explication of, and invitation to, the pedagogy of liberation as the basis for progressive activism; yet (at the level of subtext) the resonance of Freire's invitation is in large part the product of the actual employment of the method in a dialogic encounter with well-meaning, but "colonized," leftist intellectuals. This chapter explores *Pedagogy of the Oppressed* as subtextual "pedagogy of the intellectual activist," and I argue that this dualism has both theoretical and practical implications for promoting liberating social change. In sum, I inquire into the sublimated political commitments entailed in Freire's linkage between popular collective action and the revolutionary movements of the 1960s and 1970s, asking if these provide a desirable, even defensible, basis for popular democratic action consistent with Freire's theoretical commitment to popular empowerment.

The argument here proceeds at both the theoretical and practical level. I begin with a brief overview of Freire's pedagogy and its distinctive ontological and epistemological self-understanding, as a means to demonstrate the method's evident power to assist in nourishing a democratic political culture in the lives of the poor. The specific sense of democracy invoked here emphasizes the new sense of citizen efficacy and self-conscious, autonomous direction; just as it de-emphasizes, analytically, the short-term performance of newly instituted political democratic regimes at the national level. Within the logic of his pedagogy, Freire invited us to conceive of democracy as a process; that is, just as the recent instauration of civilian-led political regimes is no panacea for the problems of the region's impoverished classes, the contemporary weaknesses of these systems do not exhaust the cultural and structural reservoir of democratic meaning in Latin American societies. Instead, one can evaluate the performance of political systems—and popular political practice within these—in terms of the state's "responsiveness" to the entirety of its citizens' initiatives.[1] It is precisely in this sense that Freirian pedagogy helps to promote a more democratic political system, in assisting the poor to position themselves as citizens with the right and capacity to individually and collectively voice their preferences.

That said, however, I also argue that as a function of *PO*'s subtextual pedagogical intent, its rhetorical positioning has left a cognitive weight upon the subsequent evolution of participatory development education. Just as Freire used *PO* as an opportunity to "conscientize" his leftist contemporaries toward the commitments and self-understanding of authentic democrats, Latin American Marxism-Leninism has had a recursive influence in shaping Freire's empowerment pedagogy and its practice. In engaging one's audience in this process of consciousness raising, the educator is required to help draw the audience into a process of critical reflection by first discovering the group's "generative themes" as the baseline for the dialogic encounter (Freire, 1970, pp. 68–105; 1973, pp. 41–58). As is integral to the method, dialogic convergence between Freire and the orthodox Leninist left meant that the educator imported elements of the guiding political faith of the time into his empowerment praxis—namely, a lingering vanguardism, an attendant "mass mobilization" ideal of collective action, and a closely related statist politics. It is argued that, indirectly, this statist vision has often led to an overall impoverished and strategically inefficient notion of emancipatory politics; one that is, moreover, usually in tension with the specific goals and self-understanding of the popular organization members with which empowerment practitioners work.

Analytically separating Freire's pedagogical theory from the political (and subtextual) act of writing affords new insight into ways in which the appropriation of the method by activists is often in tension with the professed intention to promote a self-directed popular democratic political agenda. Yet, while Freirian activists' dependence upon a state-centric vision of politics is deducible from *PO,* I argue that this commitment is not constitutive of Freire's pedagogy of liberation. The Freirian ideal of mutual democratic learning and empowerment is attainable, which I illustrate through an account of an actual intellectual-community partnership in the Huasteca region of Veracruz, Mexico. The case is suggestive of how Freirian partnerships, unmediated by mass mobilization and vanguardist preconditions, allow for the mutually constitutive type of educative encounter at the center of Freirian theory. I argue that the power of Freirian pedagogy lies in its ability to promote participatory attitudes and behavior, as opposed to a specific set of predetermined strategies and outcomes; and in doing so, I outline an enriched conceptualization of popular political practice in the democratization of control over meaningful knowledge.

## FREIRIAN PEDAGOGY AS THE DEMOCRATIZATION OF KNOWLEDGE

If it is accepted that the poor cannot think for themselves—beyond the short-term need for material subsistence—others with a longer horizon of the future stand justified in deciding and acting for them. In a still influential study of political culture, for example, Gabriel Almond and Sidney Verba (1963, pp. 480–81, *passim*) argue that efficient and stable democratic governance rests upon the citizenry's belief in a myth of individual political self-efficacy, influence, and participation; albeit a belief best accompanied by actual behavior manifesting a general indifference toward politics, non-influence, and passive deference to governmental elites:

> Everything being equal, the sense of the ability to participate in politics appears to increase the legitimacy of a system and lead to political stability. . . . This point needs

some qualification. High levels of participation may have unstabilizing effects on a system. But the *sense* of competence, especially when coupled with a somewhat lower actual fulfillment of this competence, does play an important role in political stability. (1963, p. 253; p. 253, fn. 4)

This view is suggestive of the exceptional level of confidence placed in policy elites and liberal institutions by most Western analysts during the early postwar period. Freire's pedagogy of liberation had its origins in a skepticism toward this elite model of governance, and its effects upon Latin American societies in the mid-1960s: flagging economies mired in the false promises of "modernization" and the bureaucratic-authoritarian regimes that often presided over this process.

The condition of misery in which the poor live their life daily, however, is not one merely of material want; indeed much of Freire's analysis is based upon understanding its cognitive manifestations. And though Freire focuses upon this cognitive side of oppression, he expressly maintains that fatalism is a learned response to very real, objective, social and material conditions: the "fruit" of a specific historical and sociological situation, rather than an essential characteristic of the poor (Freire, 1970, p. 43). The weight of this specific and concrete history induces a "distortion of the vocation of becoming more fully human" (p. 26), through a cultural process managed and governed by specific and concrete social actors. Freire locates several specific historical forces accounting for this culture of oppression (Freire, 1973, pp. 27–34): an alienating (in the precise Marxist sense) fordist industrial economic system, overlaying an essentially feudal system in the countryside; a general cultural and social paternalism bequeathed as part of a colonial heritage, and replicated in a postcolonial history of governance characterized by an "unauthentic democracy" (i.e., populist clientelism) and conservative authoritarian backlash, or "retreat"; and socialized through the antidialogic "banking" model of education, a system of "domestication" that denies human capacities in its very pedagogical practice (Freire, 1970, pp. 52–67). All these forces coalesce to reinforce and continuously reestablish a society predicated on unequal distribution of social power.

Freirian theory thus shares both temporal and theoretical roots with dependency theory; but while the latter focuses primarily on the analysis of macroeconomic systems and the historical-structural evolution of Latin American nation-states, Freire directed his attention to the quotidian manifestations of failed developmentalist interventions.[2] These postcolonial societies, he argued, are characterized by gross inequalities of social power, a status quo enforced as much by the continuous regeneration of a pervasive "culture of silence," or collectively internalized "fear of freedom," as by force of arms or law. It is, for Freire, a state of ignorance and lethargy that results from generation upon generation of an imperceptibly learned acquiescence and accommodation to systematic economic, social, political, and cultural domination (Shaull, 1970, p. 12).

The pedagogy of the oppressed begins in this intellectual reflection, but one cannot abstractly know the condition of the poor; nor is oppression's solution a matter of mere theoretical reflection (Freire, 1970, p. 19). This requires, however, more than an assertion of the proficiency of "hands-on" observation. It entails, rather, an epistemological stance regarding the nature and production of knowledge capable of achieving the goal of cognitive liberation and a practical commitment to social change. At the base of Freire's pedagogy is the idea that for people to regain self-recognition of their humanity and dignity—that is, to assert themselves as "subjects" active in making their own history, as opposed to passive bystanders to the cultural assertions of others—they must be assisted in developing and honing the critical and reflective capacities that are constitutive of that humanity. Freire contends that all people, including the poor, necessarily objectify the world around them in order to work in it, as all people implicitly require some orienting conceptualizations to be able to act and create. This essential fact of human existence is what gives Freire confidence that the task of liberation he sets out for the poor is attainable.

It is in this initial epistemological stance, moreover, that the intellectual finds her moment, her ontological role in a collective struggle against the present dehumanizing conditions of society. The activist has skills and knowledge she can bring to bear in assisting the poor to engage in their own process of cognitive and practical liberation. But a "revolutionary leader"—Paulo Freire or anyone else—who has apprehended the need to work for liberation with the poor, has not thereby been liberated herself; rather, she has only grasped the preconditions of a collective process of liberation. A process of societal liberation, according to Freire, can only be completed through a practical engagement *with* the poor:

> We can legitimately say that in the process of oppression someone oppresses someone else; we cannot say that in the process of revolution someone liberates someone else, nor that some liberates himself, but rather that human beings in communion liberate each other. This affirmation is not meant to undervalue the importance of revolutionary leaders, but on the contrary, to emphasize their value. What could be more important than to live and work with the oppressed, with the "rejects of life," with the "wretched of the earth"? (Freire, 1970, p. 114)

The insight that leads committed intellectuals to work with the poor—that one cannot provide liberation for others, nor liberate oneself, but only in communion with others—is at the same time an epistemological admonition for intellectual-activists to be humble in their knowledge claims. This injunction applies even to the realm of technical knowledge, something the intellectual-activist may feel justified in perceiving as properly within her province as a truth that must be explained, not negotiated (Freire, 1973, p. 109). It is also an epistemological injunction in a double sense, in that it maintains that knowledge in general is socially constructed, and therefore contingent and limited; and having this social characteristic, knowledge therefore requires the participation of others to be truly useful and liberating. The intellectual must understand that her scientific knowledge is a cultural construction based on a particular moment in time and place, and thus one that must be reconciled with the cultural understanding of one's audience, which itself has its own distinctive vantage point. Given that pedagogical work at the grass roots is characterized by the encounter of very different worldviews, this means that not only the peasant or worker, but the committed intellectual herself, needs the participation of the other to further realize their initial knowledge and capacities. The poor, in sum, are not only capable of reflective knowledge; their reflections are crucial to the education of the intellectual, that is to the intellectual's liberation from her own historically conditioned understandings and behavioral inclinations.

Coming to know more in this context of partnership is not a matter of refining of one's prior knowledge, but rather of a process of discovery through a dialogic convergence with the people toward whom one is reaching out. In this way, intellectual humility prefigures the cognitive and social transformation in the people that this dialogic encounter is premised upon liberating; and it does so through a method that requires this creative capacity of exchange between a community of people with effective agency. The content of liberation thus lies within the process of critical and practical engagement itself, in the recursive rhythm of action and reflection. There is no specific, unchanging truth value behind either the peasant's or technician's particular response to the world: the goal, rather, is collectively to construct proposals for concrete action; and these proposals ultimately must prove their value—their truth—in the ability to meet the challenges from which they arose.

## THE DEVELOPMENT OF LIBERATION PEDAGOGY AFTER *PO*

In the decades following the publication of *PO* and other writings, a newly reinvigorated "social left" took up Freire's challenge to assist the poor in emancipating themselves. Freire's pedagogy rests upon a "utopian moment," a belief and trust in the capacity of people to change their world for the better, despite the obvious structural obstacles and opposing forces resistant to change. The realism of this theoretical position is not measured in terms of its conformity with what is, but rather in terms of what it can be, thanks to human action. And over time, many popular organizations energized by such partnerships have demonstrated just such an ability to continue to work on specific collective projects of community empowerment. These achievements simultaneously suggest a prima facie validation of Freire's trust in the poor to achieve proactive change, as well as the prominence given to cognitive liberation as an indispensable requisite to the struggle for social justice.

It was by an accident of history that Freire ventured into applying his pedagogical principles beyond the area of adult literacy training. Freire went to Chile in 1964 (after being exiled by the Brazilian military) to assist in the development and implementation of the government-sponsored agrarian reform program, integrating the pedagogy of liberation into rural organization training and technical extension assistance programs. It was thus under the auspices of the *Instituto de Capacitación e Investigación en Reforma Agraria* (Institute for Ways and Means and Research in Agrarian Reform, or ICIRA) that Freire's pedagogical work began simultaneously (and directly) to address both cognitive and economic forms of practical empowerment. Indeed, it was this approach Freire developed in Chile—as opposed to prior work in adult literacy, per se—that has lent to the methodology's subsequent appeal and elaboration in much of the participatory action-research independent of Freire personally.

In general terms, participatory action-research partnerships share a number of basic characteristics (Rahman, 1985, pp. 115–116): Technicians propose "catalytic initiatives" in poor communities, with the aim of promoting the self-mobilization of historically marginalized social groups. This process originates in the effort to get the poor together to collectively discuss and reflect upon their experiences of oppression, and, in exchange with development technicians, to promote critical self-awareness utilizing conscientization techniques. Upon gaining some experience with this dialogic process of collective self-discovery and critical reflection upon their circumstances, community members are invited to discuss what solutions to the problems they perceive are possible through collective action. Through these reflections, the poor move toward the formation of their own organizations, founded upon their own criteria, to pursue their own self-generated and prioritized plan of action. Once some project is defined and initiated, the people are encouraged to meet periodically, in order to review their experiences and to reflect upon their advances, their "failures," and their continuing or new needs. Such pauses becomes part of the regular rhythm of pedagogical praxis—a recurrence of action and reflection—as organization members formulate new plans of action based on their experience, revising (if necessary) their understandings and goals, to then move once again into the field of action. As members of the organization themselves become experienced in this process, they are encouraged to engage in outreach activities with other marginalized groups. This is a way to share and extend one's commitment, developing links to other communities that are similarly situated; and many researcher-activists additionally hope these links will gradually develop into federated forms of higher-level organization, and in the future link up with similarly formed federations.

The underlying premise of participatory action-research is that a "self-conscious" people are capable of incrementally, yet dynamically, transforming their environment through their own practice. Others may play a supportive role, but these cannot dominate the process. Participatory action-research claims that the means for liberating social change lie within those who are currently poor and oppressed; indeed, unlocking the capacity of critical reflection and action within the poor is the essential precondition for liberation. This is why the partnership cannot be one in which the poor passively accept the wisdom of outsiders; as silence and passivity characterize the very quintessence of the condition from which the poor need to escape. Knowledge becomes useful, empowering, precisely because the individual wins it, instead of it being given. The very process of coming to own an insight affirms the effective agency of the individual, and, in the same moment, authenticates the human worth and dignity to which he or she has been heretofore denied.

## TRANSFORMATION AND REVOLUTION

Despite the suggested affinity for promoting popular democratization as the practical foundation for social justice, participatory action-research at the grassroots level too often leaves us with a more ambiguous picture. Both sympathetic critics of participatory action-research and the accounts of some researcher-activists themselves reveal subtle forms of distrust in the self-chosen strategies of popular organizations. In practice, a tension between mutual democratic learning and the predetermined ends of action-researchers manifests itself in what some critics have identified as the latter's tendency toward "facipulation" (Pineda Pablos, 1995, p. 8). That is, the ostensible practice of an intellectual's facilitation of self-generated popular action, in reality simply masks subtle, but problematic, forms of manipulation, as activists use popular-sector organizations as the vehicle for self-defined political ends.

Activist-theorist Orlando Fals-Borda, for example, conceived of his mission as the "systematization" of local knowledge into a scientific knowledge, to be made available to the masses in their struggles for social transformation (Rahman, 1985, p. 117). Fals-Borda reported a great deal of success developing lines of cooperation with poor communities but much less success in encouraging popular-sector actors to take up his intellectual project. To his dismay, he conceded that members of his team found themselves transferring their own conception of a "popular science" to the people, instead of building it up from the people's own experience and viewed this effort as a failure:

> As historical materialism was almost an exclusive heritage of action researchers and committed intellectuals, they consequently had to diffuse it among the grass roots as an ideology. This led to the adoption as "special mediating categories" of what in a classic manner, are expounded upon as general Marxist postulates. In this manner, what was termed "popular science" had to be an ideological replica of certain general theses of historical materialism as developed in other contexts and social formations. *This is to say that groups fell victim to the worst historical form of dogmatism, that of "mimesis"* [italics added]. (Fals-Borda, 1979, p. 49)

In so advancing their own political agenda, pedagogical activists situate themselves in a nettlesome paradox. Freire alerted his audiences to the tendency revolutionary regimes exhibit in hardening into a "dominating bureaucracy," in which the impatient vanguard substitutes its priorities for the poor's (1970, p. 39, *passim*). For similar reasons, participatory action-research processes have tended to develop on the margins of formal political-institutional channels; practitioners have confessed an apprehension toward involvement with political parties and grand political projects, precisely because of what they have attributed to a crisis as much on the left as on the right. Anisur Rahman (1985, pp. 118–119), for example, argues that the contemporary historical experience with leftist vanguard movements in power has shown ascendant revolutionary regimes practicing new forms of domination, equally disempowering of the masses as their predecessors.

Although Freire argues that, in such a case, one can no longer authentically speak of liberation, he paradoxically fixed this vanguardist risk as an implicit component of social transformation. Specifically, *PO* sets forth a larger context to the utilization of his pedagogy, in which its present use is in anticipation of, and in concert with, a second stage of "revolutionary transformation" in which the people take over the machinery of the state:

> The pedagogy of the oppressed cannot be developed or practiced by the oppressors. It would be a contradiction in terms if the oppressors not only defended but actually implemented a liberating education. But if the implementation of a liberating education requires political power and the oppressed have none, how then is it possible to carry out the pedagogy of the oppressed prior to the revolution?. . . The pedagogy of the oppressed, as a humanist and libertarian pedagogy, has two distinct stages. In the first, the oppressed unveil the world of oppression and through praxis commit themselves to its transformation. In the second stage, in which the reality of oppression has already been transformed, this pedagogy ceases to belong to the oppressed and becomes a pedagogy of all people in the process of permanent liberation. (Freire, 1970, p. 36)

Here and elsewhere, Freire implied a more than metaphorical revolution, one which suggests, moreover, a statist political project as the necessary means to effectuate the process of liberation comprehensively. This discourse therein implies a structurally pre-ordained political path to the just society not much different from the one Marx laid out for a nascent capitalist Europe one century earlier. As such, it appears to be in tension with Freire's insistence on a mutually constructed theory and praxis of liberation with oppressed groups, to be determined by the emergent needs discovered within this partnership. How, then, is one to account for and resolve this internal paradox?

## PEDAGOGY OF THE OPPRESSED AS CONSCIENTIZATION: GENERATIVE THEMES FOR RELUCTANT DEMOCRATS

As articulated in the introduction, the direct audience for *PO* as text is not the oppressed themselves, but rather those professing a commitment to social justice and social transformation—namely the traditional Left. In engaging one's audience in this process of consciousness raising, the educator is required to help draw the audience into a process of critical reflection by first discovering the group's "generative themes" as the baseline for the dialogic encounter (Freire, 1970, pp. 68–105). These themes are the common elemental orienting concepts of one's social milieu, developed by people to understand the world around them; and once discovered, the educator and audience work together to initiate a self-generated new understanding of historical reality and one's place within it. This cognitive liberation is the beginning of a process of becoming a whole person who acts in concert with others to transform the world.

The above-described tension between theory and praxis within liberation pedagogy work should be seen, at least in part, as a function of the different audiences

Freire attempts to address simultaneously in his written work: that is, peasants and other historically marginalized groups who are the subjects to be reached through his method and the "committed intellectuals," for whom the method is intended as an entree into a truly progressive politics. As suggested, the surface text explication of the pedagogy of liberation is accomplished (at the level of subtext) through the actual employment of the method in Freire's effort to establish a dialogic encounter through the shared cultural idiom of Latin American Marxism. In explaining the centrality of Marxian class analysis in liberation theology, Philip Berryman suggests, similarly, that appealing to Marxism, especially in the 1960s and 1970s, was merely to speak in the vernacular. Indeed, Berryman (1987, p. 139) argues that it would been "irresponsible . . . not to deal with Marxism, since it is pervasive among Latin Americans who are concerned with social change. It is as much a part of the intellectual milieu as are psychological and therapeutic concepts in the U.S. middle class." In the same way, Freire, as educator, uses the generative themes embedded in the Marxian political repertoire as a means to assist those desirous of fighting for the poor, to come to the critical conclusion that they must therefore instead fight with the poor:

> To simply think *about* the people, as the dominators do, without any self-giving in that thought, to fail to think *with* the people, is a sure way to cease being *revolutionary* leaders. . . . In the revolutionary process there is only one way for the emerging leaders to achieve authenticity: they must "die," in order to be reborn through and with the oppressed. (Freire, 1970, pp. 113–114)

In Gramscian terms, this conversion may be seen as a strategic shift from the frontal assault on state power, or "war of maneuver," as in the 1959 Cuban revolution, to the long struggle to transform the world by working within civil society, as in a "war of position" (Gramsci, 1929–1935/1975, pp. 229–239). This less overtly contentious path to fundamental social change was to be premised on an alliance between workers, peasants, and traditional intellectuals in re-creating the world from the ground up. In contrast to Leninist notions of Party vanguardism, however, Gramsci's call for alliance was for more of a true partnership, as the building of a new social order would require the development and active participation of "organic intellectuals," leaders coming from within the ranks of the oppressed classes.[3] A war of position strategy is thus one that affirms a trust in the capacities of ordinary people to effectuate meaningful social change and also implies that, in the realm of ideas and in everyday struggles, a mass movement can force concessions from those in power. Gramsci, like Freire, thereby anticipated and theoretically prefigured subaltern class members as active participants in the making of history.

## CONSTRUCTING A FUTURE PRESENT UNDER THE WEIGHT OF HISTORY

My point regarding the dualism in *PO* is rather simple: I do not mean to suggest subterfuge on the part of Freire, nor deny the power of his insight. Yet, while successful in mobilizing and reorienting many activists to work with the poor, *PO*'s reliance on traditional Marxian categories and celebratory appeal to an ontology in the image of Ché to engage this dialogue has left a subtle, though powerful, imprint upon pedagogical activism and its relation to the organizations of the poor. The effect is subtle, perhaps, in the sense that it has not dampened the commitment of renovated leftists to a much more egalitarian political agenda. It has, nevertheless, marked these partnerships with a foundational mass mobilization vision of grand political strategizing predicated on a statist conception of politics.

By way of illustration, it may be useful to give an example of this political vision in one of its more subtle forms. In analyzing the Chilean popular organizations that developed in the wake of political and economic crises during the Pinochet regime, Philip Oxhorn argues that, while these groups represent a new form of political action and a powerful new collective identity, this "pattern" still only represents a limited phenomenon in terms of absolute numbers of member participation, as well as scope of influence:

> In order for these egalitarian and participatory patterns to begin to affect society at large, the specific organizations that embody them in the urban slums would somehow have to coalesce into a single, coherent *social movement* that can persist over time. (Oxhorn, 1995, p. 20)

Oxhorn here argues that, while popular groups may originate as a local or "territorially-based" phenomenon in the beginning stages of their development, to be politically meaningful or effective, they need to be able to aggregate into larger units in order to "functionally" represent the common needs and concerns of the popular sectors as a class. The underlying logic of this assumption rests upon a market metaphor of politics: political outcomes are the result of a pluralist numbers game in which, to win a party or group competes against others to demonstrate the power of its position through its numerical weight. As an ideal typical strategy, then, a group would seek to represent its interests as a unified pillar organization, along the lines of the labor movement. Thus, while mass mobilization strategy is congruent with the liberal notion that elected officials are ultimately accountable to citizens at the ballot box, and should therefore respect the desires of a large voting bloc, it also serves the traditional Marxist vision of constructing a universal class as the basis of a new society.

It appears, then, that even for those repositioned toward working for societal transformation within civil society, the shift has tended to be one more of strategic practice than of ontological praxis. Intellectual-activist converts appear to have been animated by the possibility of new means of struggle, while clinging to the same ultimate goal of capturing the state in order to effectuate societal liberation from a position of centralized control. This is more than a merely theoretical difference in emphasis, as there are at least two negative implications for the potential efficacy and sustainability of popular-sector organizations as a result of this vision. First, and perhaps most obvious, the vanguardist and revolutionary discourse utilized by Freire often served to invite the suspicion and fear of authoritarian elites and similarly continues to alienate some potential present-day allies. Historically, pronouncements of popular empowerment have had the effect of provoking political repression precisely because their articulation evoked the image of popular revolution, or at least the threat of "demand overload" on the fragile political system. Indeed, it was precisely this felt "threat from below" that served as the most common rationale for bureaucratic-authoritarian military intervention in South American politics in the 1960s and 1970s.[4] In the present, moreover, given participatory action-researchers' reticence to identify with traditional party activism, it is unclear how this strategy would figure into the newly democratizing political systems. In its advocacy of a "creeping" mass mobilization strategy, participatory action-research projects a discourse that expressly seeks to bring forth a new hegemonic culture, displacing existing politics with a nebulous something else. On this point, even sympathizers often (justifiably) take pause.

Beyond unnerving powerful nondemocratic opponents, a more fundamental problem emerges from an internal incongruency between intellectuals and the popular movement participants in this process. Contrary to the projected (ideological) ambitions of many activists, it has been found that participatory consciousness raising has tended to have a moderating influence on the nature of popular demands (Oxhorn, 1995, p. 296, *passim*), as was already anticipated by Freire at the time of writing *PO* (1970, pp. 17–18, *passim*). Popular sector actors appear much more concerned with "procedural," as opposed to "substantive," demands (Oxhorn, 1995, pp. 146–148, *passim*) and with promoting local autonomy and self-sufficiency, as opposed to asserting national political hegemony. Beyond the reaction of societal elites, then, the larger point is that participatory action-researchers' anxiety-causing image is based upon a misdescription of the popular politics that have tended to develop out of the mobilizations initiated through activist-community partnerships. Members of such organizations do not view their locally centered activity as a prepolitical development, but rather as part of a process only to be uncovered over time.

As Fals-Borda discovered, members of the popular classes are not drawn to the participatory action-research style of organizing for an implied promise of the direct possession of state power. Rather, groups respond with such enthusiasm to participatory organization training because of the truly novel sense of being considered as worthy, and capable of meaningful self-directed action (Huiskamp, 2000, pp. 407–416). Participants from marginalized communities tend to view the encounter as an opportunity to gain practical communication and organizing skills that will enable them to collectively pursue their own agenda of perceived needs. By way of contrast, the usual model of development programming from above asks nothing of members of the targeted community and, thus, usually ends up leaving little or no effect upon the lives of individuals or the general welfare. Participatory action-research's commitment to empowerment as democratization promises something beyond aid, and it has been this sense of deeper commitment by activists that has been the major factor in initiating interest and sustaining people's commitment to collective mobilization.

For example, in the case of *Bhoomi Sena,* a self-help movement in rural India, villagers had years of experience with paternalistic organizers, but the latter's "top-down" approach to organizing was unable to sustain the villagers' interest and commitment (Rahman, 1985, pp. 108–109).[5] When participatory action-researchers subsequently took a different tack, the training with the village created a general climate of invigorated engagement and revealed evidence of the village members internalizing a commitment to democratic and participatory collective action. Indeed, left on their own, community members expressed a desire to further decentralize the organizational structure initiated by technicians, and to introduce new mechanisms for greater power sharing to correct what they saw as a threat to the participatory element in their mobilization (Rahman, 1985, p. 111).

While technicians sometimes accede to these popular initiatives, they also often put a great deal of pressure on community members to maintain some organizational hierarchy, separating out a local "leadership cadre" to oversee community activity. This is done for the sake of efficiency—or with no particular justification at all. The reasons for creating this local vanguard are often never explained, but rather are seemingly taken as a universal article of faith. Thus, while participatory action-researchers' stated commitment to their own eventual superfluity (or at least tangency) to popular praxis is an advance from the old model of left activism, one cannot escape the fact that the reliance on a grassroots cadre to guide the people ultimately suggests a milder, though no less certain, distrust of the people. While an improvement over centralized control, it is a programmatic orthodoxy that hinges either on an idealized presumption of the inherent virtues of marginalized individuals—invulnerable to the temptations of hierarchy and exploitation[6]—or makes a considerable concession to expediency. The creation of a cadre, however, merely displaces people's alienation from their own effective agency to a different level.

Some of this bias toward hierarchical direction, no doubt, is a function of researchers' own experience of accomplishment in grassroots conscientization and organization-building, as assistance from outside the community, clearly, has been a crucial factor in shaping the ultimate outcome of successful processes of community empowerment. For even when the poor demonstrate a great deal of prior initiative and desire for proactive collective solutions to their problems, efforts prior to intellectual-community partnerships have often proved to be neither very effective nor very liberating. This observation, in turn, leads to the conclusion that popular organizations are limited in their effectiveness and meaningfulness by their limited geographic scope.

Indeed, even Francis Piven and Richard Cloward, the most vocal critics of the mass mobilization mindset of Left activists in the U.S. context, essentially accept this basic logic. Piven and Cloward (1977, pp. 1–40) argue that the mass mobilization strategy robs popular collective action of its most efficacious effect, which is "disruption," because organization (in service to a mass mobilization campaign) is not a political strategy that plays to the strengths of the poor. Their alternative prescription is to allow poor people's movements to create a sense of chaos, to be met by elite reform efforts to attempt to restore normalcy. What has been called "struggling to reform" (Tarrow, 1994), by this logic, may seem like a weak, or even accomodationist response to some; but it is held to be the best for which the poor may hope.

There are, however, two fundamental problems with the premises uniting proponents of both the mass mobilization and disruption models of popular activism. First, while paying attention to macrostructural conditions and barriers is an important part of any critical analysis pretending to anything beyond utopian idealism, one should also be cautious about letting structures speak for themselves. The participatory action-research goal to construct a "wider movement" is a goal imposed upon the experience from the intellectual side of the partnership, a constitutive marker in its discourse and method that frames all insight to be achieved by the poor.[7] There is a fine line between macrostructural investigation, on the one hand, and a tendentious historical determinism that undermines participatory action-research's ontological insight that reflective practice can structure its own opportunities. Second, and relatedly, it is one thing to argue that a strategy of national-level electoral political influence (at this moment in history at least) is not generally in the interests of local popular organizations. It is quite another to take the further—and logically unwarranted—step of ruling out localized forms of organization altogether. In sum, neither statists nor "disruptionists" ever truly consider the possibility that locally centered organization is an end in itself, and, as such, an equally important concern (i.e., in addition to the larger, national effect) in evaluating these popular political practices. Yet, it is precisely this distinction between the two parallel tracks of societal activity that is central to the self-understanding and intentional action of many popular sector organizations (cf. Oxhorn, 1995, p. 15, *passim*). And when not even considered, the synergistic implications of the effect of the local on the national cannot enter the debate.[8]

I argue, in sum, that Freire's original rhetorical framing in *PO,* and its subsequent consumption by would-be committed intellectuals, has been self-limiting in terms of the professed goal of catalyzing the poor's self-defined goals and self-generated forms of organization and concrete plans of action. Beyond critique, however, to suggest an alternative basis for the pedagogical process of liberation requires demonstrating the possibility of a defensible political project that is not predicated on a statist solution and concomitant mass mobilization strategy. In the final section, then, I highlight certain aspects of the engagement of researcher-technicians from the INCA-FAO Project—a joint pedagogical initiative between the United Nations Food and Agriculture Organization (FAO) and its Mexican government counterpart *Instituto Nacional de Capacitación Agrícola Rural* (National Rural Productivity Training Institute, or INCA RURAL)—with the *Asociación de Mujeres Campesinas de la Huasteca* (Association of Peasant Women of the Huasteca, or AMCHAC), in order to clarify my claims about the potential problems of pedagogical activism, but also to portray its greater promise. This will also serve to illustrate the argument made here regarding the importance of local democratization as an end in itself, and its defensibility as a distinct project.

## STATIST MASS MOBILIZATION VERSUS THE QUOTIDIAN UTOPIANISM OF THE LOCAL

The INCA-FAO Project was initiated in Mexico at the request of the Luis Echeverría (1970–1976) administration's larger *Proyecto de Capacitación y Organización para el Desarollo Rural* (Training and Organization Project for Rural Development, or PRODER), as part of the Mexican regime's "rediscovery of the peasant" (Grindle, 1981). INCA-FAO's general charge was to research and develop alternative rural training methodologies in order to support rural productive organizations (INCA-FAO, 1987b, pp. 1–3). Programmatically, technical teams were to work with both local-level communities and state agencies to help establish a more participatory dynamic in rural extension programs. In both instances, this was to encourage both greater efficiency and productivity in small-scale peasant agriculture, as well as achieve greater "social justice" for the peasant sector. INCA-FAO teams worked variously with regional federations of *ejidos* (peasant land cooperatives officially sanctioned by the Mexican state) in the states of Chihuahua, Oaxaca, and Sinaloa; with state food policy planning agencies at both the regional and national level; with the *Secretaría de Agricultura y Recursos Hidráulicos* (Ministry of Agriculture and Water Resources, or SARH); with the newly instituted *Banco Rural del Noreste* (Northeast Regional Rural Bank); with a regional association of urban cooperatives in Cuetzalan, Puebla; and with the loose association of locally based rural women's organizations in Tempoal, Veracruz. Five of the ten specific projects were enjoined with state administrators, and thus involved no direct grassroots work at all. Of the remaining five projects, three were with well-established regional *ejido* governance structures—part of the internal structure of the Mexican regime's official corporatist organization, the *Confederación Nacional Campesina* (National Peasants' Confederation, or CNC). This left only the association of urban cooperatives in Puebla and the loosely affiliated *Unidades Agrícolas e Industriales de la Mujer* (Women's Agricultural and Industrial Units, or UAIMs) in Tempoal as projects in which there was a significant element of direct grassroots work and participatory organization building.

In fact, it was only by accident that INCA-FAO came to work with the women's groups in 1984. INCA-FAO had originally established an agreement to work with *Unión de Ejidos Rosalina Ortega Juarez* (Union of Ejidos, or UE) in the municipal districts of Tempoal and neighboring El Higo (in a manner similar to their projects in Chihuahua, Oaxaca, and Sinaloa). The UE, however, cancelled its commitment because of internal disagreements over the nature of the goals of the project.[9] At that point, the UE president asked INCA-FAO officials if they would instead be willing to work with the newly-formed UAIMs, whose members had been experiencing organizational and funding difficulties (INCA-FAO, 1987a, p. 4). This turn of events was clearly advantageous to the UAIMs, and they welcomed the assistance at a difficult moment in their organizational development. The Tempoal project, nevertheless, turned out to be an equally profitable encounter for INCA-FAO.

Project coordinator Klaus Bethke later recalled the mutually revelatory nature of the partnership and was especially taken by his own initial experience with a conscientization exercise entitled, "A Day in the Life of a Woman" (INCA-FAO, 1987a, p. 230). Like most initial conscientization sessions, the purpose of the exercise was to promote both a sense of camaraderie among the women and to explore possible bases for a collective project (INCA-FAO, 1987b, p. 10).[10] In the exercise, the women broke down into small groups and filled out poster boards detailing their activities from when they rose in the morning until they lay down in bed at night. Coming back to discuss as a whole what they found in their small groups, the women and technicians were able to make a composite sketch of a typical day: five hours spent hand-milling *masa* and making tortillas for daily meals; three hours carrying water to the house for drinking, cooking, and bathing; two hours searching for firewood for use in cooking; two hours preparing and serving family meals (beyond making tortillas); two hours in miscellaneous tasks centered on childcare; one hour washing clothes; and two hours sewing, cleaning, washing dishes, and other miscellaneous chores. In sum, the women regularly worked seventeen-hour stints to complete their assigned domestic chores, which amounted to more than a double workday, without remuneration. This, of course, left them with little or no time for other activities, particularly the microenterprise projects they dreamed of initiating.

The lengthy and onerous nature of their domestic workload was certainly something the women had always been cognizant of in a general sense, but recounting its minutiae in this collective forum helped crystallize these dull facts into a greater insight about their lives. They very soon came to the conclusion that their first priority in practically addressing this problem was to secure funding for social-economic projects, e.g., electric or gas-powered corn mills and water pumps—which would lessen their most onerous and time-consuming domestic responsibilities and, thereby, free up time for other activities of their own choosing (INCA-FAO, 1987b, pp. 13–14).

From the perspective of the women participating in the workshops, this was something novel and animating. Equally important, however, was the reciprocal knowledge completion of the INCA-FAO team. As outsiders (and mostly men), Bethke explained, "this was an extraordinary moment of conscientization for us technicians, and forced us to reflect upon all our theories of development and emphasis on isolated [economic development] projects . . . learning that no such single project was capable of solving the women's problems" (INCA-FAO, 1987a, p. 230). It was in this group of women, in other words, that technicians were forced to encounter a perplexing and impenetrable "other." And in this confrontation with social realities disconnected from their standard intellectual experience and repertoire of action, there emerged a truly mutual process of enlightenment, and concomitant "liberation." To the benefit of all, it was clear that rural women were a class of "the oppressed" for which neither traditional Marxist nor developmentalist comprehensions had easy answers, no standard strategy of action to engage, nor any certain endpoint toward which to aim. Precisely because the women's perceptions of reality were disconnected from the preconceptions of the technicians, the latter were forced into a dislocating confrontation with their core assumptions.

In the AMCHAC women's vision of revolutionary social change, the locus of meaningful activity is centered in the individual UAIMs and communities. This is not to deny the importance of their commitment to the public intercessions the Association performs on the local, regional, national-state, and even international levels (Huiskamp, 2000, pp. 407–410). Still, the impetus for collective mobilization was to begin in the communities, and the radical utopian vision the women have for group action is premised on creating a dynamic and more self-sufficient space of living. Specifically, they seek to reclaim the community as a place where their children can live, learn, grow, and want to stay and where they themselves, their spouses, and children can work and prosper. They do not want to be dependencies of a clientelist state, but rather to establish the conditions that would allow them to contribute in and to national life from where they work.

While the AMCHAC microenterprise cooperatives necessarily work within the logic and constraints of the market system, their productive activities are informed by collectively formulated family, group, community, and gender concerns rather than an abstract logic of profit maximization. Their activities are primarily local and small in scale, but in small ways they change the boundaries and meanings of the system locally by virtue of their collective identity and collective action. The women possess a deep intuition that projects like these, which build the infrastructure of the community and social capital—networks of cooperation and collective self-sufficiency—are essential to their goal of saving, or re-creating, the *ejido* as a viable social and economic space. Members of the UAIMs are not oblivious to other problems in the community and the impact of larger social forces in undermining their meager existence on the margins of Mexican society. These concerns are what motivated them to engage in collective action in the first place and are also why they participated in regional forums seeking solutions to the changing opportunity structure with the state's fait accompli of *ejido* privatization under the Salinas de Gortari (1988–1994) regime. At the same time, however, the women also seem to instinctively realize that no community development is possible—nor worth the effort—without some larger social purpose beyond work: a sense of belonging, a sense of place.

This is the essence of the quotidian utopian vision elicited from a Freirian process: a patient, deliberative, reflective—and yet concrete and pragmatic—commitment to transformation. The AMCHAC women's work entails an ambitious revisioning of the fundamental bases of social, cultural, economic, and political life, especially, and precisely, given an objective appraisal of their resources, life experience, and "reasonable expectations," borne of historical and cultural memory. And yet, based on practical action, specifically on concrete steps taken toward the gradual accretion of small victories, the women continue working ever closer to the realization of their goals.

## CONCLUSIONS

The Tempoal project, in fact, had been nearly abandoned before it ever started, as few members of the INCA-FAO Project as a whole were interested in working with "a bunch of women."[11] Some of this reluctance may be imputed (correctly) to a general sexist dismissal. Still, a not insignificant explanation for this response was an ideological intuition making technicians aware that "rural housewives" are not the forbearers of the "universal historical class" and therefore not in sync with the politically committed Marxist intellectual's larger sense of purpose and goals. Given no prepackaged set of solutions to the "problems of women," especially rural women, the technicians who did come to work in Tempoal were forced to truly search for the UAIM members' generative themes, to listen to how the women understood the problematique of their reality and their place within it. They were forced to begin with the experiences and understanding of the women themselves, as opposed to their foreordained class interests. And from this less-mediated initial point, they had to work in concert with the women, working backwards toward the development of an organic political strategy that could meet the needs of an ongoing strategic practice.

This is strictly what each Freirian "partnership" should entail, flowing from the metatheoretical stances of Freirian pedagogy itself. Moreover, this should be fairly clear from participatory action-research's ontological and epistemological commitment to history's contingency, and its amenability to alteration through conscious and reflective collective action. Only if intellectuals are willing to critically reenter their own historical reality—the achievement they ask of the oppressed—is the negotiated exchange of knowledge capable of producing a democratic outcome. And unless it is a democratic outcome that is being sought, activists lose much of their essential moral justification. By virtue of this less-mediated encounter, the technicians perhaps went away with a somewhat more enlightened understanding of their own limits. It is clear, however, that the Tempoal project itself was allowed to develop along a much more unique trajectory than if, as initially planned, the technicians had worked with the women's male counterparts.

In reading PO as both pedagogical explication and pedagogical encounter, the argument is not that Freire necessarily perceived PO as the same type of dialogic encounter with reluctant leftists that characterized his work with illiterate peasants and urban workers. The point, rather, is that PO assumed this form in a de facto manner. Freire saw in Marx some potential for a knowledge to help perfect his own insights and moral commitments and to inform his practical and theoretical work (Freire, 1996, pp. 86–87). But whether for his own liberation (in concert with others), or more directly (if not fully self-consciously) to bring activists to a praxis which would enable them to pursue their own ontological mission (by helping others achieve to achieve liberation and social justice), the basic dialogic process of convergence is the same.

There are, then, at least two ways to evaluate the effects of Freire's dialogical conversion with Marx or Freire's Marxian (mainly Leninist) activist contemporaries.

The first is to declare that the resultant appropriation of Freirian pedagogy, informed by a dogmatic rhetoric of merely political revolution, was predetermined to fail in its objectives. That is, the pedagogical dynamics underwriting a successful grassroots encounter between committed educator and the poor, are quite different than those required to present one's case to someone with the same essential socioeconomic and cultural background. Utilizing the pedagogy of the oppressed in the latter instance, then, is not merely superfluous, but counterproductive. In addressing one's sociocultural peers, the circuitous route to knowledge exchange engaged in with the poor may actually hinder the intended audience's ability to reflectively reenter those understandings they take as second nature.

On the other hand, if Freire's PO had been written any other way, it might never have achieved the depth of resonance with its audience that it did; and thus we might not have ever witnessed the emergence of pedagogical practice as an avenue of committed sociopolitical activity in Latin America and elsewhere. Even for someone critical of the actual practice of participatory action-research, it is sufficiently clear on its face that an errant pedagogy of liberation is a welcome alternative to a self-conscious and unapologetic vanguardist politics—not to mention the status-quo enforcing practices of traditional development work and party politics. In other words, a second way of evaluating the results of Freire's discourse with the traditional Left in PO is to recognize it as part of an ongoing process of dialogic encounter. In this case, one committed to the goals of the process registers his reflection concerning the existence of an error and its source, submits the reflection for collective evaluation, and thereby moves the process along within the strictures of its organic processual rhythms.

This second interpretation calls for one to see paradoxes, or "tensions," as "fertile" points of discursive reflection "that can continue to inspire and energize our work" (Mallon, 1994, p. 1506). Siding with liberation pedagogy, then, is not merely a matter of choosing a second-best option. The ontological and epistemological premises underlying Freire's theoretical expositions and pedagogical work allow for—or rather demand—moments of reflective pause as a means of verifying or disproving the validity of one's knowledge and practical course of action. While the process of collective reflection provides "objective" bases for guiding action, these collective truths are necessarily held as conditional and contingent, something open to adjustment in light of emerging realities. Moreover, the implications for altering practical activity and theoretical understanding revealed within these "emerging realities" may be positive or negative (or perhaps more likely, both positive and negative) as a group's very successes will pose new challenges that mandate new strategic and tactical emphases. Indeed, if Freirian-inspired pedagogical work cannot expect such positive developments, the whole enterprise makes no sense.

Freirian-inspired praxis is not predicated upon easy access to mechanical, unchanging truths; indeed, it requires a constant questioning of its motives, assumptions, and activities to remain faithful to both its theoretical and political commitments. The encounter between AMCHAC and INCA-FAO is suggestive of

Freirian epistemological and ontological claims in their most profound sense: that is, in the ability of the emergent interests and practices of the poor to offer a rich, unconsidered model of democratic action and self-understanding that might never have otherwise emerged. The AMCHAC women are inspired by a vision of an altogether different world and yet one firmly anchored in the reality of this one. Their vision is utopian in its sense of shared optimism regarding the capacity of ordinary people to shape their world, but it is a confidence borne of their own experience in doing so. That they have committed themselves to a process of proactive change, rather than any specific endpoint, cannot be overemphasized. The idea of process gives one the hope that small steps can matter and the courage to engage oneself, as small steps are less alienating than grand visions of the future, marshaled into existence from above. Moreover, a commitment to process also leaves one open to the creative capacity of the process, of the collective energies of a people united by a cause, a reason, a social force, outside immediate and personal interests. It also cautions people not to settle for received, whole-cloth ideological visions, but rather to keep searching, a day at a time, for a better solution, a better life, in unison with others committed to the same goals of justice. It is precisely in this sense that the process itself is an end of action, as well as a means to specific ends. The collective commitment to this process facilitates and exercises virtuous human activity—the very realization of being human, of reclaiming one's ontological role as a social actor in history.

The matter of judging the relevancy, or "success," of such action cannot be justly posed as to whether it eradicates poverty, misery, and injustices of other stripes. What other real historical, political, or economic organizational principle has done so? What other option lurks on the horizon with such a promise? There may exist a whole range of strategies and opportunities to be seized in the pursuit of a more just and humane society, some perhaps capable of producing more immediate results and objectively greater degrees of social change. But even if these existed, and were politically feasible to implement, they could never substitute for these locally based endeavors, chosen and pursued by the people they are intended to effect.

*Notes*

1. In making this distinction, I borrow from Jonathan Fox's (1994) conceptualization of democratization as the gradual "erosion of authoritarian clientelism," and a greater respect for citizen rights, especially for citizen's "associational autonomy."

2. Like most dichotomizations, this is a false one. In "Education as the Practice of Freedom," Freire (1973, pp. 21–32) goes to some great lengths to develop an historical-structural account of the macrosociological, economic, and political evolution of the "colonized mentality" in Brazilian society, which he sees at the root of oppression and the "culture of silence." Moreover, Freire's actual account, like those historical accounts underlying the theory and praxis of kindred liberation theologians, draws quite liberally from dependency theory critiques floating around various Latin American intellectual circles at the

time. *Dependistas* Cardoso and Faletto (1969/1979), in turn, understood their work as necessarily having practical implications for concrete struggles of liberation. See also Leonard (1990) for a discussion of the "family resemblances" between dependency theory, Freirian pedagogy, and liberation theology.

3. For Gramsci's discussion of traditional versus "organic" intellectuals, see 1929–1935/1975, pp. 5–23, *passim*.

4. The use of the military metaphors in Gramsci's terminology of the "war of position" is likewise regrettable, as the terminology has often served to energize a conservative backlash to Gramscian theory. Regrettable, but additionally misleading, is the type of collective practice he envisions in a war of position, which has little to do with conventional guerrilla warfare; indeed, Gramsci considered the early Christians to be the most successful example of a counterhegemonic movement. (See McLellan, 1987, p. 114.)

5. For a discussion of other South Asian participatory action-research cases, see De Silva, Mehta, Rahman, and Wignaraja (1979) and Tandon (1980.)

6. See Ellis (1996) for a similar argument regarding the North American New Left's devolution into a manipulative vanguard politics. The difference between Ellis's argument and the one presented here is that Ellis (p. 147, *passim*) conflates what he demonstrates as the "romanticized vision of the poor" with the very possibility of a popular egalitarian politics.

7. This is not to deny that there are individuals and communities who do come to conclusions in line with participatory action-researchers' understanding of the natural trajectory of organization building and outreach. I concede, in other words, that some might come to pursue a mass mobilization strategy independent of the preconceptions of their technician partners. My point here—beyond empirical evidence from researchers' accounts themselves, and other sources, as to the reluctance these groups show to such a project—is that, given these intellectual predilections and the formative influence technicians have upon shaping the conscientization experience, it would be difficult to know if this were, in fact, an independent conclusion.

8. This issue is more fully considered in Huiskamp, 2000.

9. Klaus Bethke, personal communication, January 25, 1994.

10. Following Freirian insights, these mainly verbal and pictorial exercises were also a concession to the group members' skill bases, and the special requirements for working with illiterate and semiliterate communities.

11. A former INCA-FAO technician, personal communication, February 6, 1994.

## References

Almond, G., & Verba S. (1963). *The civic culture: Political attitudes and democracy in five nations*. Princeton, NJ: Princeton University Press.

Berryman, P. (1987). *Liberation theology: Essential facts about the revolutionary movement in Latin America—and beyond*. New York: Pantheon Press.

Bethke, K. M. (1989). *Rural development for and with women: The case of Tempoal, Veracruz*. (United Nations Development Fund for Women, internal report). Mexico: UNIFEM.

Cardoso, F. H., & Faletto, E. (1969/1979). *Dependency and development in Latin America*. Berkeley, CA: University of California Press.

De Silva, G. V. S., Mehta, N., Rahman, A., & Wignaraja, P. (1979). Bhoomi Sena: A struggle for people's power. *Development Dialogue, 2,* 3–70.

Ellis, R. J. (1996). Romancing the oppressed: The New Left and the left out. *The Review of Politics, 51*, 109–154.

Fals-Borda, O. (1979). Investigating reality in order to transform it. *Dialectical Anthropology, 4*, 33–56.

Fox, J. (1994). The difficult transition from clientelism to citizenship: Lessons from Mexico. *World Politics, 46*, 151–184.

Freire, P. (1970). *Pedagogy of the oppressed*. New York: Continuum.

Freire, P. (1973). *Education for critical consciousness*. New York: Continuum.

Freire, P. (1996). *Letters to Cristina: Reflections on my life and work*. New York: Routledge.

Gramsci, A. (1929–1935/1997). *Selections from the prison notebooks* (Q. Hoare & G. Nowell Smith, Eds. & Trans.). New York: International Publishers.

Grindle, M. S. (1981). *Official interpretations of rural underdevelopment: Mexico in the 1970s*. Working Papers in U.S.-Mexican Studies, 20. La Jolla, CA: Program in U.S.-Mexican Studies, University of California, San Diego.

Huiskamp, G. (2000). Identity politics and democratic transitions in Latin America: (Re)organizing women's strategic interests through community activism. *Theory and Society, 29*, 385–424.

INCA-FAO. (1987a). *Asesoria a organizaciones de mujeres campesinas en Temporal, Veracruz: experiencias y resultados*. Serie de publicaciones finales del PRODER, documento 5. México, D. F.: FAO/PRODER.

INCA-FAO. (1987b). *Desarollo rural y capacitación: una propuesta metodológico alternativa*. Tomos I & II. (México, D. F.: FAO Programas Educativas.

Leonard, S. T. (1990). *Critical theory in political practice*. Princeton, NJ: Princeton University Press.

Mallon, F. E. (1994). The promise and dilemma of subaltern studies: Perspectives from Latin American history. *The American Historical Review, 99*, 1491–1515.

McLellan, D. (1987). *Marxism and religion: A description and assessment of the Marxist critique of Christianity*. New York: Harper.

Oxhorn, P. D. (1995). *Organizing civil society: The popular sectors and the struggle for democracy in Chile*. University Park, PA: Penn State University Press.

Pineda Pablos, N. (1995). *The empowerment approach and community-based economic development: A critique*. Unpublished manuscript.

Piven, F. F., & Cloward, R. A. (1977). *Poor people's movements: Why they succeed, how they fail*. New York: Vintage Press.

Rahman, M. A. (1985). The theory and practice of participatory action research. In O. Fals-Borda (Ed.), *The challenge of social change*. London: Sage.

Shaull, R. (1970). Foreword. In P. Freire, *Pedagogy of the oppressed*. New York: Continuum.

Tandon, R. (1980). *Participatory research in Asia*. New Delhi: Centre for Continuing Education.

Tarrow, S. (1994). *Power in movement: Social movements, collective action and politics*. Cambridge: Cambridge University Press.

Weiler, K. (1996). Myths of Paulo Freire. *Educational Theory, 46*, 353–372.

*Jill L. Haunold*

# IDLE HANDS ARE THE DEVIL'S WORKSHOP: A HISTORY OF AMERICAN CHILD LABOR AND COMPULSORY EDUCATION; EMANCIPATION OR RECONSTITUTED OPPRESSION?

THE CARICATURE OF child labor in America has often been only that of the sensationalized and stereotypical, unkempt factory child or juvenile street "arab" (Riis, 1971). Photos and stories describing exploited and oppressed sweatshop children of the late nineteenth and early twentieth century are grim. The analysis of the historical data is often paternalistic in its view. However, an examination of the history of child labor set independently from other oppressed groups works to frame my argument that today's schools are an extension of this exploitation and act as tools of further oppression.

This chapter will focus on child labor's unique position in United States history. Giving children their own historical forum, based on their unique humanity rather than as a subcategory of other oppressed groups, provides a different lens from which to view today's schools and children. This may be one step toward abolishing current child oppression and exploitative practices. The history of child labor in its various settings and the complexity of the fight for child labor laws cast a critical light on the cultural and social aspects of how and in what ways we value or devalue children.

In order to set the stage for the arduous fight against child labor, there must first be an examination of the conditions under which children labored. Children in America labored in environments that simultaneously required their youthful vigor and made them old before their time. Children toiled in the southern cotton mills, northern glass factories, isolated coal mines and urban cigar box sweatshops. Young workers were street salespeople and produced such products as plastic flowers and decorative lace work on expensive shirts in their tenements as "home-work."

The history of American child labor is messy. There was no one child labor problem. The battles for laws to limit and regulate child labor were fought in fits and starts. The war against child labor was, at last, won not with unanimous agreement on child labor laws but through renewed institutionalization and enforcement of mandatory education.

Traditional culture, economic necessity, and religious values all contributed to the difficulty of the efforts to eradicate exploitative industrialized child labor practices. Adults were, and are still, ambivalent regarding child labor. Horatio Alger stories, popular at the turn of the century, have become American folktales of men who began to labor as boys and made their way to riches through honesty and hard work.

A common value held by the dominant culture regarding the poor was that "idleness, being the devil's workshop," would lead to a life of laziness and moral turpitude. Criminal pursuits would follow a youth filled with unguided play. This value is demonstrated even today by the carefully controlled leisure time of middle-class American children (Ferguson, 1999).

American industrialization had a new and caustic effect on working children. Girls and boys typically toiled at different types of work and work places (Byerly, 1986). However, the effect was the same. Their bodies and minds were numbed with pain, fear, and fatigue. They trudged, sleepwalking, to work twelve-hour days, six days a week. Often, children fell asleep in doorways, unable to make it home before they succumbed to the grip of exhaustion. The general narratives of children comprised stories of the harshness of life, each individual setting of which had its own specific horrors (Markham, 1969). Children filled the least-desirable, lowest-skilled, and thus lowest-paying jobs in America (Holleran, 1997). Southern millwork was one such job. The adults who worked the mills as children best describe their lives:

> My first job in the mill was terrible. . . . I didn't like it, it was too hard.
> But don't even bother asking what the air was like in the mill because you don't want me to get all riled up in telling you. But I've stood and wound, and you have to stand in one place for that, and the lint would be up over my ankles. . . . I used to have coughing spells, coughed 'til I spit blood, . . . . (Byerly, 1986, pp. 181–188)

> I was eleven and my sister was ten when we went to work in the mill. The girl that trained me was younger than that. I stayed with her, her a-learnin' me, for about two weeks, and I didn't get nothing for it. . . . We went in at six in the morning and got out at six at night. I worked two weeks and my first payday I drew $2.50. The biggest portion of the spinners was kids back then. . . . We'd go out there behind the mill at the warehouse and us girls we'd build us a little playhouse until they'd whistle for us. . . . Just nothing but children. (Byerly, 1986, pp. 62–65)

Considering the number of child workers employed, there were few large-scale events at the time calling public attention to the issue, and, notably, when adults did express any concern, it was over the cheap labor of children taking jobs away from adult males rather than interest in the children themselves. Mother Jones and her March of the Mill Children was one exception (Jones, 1925/1969).

Thirteen percent of the labor force unemployed from the Kensington Mill workers strike in 1903 were children, many under the age of ten. Mother Jones decided that, in order to gain public sympathy for the plight of these children, the public had to see for themselves what laboring had given them. She marched through the country and cities with her little army of mill children, these "stooped little things, round shouldered and skinny, some with their hands off, some with the thumb missing, some with their fingers off at the knuckle" (Jones, 1925/1969, p. 70). Mother Jones' goal was to make the lives of those children the personal problem of every man, woman, and child along the way.

Second to the mills in the numbers of children used, glass factories employed almost 8,000 children, mostly boys, or 13 percent of all glass workers in the country. In temperatures of up to 140 degrees, boys ran twenty-two miles in eight hours, all the while inhaling the microscopic solidified chards of glass. Often imprisoned by barbed wire fences, most of the boys became accomplished drinkers by the time they reached the age of ten (Markham, 1969).

Dark coal mines pressed 24,000 children into service legally, with an additional ten thousand working illegally. Most of these boys worked in what was described as a "bumping river of black fog" called the "breakers" (Markham, 1914/1969, pp. 106–107). In the mines, the chances of surviving a serious accident were even less than other settings (Trattner, 1970).

Box factories employed numerous children because of the nature of the work. The box-making industry was unique in that the machinery was relatively light and required a minimum of construction requirements for the buildings that housed them. Workers and machinery were stacked upon one another, floor after floor, in buildings so unsafe that many collapsed with all inside (Markham, 1914/1969). The boxes made were primarily those used to contain cigars. The machines used in this industry stamped out the material with large cutters. Typically, girls were employed to glue the fancy paper covering onto the boxes. Only small human hands possessed the dexterity required for this work. The glue, whose smell permeated the air in these factories, hardened quickly to the girl's hands in winter.

One of the advantages of child labor for employers was that, on their own, children rarely organized or struck, as they were not formally a part of any union. An exception to this was the mining industry. When the adult men struck, the boys would follow them off the job since they were often father and son.

An example of spontaneous striking of children was cited in Edwin Markham's 1914 *Children in Bondage*. While Markham does not give a date, he cites an incident when 200 box-factory girls struck during the Christmas season in New York because, at the height of the season, the master had declared a wage cut of 10 percent, reducing their wages to thirty-five cents a week. The mini-strikers organized others not to return to work for the reduction in pay. Children were stationed to maintain a watch on the street to keep scab children away from the factories. The strike was broken by the city police and fifty-seven small girls were arrested. That the girls were easily downed is not surprising. What is perhaps significant is that this strike was entirely organized by young girls in an industry where there were no adults.

Much of child labor was not visible to the typical middle class American. Most people did not see into the mills, box factories, and coal mines. But one form of child labor was observed daily by millions of Americans: street workers, the vendors, and "newsies." The common experience of interacting daily with street children may well have served to extend the existence of child street labor. In addition, there was a romantic notion that these boy workers were supporting their poor widowed mothers.

When Edward Clopper conducted a study for his 1912 doctoral dissertation, he found that, in actuality, out of a total of 1,752 Cincinnati newsboys, only 239 were fatherless, and 1,432 still lived with both parents. Clopper did the first research on children who were sent to work early and their later criminality. Prior to his work, it was commonly held that working hard as a youngster helped the child gain necessary skills for becoming a successful adult. Norms regarding busy and industrious children were strong however, and even Clopper believed that there was good work and bad work for children. "Developmental work is desirable for children, injurious work is not. Proper work is disciplinary and educational. One is necessary to the building of physique and character, the other must be suppressed" (Clopper, 1912/1970, p. 116). As a member of the Child Labor Committee, Clopper would go on to produce many pamphlets on the ills of child labor.

As early as 1832, child labor had come under attack. At a convention that year, the New England Association of Farmers, Mechanics, and Other Workingmen condemned industrialized child labor because children needed healthy recreation and mental activity. Labor unions, noting that competition in the form of cheap child labor depressed wage scales, sought to obtain a shorter workday for children and later a minimum age for children to begin work (Trattner, 1970). By 1836, Massachusetts led the states in barring children under fifteen from jobs in manufacturing unless they had attended school for as least three of the preceding twelve months. The leading maxim was that the best child labor law was compulsory schooling (Kauffman, 1992).

The number of children working continued to increase as the trade unions' motives were publicly called into question. By 1900, an increase of over one million children in the labor force over the preceding thirty years brought the figure to almost two million child laborers, not including working farm children and children working illegally. As public awareness of the issues of child labor became heightened through the pen and photographs of Jacob Riis and Lewis Hine, social workers and other citizens began demanding government intervention.

The National Child Labor Committee was founded on 15 April, 1904, at Carnegie Hall in New York. Charter members included populist and racist South Carolina senator "Pitchfork" Ben Tillman, and Episcopal clergyman Edgar Gardner Murphy of Arkansas. These, along with others, and perhaps not coincidentally, rich northerners such as John D. Rockefeller, J. P. Morgan, and Andrew Carnegie, began the paternalistic style that was to mark the committee's actions throughout its existence. The committee first viewed its mission as one of prevention and public education, not one of promoting legislation. In this way, the original members of the committee believed that they would influence local initiatives and sentiment toward the abolition of child labor. The place where they would launch their initial attack would be the coal mines of Pennsylvania (Trattner, 1970).

The Committee began its crusade by publishing and circulating reports of investigations of child labor in the mines. Mine operators took a dim view of this activity. Pennsylvania's commissioner of labor blamed child carelessness or irresponsibility for most mine accidents. The remedy was the release of all such errant youth. These declarations could not indefinitely hide the conditions under which these children were working. By 1911 the sixteen-year-old minimum working-age limit was extended to Pennsylvania's bituminous mines (Trattner, 1970).

The Committee next attacked the glass factories. The glass industry argued that child labor was a necessity to its survival. In their paternal benevolence, glass manufacturers sought to provide the required early training to the young so they would be good glass workers as adults. The life expectancy for these good adult glass workers was forty-one. Public sentiment at the time was still on the side of the glass manufacturers. Business continued to win against any attempt to abolish child labor or improve conditions in these factories (Trattner, 1970).

A parallel fight was being fought in the southern cotton mills. The southern mill employers held an advantage in that they typically owned the homes in which the employees lived. Parents and children in mill towns would, not surprisingly, come out publicly in favor of the mill's child labor practices. Continuing to argue that restricting child labor would leave poor widows no means of support, the southern mill owners successfully fought any child labor reforms for several years to come.

It was during these early battles that the committee began to put forth the argument that the most detrimental effect of child labor was that it kept children from receiving an education. Alexander McKelway, a founding member of the committee and a white supremacist, put forth an ostensibly moral argument. He contended that educating White youngsters was essential to the maintenance of the prosperity of American Whites, suggesting the import of non-Whites to work in the southern mills (Trattner, 1970).

The committee's focus remained on local laws and public awareness, but in 1903 it began gathering support for a federal children's bureau. As the committee continued compiling evidence that related child labor to deviance, public support rose for the cause. State laws regulating the labor of children had passed by 1910 but remained minimal and largely unenforced.

The committee came to believe that only federal legislation would be effective. With continued stiff opposition from the South, the committee began to fight on the federal level. Reformers began looking toward a revision of the Constitution. It was mid-1924 before Congress finally approved the proposed amendment.

This action revived strength in the opposition. A vicious propaganda attack was launched. The National Association of Manufacturers, supported by Catholic leaders and farmers, made their priority the defeat of the amendment in 1924. They believed that they had already lost their liquor and women by constitutional amendment and would soon lose their children if they did not fight. Working-class Catholics argued that this was simply another ploy by which government sought to take the right of parents to educate and guide their children as they saw fit, and they too fought to put it down. This propaganda campaign increased the public perception that "spinsters, lesbians, and Reds" were leading the push for the child labor amendment (Kauffman, 1992, p. 153). The Child Labor Amendment was defeated in Massachusetts on November 4, 1924.

The numbers of poor children in industrialized early nineteenth-century America were increasing. It was progressive educators, however, who turned the tide of the child labor battle. Compulsory education became widely viewed as the best road to eradicating child labor. Education reformers saw public education as of little use if parents in poverty were allowed a choice in sending their children to the factories instead of school. First, cities like New York, and then states, began to do what was viewed as usurping parental rights, requiring that they send their elementary-age youngsters to school instead of to work. Middle-class educators viewed public education, and enforced schooling, as a solution and these children's only hope.

The apparently altruistic motive of free education for all became clouded with more sinister motives. It was widely and successfully argued that providing for the maintenance of the democratic experiment required that the populace be educated to some extent. However, the eradication of some of the undesirable characteristics of the foreign-born was also seen as a justifiable reason for a mass inoculation of Americanized education. For native-born Protestants, this meant the purging and prevention of foreign languages, culture, and religions. Compulsory attendance laws had been in place in twenty-four states since the 1880s. Though rarely enforced, the precedent had been established, and it was not a difficult leap to enforcement as public sentiment rose in support of doing so (Butts, 1978).

The labor unions breathed new life into the amendment in 1933. During the Depression, children were seen once again as taking jobs from men. Every state had compulsory school attendance laws for youths up to age fourteen. The Codes of Fair Competition adopted by businesses in 1933 dealt the final blow to child labor practices. Between July and December 1933, more than 150,000 children between the ages of sixteen and eighteen were removed from industry or hazardous occupations. In 1934 these codes were extended to paperboys in large cities (Kauffman, 1992).

The Child Labor Amendment did not survive the 1930s and, surprisingly, neither did child labor in the same way that it had thrived during the previous fifty years. Trattner (1970) attributes this success to slow but peaceful reform. I contend that, while the grim and sensational aspects of child labor have been mitigated, there was essentially little in the way of reform, and children have not been emancipated.

The history of child labor demonstrates that children's marginalization is so institutionalized and complete that their invisibility and lack of consideration in their own history is unnoticed and considered a demonstration of peaceful change, a change that took over one hundred years to move in what is, arguably, a circle.

How childhood is conceptualized by a society reflexively creates who children are; this in turn recreates society's conceptualization. Children are a powerless group. Their powerlessness is not limited to their size. The powerlessness of children is by definition. Children hold a subordinate position and are restricted in every sense in which they can participate in society. As demonstrated by the events of child labor history, two million workers were afforded no voice in their lives, were essentially slaves, and have gone unnoticed in their relative absence from their own history.

Aristotle contemplated the effect slavery had on humanness. Slavery, he said, makes people less human because they are unable to make choices, deliberate, or exercise control over their lives. As such, the most effective way to motivate slaves is to offer them freedom as a prize sometime in the future (Ciulla, 2000). The freedom "carrot" that children have always been promised is adulthood.

The failure of adults to clearly conceptualize children as more than objects will continually lead to their confused and inadequate admittance to humanity. The consistent portrayal of children as passive objects and victims of influences, unable and unwilling to resist is ironic given the historic evidence to the contrary. Very young children held down jobs, acted responsibly toward family, and acted collectively. At the same time that their humanity was ignored, children were demonstrating their own agency.

The common belief that children are simply not competent to know what is best for them persists. This perception stems from the adultcentric and developmental view that childhood is simply a stage in becoming a competent adult (Mason & Steadman, 1996). Adults define humanity as the state of adulthood. Therefore, children are in the process of becoming human. This not-quite-fully-human argument has been utilized as the rationalization for atrocities to marginalized groups throughout history. Child labor reform arguments reflected the Darwinian view that that which did not kill the children, simply made them stronger, in effect, culling out the weak and leaving only the strongest to become adults and reproduce. Children are developable.

The Oxford English Dictionary defines the word "develop" as "to unwrap, disentangle, to rid free or to unfold." As a constructivist, portions of this definition are intuitively appealing to me. However, it is the "disentangle and to rid" portion of the definition for development that continues to be used as a tool of oppression, with childhood considered an unpleasant, yet repairable, stage. The implication is that we have arrived when we grab the brass ring of adulthood. The realization of the lie and the Sisyphus-like reality of adulthood is a terrifying awakening.

American pygmalionism and capitalism have created schools whose purpose has become to build the new ideal American worker. In addition to acting as a labor force reservoir and dam, training the child for work is the business of schools. The implication of the student-as-worker model for the young prototype employee is that the only aim of education is to get a high-paying job and that the only role worth playing is that of the adult worker. Once the values of the oppressors are adopted, only one identity is of perceived value (Freire, 1972).

Children have been used as fuel for the economic fire, first as workers, then as potential workers, and now, in perhaps their most important role, as consumers. Young workers have money to spend; adolescent consumers are a boon to the economy. Schools have taken seriously their role in educating for consumerism and capitalism. School boards and administrators have negotiated lucrative vending and advertising contracts. Schools receive goods in trade for advertising and point with pride to their students who punch a time clock as evidence that they are fulfilling their obligation to produce good citizens.

Critical educators have correctly challenged this practice. Henry Giroux recently questioned what is becoming an all-out attack on youth in his piece, "At War Against the Young: Corporate Culture, Schooling and Politics of 'Zero Tolerance'" (Giroux, 2000). As critical thinkers, it is time for us to begin to define critically and put forth a serious theory of ageism. I use the term as it is defined in the Oxford English Dictionary: "Prejudice or discrimination against people on the grounds of age; age discrimination."

Nonwestern cultures have viewed children as "little people," quite a different metaphor than the common American term "little monsters." Childhood is a social construct and not biologically founded. Parallels can be drawn between past views of women as subordinates and those of children, based on biology versus a social paradigm.

If we accept our goal as the emancipation of all living beings, perhaps we must begin with the emancipation of young humans. If we are to emancipate the young, the critical discourse about youth and school must include that of children as an oppressed group.

The point to be made through the preceding historical account and analysis is that, in the crusade to abolish child labor, a new and perhaps more insidiously dangerous socially constructed conceptualization of childhood was created. Two million child laborers worked responsibly in conditions that no human should have to endure. However, they lived their human lives individually and communally, fought for what they believed in, and died. Children were then forced into compulsory institutionalization without a vote by racist paternalistic males in a system of "zero tolerance" where for seven hours a day they are, as Michele Foucault noted, "observed" and must request permission to go to the bathroom (Foucault, 1970). Children in schools are herded, guarded, watched, tested, and developed.

Because children and adults in the poverty of industrialized America were unarguably working in abominable conditions, the motives and methods of those fighting to remove children from these conditions have garnered little serious critical consideration and dialogue. It is my contention that these assumptions about childhood are the foundations of today's schools, and that left undeconstructed, these foundations are essentially still in operation and actively oppressing children. In failing to critically examine these oppressive and socially unjust underlying assumptions, views, and practices of those whom history has held up as the champions of the abolition of child labor, we have simply removed the young from one form of tyranny to another.

## References

Butts, R. F. (1978). *Public education in the United States*. New York: Holt, Rinehart and Winston.

Byerly, V. (1986). *Hard times cotton mill girls*. Ithaca: ILR Press, New York State School of Industrial and Labor Relations, Cornell University.

Ciulla, J. B. (2000). *The working life: The promise and betrayal of modern work*. New York: Times Books.

Clopper, E. N. (1921/1970). *Child labor in city streets*. Introduction by Louis A. Romano. New York: Garrett Press.

Ferguson, A. (1999, July 12). Inside the crazy culture of kids sports. *Time Magazine, 52*–60.

Foucault, M. (1977). Discipline and punish: The birth of the prison. Harmondsworth: Penguin.

Freire, P. (1968/1972). *Pedagogy of the oppressed* (M. B. Ramos, Trans.). New York: Herder & Herder.

Giroux, H. (2000, May/June). At war against the young: Corporate culture, schooling and politics of "zero tolerance." *Against the Current, 86*, 17–21.

Holleran, P. M. (1997, fall). Family income and child labor in Carolina cotton mills. *Social Science History, 21* (3), 287–320.

Jones, Mother. (1925/1969). *Autobiography of Mother Jones*. New York: Arno.

Kauffman, B. (1992). The child labor amendment debate of the 1920s; Or Catholics and mugwumps and farmers. *The Journal of Libertarian Studies, 10* (2), 139–169.

Markham. E. (1914/1969). *Children in bondage*. New York: Arno.

Mason, J. & Steadman, B. (1996). The significance of the conceptualization of childhood for promoting children's contributions to child protection policy. http://www.aifs.org.au/external/institute/afrcpapers/mason.html

Riis, J. (1971). *How the other half lives: Studies among the tenements of New York*. New York: Dover. (Original work published 1901.)

Trattner, W. I. (1970). *Crusade for the children: A history of the National Child Labor Committee and child labor reform in America*. Chicago: Quadrangle Books.

Williams, T. T. (1994). *Pieces of white shell*. Albuquerque: University of New Mexico Press.

*Ricky Lee Allen*

# WAKE UP, NEO: WHITE IDENTITY, HEGEMONY, AND CONSCIOUSNESS IN *THE MATRIX*

*THE MATRIX* IS a critically acclaimed film that has achieved cyber-cult status since its release in 1999. As evidenced by the scholarly attention to *The Matrix* (e.g., Zizek, 1999), there are critical theorists who are excited about the way that the directors, Andy and Larry Wachowski, allow us to experience reality as it is seen through the likes of Jean Baudrillard and Marshall McLuhan. The Wachowskis brilliantly use images of silencing, hegemony, consciousness, identity transformation, and counterhegemony to represent life in a repressive regime.

However, beyond traditional critical theory concepts, there are other systems of imagery than can be seen from ideological paradigms that are generally not considered to be members of the critical pedagogy community. For example, populist Christians argue for seeing the movie as a parable of the Second Coming of Christ. In contrast, Black nationalists contend that the movie is another example of white supremacy in that Neo, the main protagonist, represents a white Jesus who liberates the Black characters of the movie rather than depicting the Black characters as their own savior. Looking at the film through the lens of critical whiteness studies, the film reasserts the centrality of white authority when it shows Neo's white body as the only one that escapes the social structures of oppression. What follows are a polysemiotic analysis of the film and a furthering of the dialogue on what counts as "critical pedagogy."

## A CRITICAL THEORY INTERPRETATION

There are a few key concepts that occur frequently in the writings of critical theorists. Through these concepts, the discourses of critical theorists have described particular mechanisms within the capitalist system that both produce and reproduce social inequality. As students of critical theory, the Wachowskis constructed both plot and imagery from its concepts

## ALIENATION

The main character, played by Keanu Reeves, lives a double life. By day, he is Thomas Anderson, a white, middle-class corporate employee writing code for Metacortex, a major software firm. By night, he is Neo, a slightly Gothic computer hacker. One of his hacking activities involves keeping tabs on the famous hackers, Trinity and Morpheus. One night, Neo receives an unsolicited message on his computer screen that says he should "follow the white rabbit," an allusion to *Alice in Wonderland*. An instant later, he hears a knock on the door. He opens the door to find a group of young Goths who have dropped by to "buy some code." It just so happens that there is a woman in the group with a white rabbit tattooed on her shoulder. Following the directions from his computer, he goes with the Goths to an S&M club. At the club, he meets Trinity, a slightly androgynous white woman, whom he quickly recognizes as the famous hacker that he has been reading about on the internet. In their first dialogue, we learn of Neo's alienated existence when Trinity whispers in his ear. She tells him that she knows why he is a loner and hacker, and she does so in a way that suggests that she is driven to find the answer to the question, "What is the matrix?" It is Neo's drive to understand this question that frames his desire to meet Morpheus, whom Neo believes will give him the answer to his question. Trinity knows that Neo can see deep contradictions in how he lives trapped within the restrictions of a corporate world.

Trinity's words reveal that she understands Neo's state of psychological conflict. She knows that he can see deep contradictions in how he lives trapped within the restrictions of a corporate world. Neo earns a living by constructing software for Metacortex, but he spends his nights deconstructing that same global network of code, trying to unravel the web that he himself has helped to create. Neo struggles to reconcile his two selves, the rebellious computer hacker and the dutiful corporate employee. Rather than continue with the contradictions, he seeks out in his own haphazard way other hackers, such as Trinity, not realizing that his virtual activities would lead to an actual face-to-face meeting. Trinity provides a powerful sense of direction for someone like Neo. Having been through the process of alienation and finding a new identity, she knows exactly what to say to him in order to have him connect with her on an affective level. Even though he just met her, he willingly follows her on a journey that takes him away from the intellectual and moral morgue that is Metacortex. In this scene, the Wachowskis establish her as Neo's guide on a journey into a realm where his felt contradictions are ultimately resolved.

However, this journey of discovery does not begin right away. Instead, Neo lingers for a while longer in the corporate world. The morning after his meeting with Trinity, he arrives late for work. His boss, Mr. Rhinehart, reprimands Neo for his tardiness. The scene is set in a very executive-looking office with a panoramic view of a generic metropolitan downtown area. Mr. Rhinehart tells him that he needs to follow the rules, be a team player, and fulfill his corporate function. With all the coldness of someone who seems completely oblivious to the experience of alienation, Mr. Rhineheart calmly laments the necessity of unquestioned compliance with company morals. Exhibiting the kind of reasoning one finds in a totalitarian regime, he says, "If one employee has a problem, then the company has a problem." In other words, if one employee does not think and behave in the ways dictated by the company, then the management will see that employee as a threat to the value and stability of the company. In a funny yet powerful moment of filmmaking, a pair of window washers clean Mr. Rhinehart's windows from a scaffold positioned outside. During the exchange between Neo and Mr. Rhinehart, the window washers make noises with their squeegees that can best be described as the high-rise equivalent of running one's fingernails across a chalkboard. These irritating sounds are suggestive of the psychological trauma Neo endures during his boss's lecture and, for that matter, on a daily basis in the corporate culture of Metacortex. Thus, Neo's alienation, that is, his feeling of being constructed as an outsider or an alien to a dominant culture, is grounded in his interactions with corporate managers like Mr. Rhineheart. His alienation, at least as presented by the Wachowskis, is an emerging class-consciousness of his Othered position within the hierarchies of high-tech capitalism. As far as I can tell, this is the only scene that the Wachowskis offer as an explanation as to why Neo feels conflicted about his corporate life. Through the critical theory lens, the rest of the film deals primarily with how he resolves his (class) identity crisis.

## HEGEMONY

Hegemony is a social condition in which relationships of domination and subordination are not overtly imposed from above, but are part of consensual cultural and institutional practices of both the dominant and the subordinate (Freire, 1970/1993; McLaren, 1994). In a system of hegemony, complicity with the cultural and institutional norms of everyday life produce subtle, yet devastating, effects for the oppressed. Hegemony creates a type of consciousness among many of the oppressed that either blinds them to the reality of their own oppression or paralyzes them to the possibility of organizing against the structures of oppression (Freire, 1970/1993).

Hegemony is a common theme in *The Matrix*. There are many references in the film to the masses living out their daily lives blinded by their false sense of reality. Adding a science fiction twist to a critical theory critique of high-tech capitalism, the Wachowskis represent reality as a nightmarish tale of evolution gone terribly wrong. From Morpheus, we learn the history of humankind's fall from the top of the evolutionary ladder. In this postapocalyptic world, all life, including humans, is ruled by a master race of robotic beings. These robotic beings evolved out of the efforts of high-tech capitalists to produce "artificial intelligence." Unfortunately, the robotic beings, as evolutionary descendants of humans, were programmed with a trait that humans themselves had almost perfected before their demise: the keen capacity to exploit other humans. The humans tried everything to stop the robots from achieving global supremacy. For instance, the humans scorched the skies in an attempt to deprive the machines of the solar energy that they needed to fuel their bodies. The robotic beings responded by evolving the ability to use the bio-electricity that is naturally found in human bodies. They learned to "farm" humans in enormous, biotechnical fields. Rather than relying upon the sun, robotic beings simply drop by the human farm to get a new human-powered battery pack to insert into their mechanical bodies. Of course, the irony is that humans have spent much of their history trying to find fuel for their machines. Now, in this new, post-human world, *they are the fuel* for their machines.

In the human fields, the bodies of humans are grown inside of biomechanical wombs, which eventually serve as fuel cells. At the same time, the minds of these humans are under the illusion that they are living as normal citizens in the "real world" of the late twentieth century. Since they are not able to physically leave the womb, they dream that they are freely moving about the world, never realizing their horrific predicament of enslavement. The dreams serve the purpose of keeping their bodies stationary and docile within the womb, unable to act against their oppressors. In this state, their bodies have no possibility for radical agency. Thus, as this representation of entombed and unconscious humans suggests, one way that hegemony operates is in its ability to deny humans real knowledge of how their bodies are located within social and historical hierarchies. If oppressed people gain true knowledge of how their bodies are situated in the world, then they might be more likely to take action to change their situation. Instead, what we see in *The Matrix* is that false images of reality help to construct modes of thought and behavior that maintain the status quo—a status quo that, if the oppressed, and possibly even the oppressor, were directly confronted with it, would likely be nauseating and traumatizing. Agents Smith, Johnson, and Brown, the primary antagonists, represent those who actively surveil the hegemony of the matrix and guarantee that few see reality for what it is. Meanwhile, the humans dream their way through a living death inside a necrophilic womb that provides both an umbilical cord for their false sense of self and a coffin for their humanity.

## SILENCING

One method of maintaining hegemony is by silencing those voices that seriously challenge the validity of the hegemonic view of the world. Silencing works to deny alienated Others access to critical discourses and collective agency. The Wachowskis present the process of silencing through at least two visual metaphors. The first is when Agents Smith, Johnson, and Brown apprehend Neo and take him to what looks like an interrogation room at a police station. Agent Smith conducts the inter-rogation and forces Neo to choose between Thomas Anderson, his corporate self, and Neo, his hacker self. Refusing to answer, Neo defiantly gives Agent Smith the middle finger. The agents respond by making Neo's lips seal shut, rendering him un-able to speak. At this point in the film, Neo becomes more than an isolated and indi-vidualistic hacker. He is close to participating in the collective agency of the resis-tance movement and has already spoken to its key leaders, Trinity and Morpheus. In this scene, Neo learns that those who monitor the normative order will vigorously defend it against any verbal or physical attacks on its legitimacy (Freire, 1970/1993).

The second visual metaphor that depicts silencing occurs when the machines called "sentinels" surveil the underground tunnels where the Nebuchadnezzar (the resist-ance movement's spaceship) travels. Although the tunnels are usually a good place to hide from the machines, the crew continuously watches for the squid-like sentinels who patrol the inner world of the tunnels. Like a mechanical death squad, the senti-nels are looking to catch and kill human resistors. The crew of the Nebuchadnezzar has learned that they can avoid the wrath of the sentinels by being silent; the sentinels only attack when they hear the voices of the resistance. In critical theory terms, the sentinels represent the silencing behavior of those who are not critical of hegemony and not conscious of their role as oppressors (or, as the oppressed who represents the oppressor). Within the territory of the oppressor, such as the borderworld of the tunnels, being silent is one way to avoid confrontation. This kind of avoidance is not always optimal, because it means that hegemony will persist. However, in the context of the film, the avoidance fits because battles are chosen within the scope of a larger movement. Besides, the sentinels would kill them if they speak. So, the implication is that, in some cases, silence is purely a means of survival within a brutal regime, and a contingent tactic within an organized resistance and/or revolution.

## CONSCIOUSNESS

In critical theory, consciousness describes a state of mind that acts upon an awareness of the circumstances and mechanisms of oppression. In contrast, false consciousness is a "negative" state of mind that is oblivious to how hegemony causes blindness to oppression. It is characterized by a disjuncture between one's imagined view of the world and the real conditions of social relations; a person with false consciousness lives inside of the map, and not the territory. In part, *The Matrix* is a story about Neo's coming to consciousness of the objective conditions of the matrix (Lloyd, 1999). He gains an awareness of the ideological blindnesses that the matrix has created in his and other's perceptions of reality. The theme of consciousness is deep-ened through frequent use of related terms such as "the dreamworld" and "virtual re-ality," both of which stand for environments that are conducive to the construction of false consciousness. In the discourse of critical theory, to be "living in a dream-world" is to be unaware of the everyday conditions that have been produced and re-produced by oppressive systems of hegemony, such as capitalism. Neo's realization that humans are not comfortable, normal, middle-class citizens, but are instead slaves to technology and capitalism is, in the criticalist view, the central epiphany of the movie and is one of the main messages directed at the viewing audience.

## IDENTITY TRANSFORMATION

When people lack a critical understanding of their reality, apprehending it in frag-ments which they do not perceive as interacting constituent elements of the whole, they cannot truly know that reality. To truly know it, they would have to reverse their starting point: they would need to have a total vision of the context in order subse-quently to separate and isolate its constituent elements and by means of this analysis achieve a clearer perception of the whole. (Freire, 1970/1993, p. 85)

One of the more dramatic sequences in *The Matrix* depicts Neo's birth into a new identity, or a new state of being. The new identity that he emerges with is one that is conscious and critical of the whole that has been created. This part of the story begins when Neo meets Morpheus, the leader of the resistance movement, for the first time. Morpheus offers Neo two pills. The blue one will maintain his false consciousness about the state of humankind; the red one will show him the reality that is. Neo swallows the red pill and prepares for his trip into reality. While he sits in a chair waiting for the pill to take effect, he sees his reflection in the mir-rored wall. The mirror metaphor represents, as it often has in Western philosophy, an examination of both an individual self and a group self. This critical self-examination occurs when society reflects back an image that does not match the image that your were expecting. In this instance, Neo enters his trip into reality with a fragmented or alienated sense of self; that is, his understanding of himself differs from what others are telling him about who he really is. He is unsure of his identity, his purpose, and his place in the world. As he gets closer to his encounter with reality, his image in the mirror turns from fragmented to whole, a foreshad-owing of the clearer perception of reality that he will gain on his journey. At this point, the camera view literally goes down Neo's throat in a symbolic rendering of the reconnection of the mind-body split that he has been experiencing. This be-gins the journey of achieving a true (or less false) sense of self (Kuhlmann, 2000) and a more humanized and alive state of being (Freire, 1970/1993).

Once consciously situated and awake in the real, post-human world, Neo emerges from his artificial, necrophilic womb. Looking like a baby who has ges-tated for thirty years, his body is smooth and hairless; yet he is a full-grown man. He has multiple black cables attached to his back that have served to placate both his body and mind. Restrained by these cables, he struggles to rise out of the pink and viscous amniotic fluid and manages a horrified glimpse out at the sea of pods filled with human bodies. As he tries to get his bearings, a machine that surveils the human fields, a farmer of sorts, notices that he is conscious, that his mind and body are reconnected and able to see reality. Realizing that he will no longer be satisfied with lying silently in the womb, the machine grabs him by the neck, and the many cords are released from his body. The final cord to go is the large plug inserted in the back of his head, an obvious symbol of hegemonic thought control. The machine pulls out this plug, and Neo's body is literally flushed into a sewer that drains the fields of human waste. What this scene suggests is that Neo's new consciousness inhabits a social identity, a culturally recognizable state of being, which is perceived as antithetical to the maintenance of the matrix. The mere acts of standing and seeing mark him as a threat. In other words, seeing and accepting reality for what it is has as a cost that the person with this critical consciousness will now be identified as an Other. In this case, Neo used to imagine that he was a normal part of society. Once he learned that this normalcy was complicitous with society's dysfunction, he was identified as the dysfunctional one. The lesson learned is how power operates through hegemony. One learns that you can remain safe and comfortable in your artificial womb by remaining silent.

## COUNTERHEGEMONY

Gladly, the Wachowskis avoid the fatal flaw that most directors make when telling stories about heroes in pursuit of justice and social change. They do not depict Neo's quest as that of an isolated individual toiling in complete anonymity against all odds. Instead, they effectively show how those in the resistance movement help him to actualize his new, revolutionary self.

> We can legitimately say that in the process of oppression, someone oppresses someone else; we cannot say that in the process of revolution someone liberates someone else, nor yet that someone liberates himself, but rather that human beings in communion liberate each other. (Freire, 1970/1993, p. 114)

After rescuing Neo from the sewers of the human fields and taking him to the Nebuchadnezzar, the members of the resistance movement educate him on the discourses and actions that they have developed over time in their revolution. The counterhegemony process that the Wachowskis show us is focused on a reconstruction of Neo's understanding of himself, others, and the world. This educational process is consistent with that described by critical pedagogists.

> Conversion to the people requires a profound rebirth. Those who undergo it must take on a new form of existence; they can no longer remain as they were. Only through comradeship with the oppressed can the converts understand their characteristic ways of living and behaving, which in diverse moments reflect the structure of domination. (Freire, 1970/1993, p. 43)

Neo's reeducation begins with the assistance of Tank, a human who was born free of the matrix in the human-controlled city of Zion. Given that he never lived inside of the illusionary world of a biotechnical womb, Tank symbolizes the noncolonized of the oppressed. In the initial phases of Neo's reeducation, Tank, as teacher, downloads software program after software program into Neo's cerebral cortex through a skewer-like plug inserted into the base of Neo's head. Each program that is downloaded into Neo's brain contains the information and survival skills that he will need to fight the surveillers of the matrix, particularly the agents. In this pedagogical scene, software is a metaphor for the linguistic and ideological structuring of consciousness. Since software is coded in language, it represents the linguistic systems of humans that form their conceptual and ideological systems. These are the systems that shape human perception and structure consciousness. Thus, if one obtains new software, the result should be new types of thought, awarenesses, and actions. The reeducation of Neo is suggestive of critical education pedagogies that explicitly challenge the hegemony found in those with colonized and colonizing mentalities. The struggle for a critical consciousness is waged through discursive engagements with those who have been decolonized, or never were colonized (Freire, 1970/1993). Much like installing new software on a computer, new ideologies are learned in the critical education process that provides discursive strategies to resist hegemony while also enabling the further transformation of others who are yet to be decolonized.

The notion of agency constructed by the Wachowskis is unique in that it links the cyberculture metaphors of hacking and system failure. Those who hack against the matrix are those who exhibit an oppositional form of agency. Those who do not hack are those who stay within the illusion of the matrix and exhibit a conformist type of agency. Many pivotal moments in the film focus on the choices Neo makes about hacking against the matrix. He makes minor choices early on in the film by choosing to do small-time hacking from his apartment and selling code (the equivalent of being a drug dealer). But later in the film, he must make choices that stand to influence the future of the resistance movement. One common theme the Wachowskis address is how Neo's choices are reasoned through his understanding of fate. In critical theory, a belief in fate can be seen as a problematic acceptance of oppression. For instance, when the oppressed see their circumstances as the product of fate, they most likely will not organize to change those systems that oppress them (Freire, 1970/1993). Seemingly unable to participate in a state of critical agency, they exist in a psychological condition called *fatalism,* which is marked by hopelessness for a more humanizing world (Freire, 1970/1993). Critical theory and critical pedagogy are discourses that strive to work against fatalism. They argue that the oppressed and their allies can choose against fate and create actions of resistance, rather than accepting the judgment rendered by oppression.

This tension between critical agency and fatalism provides the context for a key turn in Neo's development as The Chosen One. At one point in the film, Morpheus is taken hostage by the agents and faces a certain death. Instead of allowing Morpheus to die as a martyr for the cause of the resistance, Neo decides to go against what appears to be fate and attempts to save Morpheus. His newly found ability to choose against fate is influenced by his decoding of the words spoken to him by the Oracle. She said to him that he would remember that he does not believe in fate. Driven by a profound sense of optimism, Neo, along with Trinity, saves Morpheus and his legacy as The Chosen One takes on larger than life dimensions.

## THE CHOSEN ONE?

Many of the conceptual elements common to critical theory are exemplified in *The Matrix*. However, there is an aspect of the movie that escapes a critical theory lens: Why is there a preoccupation with whether Neo is "The Chosen One"? In the criticalist tradition, the idea of an individual hero like Neo, an oppressor who rises to lead the oppressed, would likely be subverted to the power of a collective insurgency by the oppressed themselves (Freire, 1970/1993; Miller, 2000). If the Wachowskis were constructing their film solely on the backs of critical theorists, then this is an unlikely turn in the plot. Noted critical theorist Slavoj Zizek (1999) states that the film is "like the proverbial painting of God which seems always to stare at you, from wherever you look at it: practically every theoretical orientation seems to recognize itself in it" (¶ 1). That is why it is also important to look at other realms of interpretation in order to more fully decipher the messages of *The Matrix*.

## A POPULIST CHRISTIAN INTERPRETATION

The populist Christian interpretation focuses on the depiction of Neo as The Chosen One. In this view, the film represents a deep and vital message about the current condition of the Christian faith. In fact, just looking at the list of names chosen for the characters tells us that the Wachowskis systematically relied upon Christian theology in constructing the narrative. For example, the name "Neo" is religiously significant. Jesus Christ is the savior figure of the Christian faith. The name "Christ" has a Hebrew root that means the "anointed one," or, put another way, the "chosen one" (Tharps, 1999). So, Christ was the chosen one who saved humankind from its sins, much as Neo saved humankind from its self-imposed enslavement in technology. "Neo" is an anagram for "one." Additionally, the term "neo" means "new," or, in other words, he is "the new one" or "the Second Coming" of Christ that is talked about in populist Christian discourse. In the first scene that we see Neo, a redheaded, Gothic-looking man even refers to Neo as his "own personal Jesus Christ" (Schuchardt, n.d.). Further along in the film, there is more direct confirmation of the Second Coming parable. In a conversation with Neo, Morpheus alludes to Jesus when he says that there was once a man born inside of the matrix who "freed the first of us and taught us the truth." After the death of this man, an oracle claimed that a second man would come to free the rest. Morpheus reveals that he has spent his life looking for this second man, The Chosen One. Morpheus' behavior towards Neo suggests that Morpheus believes that Neo is The Chosen One. The implication is that the man who was born inside the matrix was Jesus. Also, Morpheus is telling us how he has committed himself to finding the new savior, the Second Coming. His last sentence implies that he believes that Neo is this new savior, The Chosen One.

Moving to other characters, the name "Trinity" in Christian theology refers to the father, son, and Holy Ghost, who are represented in the film by Morpheus,

Neo, and Trinity respectively. The spaceship of the resistance movement is called the "Nebuchadnezzar." Nebuchadnezzar was the Babylonian king who searched for the meanings of his dreams. Morpheus, the Greek god of dreams, is the name of the leader who runs the Nebuchadnezzar (Hussain, 2000; Tharps, 1999). Also, Morpheus is like John the Baptist in that he spends his life searching for a chosen savior (Harvey, 1999). The members of the resistance visit an oracle to have their dreams interpreted. Not so obvious by name, but by his function in the plot, is Cipher. He is a Judas character, a traitor, who chooses the evil of the matrix and betrays Morpheus. Cipher makes his "deal with the devil" over a steak dinner. Additionally, there are frequent references to a city of free humans called "Zion." Christian theology says that Zion is the place where true believers will reside after human sin leads to the apocalypse of the earth (Hussain, 2000; Tharps, 1999). And, finally, there is a character named Apoc, which is short for "apocalypse."

Moving deeper into the plot, Neo's birth into a new consciousness and identity represents something different to the populist Christian writers. As I have suggested, his coming to understand himself as The Chosen One is a story about the Second Coming of Christ, which, according to Christian theology, is to take place after the apocalypse. To understand this view, some of the key events of the film that I have already discussed through a criticalist view need to be reinterpreted. For instance, Neo's change of consciousness, in a populist Christian perspective, is read as his realization that all humans are slaves to sin, as opposed to high-tech, global capitalism. We are all born into a world of inescapable, original sin, or so the logic goes. Neo's birth scene represents his salvation and acceptance of Christianity. As he stands covered in the sticky, pink substrate of the biomechanical womb, he is "born again"—maybe, this is another reason why he is called Neo.

The members of the resistance movement wonder among themselves whether Neo is The Chosen One. They seem to have only vague notions of what a person must do in order to be The Chosen One. However, they do seem to believe that, for Neo to prove his chosenness, he must face the forces of evil, represented by the agents, mano a mano in a battle to the death. He passes this test in a resurrection scene that symbolizes to populist Christians the Second Coming. In this scene, we see Neo die after the agents shoot him several times in the chest. There is blood on the wall, and the heart monitor that is connected to his real body, back on the Nebuchadnezzar, flatlines. Seconds later, he is miraculously resurrected by Trinity. When Trinity sees that his material body has died, she leans over him, tells him that she loves him, and kisses him on the mouth. Then, back in the world of the matrix, he rises from the dead, having been saved by the love of a "true believer" who embodies the Holy Spirit. Additionally, his mind and body are no longer the same as they were before his death. He is transformed into an infinite, supernatural being with none of the apparent limitations of human weaknesses or flaws (Schuchardt, n.d.). He is no longer inside of and constrained by the matrix. Instead, he is above and beyond it. He achieves a state of omnipotent knowledge that makes the illusions of the matrix transparent. This new vision enables him to see straight through to the raw, green codes that encrypt the digital images of the matrix. The agents fire bullets at him, but the bullets stop and drop to the floor because he is no longer a being restricted by the human dimensions of the matrix's rules. In one last great refusal to abide by the authority of the matrix, he leaps inside of the body of Agent Smith, splitting him open in a symbolic dismantling of the technological world and worldview that has alienated humans from being true believers of Christianity. Neo thus stands as a model of both saved and savior. He is presented to us as a religious reference point in that if *he* can be saved, then so can those in the audience. In the final scene, he even flies through the air and veers sharply towards the audience, hinting that he is going to "do" them just as he "did" Agent Smith (Schuchardt, n.d.).

The Wachowskis purposefully borrowed from Christianity to establish much of the plot. Warner Brothers even released the film on Easter weekend of the last year of the millennium (Schuchardt, n.d.). One aspect that I find interesting about the use of Christian parable is that there is a moral link to critical theory. Since critical theory emanates from Western culture, Western critical theorists cannot completely escape the Christian-dominant culture in which they have been immersed. Rather than trying to completely detach themselves from Christianity, some criticalists choose to embrace the more progressive moral and political endeavors commonly associated with some forms of Christianity, such as alleviating human suffering, siding with the disempowered, and transforming the world through a deep love for all humanity (Freire, 1970/1993). If we look at the words of Paulo Freire, arguably one of the most important figures in the history of critical education, we see numerous connections between critical theory and the more radical elements of Christian theology. Freire believed that the oppressor is blind to the effects of oppression and can only be changed through the love and humanity of the oppressed (Freire, 1970/1993). In *The Matrix,* the resurrection scene represents not just Neo's transformation into a savior, but also his transformation into a leader who works for and with the oppressed. As a white male, Neo is the oppressor in relation to Trinity, who symbolizes the oppressed in a patriarchal context. Trinity expresses her critical agency in the form of love towards an oppressor figure whom she sees as having the potential to be a revolutionary leader.

> [I]n the revolutionary process there is only one way for the emerging leaders to achieve authenticity: they must "die," in order to be reborn through and with the oppressed. (Freire, 1970/1993, p. 113–114)

Through Trinity's love and the help of the other crewmembers, Neo dies and is reborn as a revolutionary figure who fights against the oppression caused directly by the dehumanizing force of the robotic beings, and indirectly by the human society that built them. Neo dies in the mortal sense, but he also dies in the sense that he puts to rest his former hegemonic self to become one with the resistance movement. He relinquishes any ties to his former privileged identity, and is reborn as one who is only for the revolution, a revolution whose goal is to liberate all humans from enslavement to oppression.

However, the links that Paulo Freire enables us to make between critical theory and progressive Christianity should not be confused with what the populist Christians believe. The populist Christian perspective contains serious omissions of the real issues of oppression that exist in contemporary society. What troubles me the most are the blindnesses, particularly color-blindnesses, represented in this view. It is difficult for me to understand how anyone can watch this movie and avoid issues of race, class, and gender. Yet, none of the writings that I have encountered from the populist Christian perspective on *The Matrix* discussed any topics related to identity and power. If we are to accept the assumption of the populist Christian view, then the crew of the Nebuchadnezzar embodies those who are saved and will make it to Zion. Thus, they stand as models of the saved. However, closer examination reveals a strange inconsistency. If we look at the crewmembers, they do not reflect the demographics of the populist Christian population. The crew of the Nebuchadnezzar consists of three Black men, one woman named "Switch" (implying that she is bisexual), and a slightly androgynous white female who doesn't exactly look like the type to vote Republican. Are we supposed to believe that populist Christians think that these are the children of Zion? Something tells me that the answer is "No." In fact, these are the kinds of people that the populist Christians so often denigrate or label as "sinners" for their so-called "social deviancy." It seems as though, in this interpretation, there is a complete disregard of, or obliviousness to, the mind-body split that so much of the film tries to counter. The writers appear to believe that the production, organization, and stratification of bodies do not matter for their larger Christian project of salvation. It is at this juncture that I believe many criticalists, even those who see themselves in alliance with Christianity, would most likely part company with populist Christian ideology. After all, criticalists tend to believe that it is their moral and spiritual duty to unseam those systems and perspectives that perpetuate oppression, such as white racism, patriarchy, and capitalism.

The criticalists have their critics as well when it comes to issues of identity. For example, many scholars working in the field of ethnic studies find that critical theorists and critical pedagogists do not talk in specific terms about identity. In other words, rather than merely mentioning that racism is a problem, these scholars argue that racial systems of oppression, such as whiteness, need to be thoroughly examined and extensively critiqued. Next, I move on to those who look more closely at the film through an emphasis on Black racial identity and a critique of white racism.

## A BLACK NATIONALIST INTERPRETATION

In the Black nationalist perspective, the problem of whiteness is a central focus of critique. From this view, the film is not a story of empowerment, but one of potential disempowerment. However, before discussing this concern, I will first present those parts of the film that positively coincide with a Black nationalist ideology. First of all, the Wachowskis do depict people of color in a fight against white power. One author commented that the agents look like representatives "of a Republican administration" (Thomas, 1999). The film appears to pay attention to who is actually oppressed in the U.S. and having that reflected in the crew of the Nebuchadnezzar. Blacks, women, bisexuals, and non-macho men were all portrayed as comrades in a collective struggle. Second, two Black characters, Morpheus and the Oracle, are represented as being incredibly wise. As a working-class, older, Black woman, the Oracle is the person most valued by the resistance movement for her insights into knowledge, truth, and destiny. By depicting the Oracle as a Black woman, the Wachowskis imply through imagery that the root of wisdom, both past and present, is African and female in origin. Also, it coincides with more recent trends in radical philosophy that contend that a systematic search for knowledge should begin with the wisdom of poor women of color since they have the most experience with navigating multiple forms of oppression (Collins, 1990). The Oracle is particularly sagacious when it comes to questions of identity. On the wall of her kitchen, she has a plaque written in Latin that says "know thyself." This is an allusion to the identity development process that Neo is going through. The Oracle's words and demeanor make it seem as though she is very experienced when it comes to developing a positive sense of self. Her social location as an African American woman gives the scene legitimacy.

> Who are better prepared than the oppressed to understand the terrible significance of an oppressive society? Who suffer the effects of oppression more than the oppressed? Who can better understand the necessity of liberation? (Freire, 1970/1993, p. 27)

In contrast to the Oracle, Neo, as a middle-class white man, struggles throughout the film in his quest to "know thyself." Neo's struggle is understandable since he has not experienced the dehumanization of racial oppression, save for his trouble with the corporate culture of Metacortex.

Despite its positive aspects, the film ultimately offers a disempowering message. As previously discussed, Neo is presented as a Jesus figure. However, it is important to contextualize him as a *white* Jesus figure. Much like the European representation of Jesus Christ as white instead of Black, the Wachowskis construct Neo as another white savior figure who is the liberator of Blacks (and the other oppressed peoples of the Nebuchadnezzar). They argue that the white Jesus figure has historically been used to limit the agency of Blacks in their attempts to be self-determined and free themselves rather than waiting for whites to change. Neo is the only one who achieves the status of The Chosen One and gains superhuman powers to fight the agents. Given the ongoing condition of colonization that exists in the U.S. and around the world, the psychological effect can be that the oppressed learn that they need to look to the oppressor for salvation. Paulo Freire (1970/1993) argues that the best situation is for the oppressed to believe in their own empowerment:

> Although the situation of oppression is a dehumanized and dehumanizing totality affecting both the oppressors and those whom they oppress, it is the latter who must, from their stifled humanity, wage for both the struggle for a fuller humanity;

the oppressor, who is himself dehumanized because he dehumanizes others, is unable to lead this struggle. (p. 29)

To add insult to injury, the Wachowskis even show Neo gaining most of his transformative knowledge from direct, dialogical interactions with Black people. Three Black characters, Morpheus, Tank, and the Oracle, are the primary teachers in Neo's reeducation process. Yet, their radical knowledge elevates Neo to a status beyond their own. S. F. Thomas (1999) points out that this is similar to what happened in the emergence of European civilization. He argues that "civilization" was brought to Europe through the Moorish occupation of Europe during the period between the eighth and fifteenth centuries. The film alludes to this fact when Agent Smith tells a shackled Morpheus that "your civilization is now our civilization," thus indexing the co-optation of Moorish culture and the subsequent enslavement of Africans under global white supremacy (Thomas, 1999).

I take the Black nationalist perspective as a personal and collective challenge to see what I, as a white person, and other whites can do to be allies in the fight against hegemony, particularly white racist hegemony, without simultaneously playing out a problematic savior role on center stage. Towards this end, I do have a minor, sympathetic critique of the Black nationalist view. In contrast to what I typically see in the discourse of Black nationalists, I still have hope for the possibility that more whites can come to an understanding of the realities of white racism without having to be the hero figure for people of color. Neo represents the oppressor on the crew of the Nebuchadnezzar in that he is a middle-class, white man. It is unlikely that a member of the oppressor group, such as Neo, will be the primary liberator of the oppressed. Instead, he can only liberate himself and other oppressors in dialogical collaboration with the oppressed. What this means is that I do believe that a white person can be a savior, but of other whites in terms of helping them transform their white consciousness towards one that works for the abolition of whiteness and white supremacy.

## A CRITICAL WHITENESS STUDIES INTERPRETATION

All three of the interpretive frames that I have presented thus far are limited and limiting. Each deals with the problem of whiteness in ways that leave untheorized the role of white radicalism in the abolition of white racism (see Giroux, 1997). The criticalist view pays no specific attention to whiteness. The populist Christian view does not even see whiteness. And, the Black nationalist perspective is mainly focused on the self-determination of Blacks and not on the transformation of whites. Given these limitations, what type of interpretation of *The Matrix* would provide critical insights into the chronic presence of whiteness and the possibilities for white transformation?

In the final analysis, the film overprivileges the imagery of class alienation to explain Neo's quest for a new identity; the idea that Neo's original alienation stems from his place of work is unsatisfying. As previously discussed, the only time the

Wachowskis give us a glimpse of Neo's alienation is when his boss at Metacortex lectures him. Without doubt, Neo's experiences at Metacortex were alienating. However, I do not believe that this was the only time in his life when he noticed the presence of alienation, whether it was his own or someone else's. Moreover, I do not believe that the other crew members of the Nebuchadnezzar were alienated by their jobs. I say this because class is not suggested as their primary oppression. For the other crew members, the Wachowskis' imagery suggests that patriarchy alienates the white woman, heterosexualism alienates the bisexual, and whiteness alienates the Black men. I believe this because I was given no scenes that showed their reasons for questioning the matrix. Instead, we are to assume that they are obviously alienated by the matrix because we can readily see their marginalized identities. In contrast, Neo is a white, middle-class man with a well-paying job. If the scene with his boss were not included, would anyone understand why a white, middle-class man, who represents power and privilege, would feel alienated?

Like any white man, or, for that matter, any human, Neo's experiences with the social world are situated within multiple and intersecting systems of oppression, not just within the singular totality of capitalism (Collins, 1990). For example, a person can be the oppressed within a capitalist system of oppression, yet also be the oppressor within a racial system of oppression. Both occur simultaneously, even though the person is standing in the same place and in the same body. Such is the case for white men who are not members of the capitalist class. Neo is a low-tier, middle-class worker who is exploited for his labor to make money for the capitalist owners of Metacortex. However, he is also a white person and thus a member of a racial group. His experience in the world is necessarily racial as much as it is classed. What if we read his alienation at work as a realization that the rules of corporatization are morally wrong because they systematically privilege white bodies to the exclusion of people of color? In other words, Neo's growing criticism of the system may stem from his awareness that corporations are a way for whites to unfairly control and exploit the people and property that they colonized during European imperialism (Mills, 1997). Why couldn't his emerging outrage at white racism, as structured in the public and private sectors, be the reason for his identity crisis?

Would Neo really need to go through all that he goes through in the movie only to realize his own oppression, that is, class oppression? It would seem to me that his class alienation would be more readily apparent to him and more easily understood by him, but the film depicts a tremendous and complex struggle waged in cooperation with Blacks and women. Throughout the film, he is looking for an understanding of the world for which he does not yet have a discourse. This means that he is looking for something that is very difficult for him to comprehend and embrace. Whites, particularly white men, are much more likely than people of color are to explain the world in terms of a singular notion of social class (Collins, 1990). Those in the position of oppressor, like white men, tend to have a very difficult time expressing and challenging their oppressor experiences (McIntosh, 1997; Tatum, 1997). Neo may be oppressed within the corporate world, but he is simultaneously the oppressor within other totalities such as race. Because white men do not have to worry about their race in the culture of work, they seem to have a difficult time talking about their whiteness. They typically have little understanding of the social construction of whiteness, white thoughts, and white bodies (Tatum, 1997). They do not have to think about their racial position in the world because they can move about the territories of whiteness as a so-called normal human being. After all, it is quite significant that it is Neo, a white man, who is the main protagonist of the movie. He is the white figure who is juxtaposed against Morpheus, the main Black figure, and the rest of the crew of the Nebuchadnezzar. For me, there are constant reminders that it is a white body going through this transformation. His white identity and the larger totality of whiteness, as a broad social context, must be vital to the meaning of the film and more central to any interpretations of it.

A critique of *The Matrix* from a critical whiteness studies perspective means that I must first give the Wachowskis the benefit of the doubt. For the sake of argument, let's say that the Wachowskis intended for Neo's whiteness to be important to the story. I say "for the sake of argument" because I do not feel that the Wachowskis borrowed from critical whiteness studies, as I am positive that they did from critical theory and Christian theology. And, let's say that they intended to weave in a critique of whiteness and a method for intervening in white racism. Given these starting points, what critique of whiteness does the film have to offer? And, what are the limitations of this critique for an anti-racist pedagogy? There are at least two obvious allusions to whiteness. The first occurs in the scene where we first see Neo. One of the people he sells code to says, "What's the matter, Neo? You look a little whiter than usual." Another of the more obvious allusions to whiteness occurs when the agents take Morpheus hostage. During a fight between Morpheus and Agent Smith, Morpheus tells Agent Smith, "You all look the same to me." His humorous comment is a sarcastic turn of the white supremacist notion that all people within a particular group of color look the same. However, I am not sure whether Morpheus means that all whites look the same or that all agents look the same, since all of the agents are white. Nevertheless, what I am sure of is that the consequences of his statement are far from humorous. Immediately following his comment, a defenseless Morpheus is brutally beaten by a group of police armed with nightsticks in a sickening image taken straight out of the Rodney King case in Los Angeles. Subsequently, he is placed in a makeshift pair of handcuffs that have a resemblance to shackles, thus conjuring up dual notions of African Americans' enslaved past and imprisoned present. This scene demonstrates how the repressive forces of whiteness react and have reacted to Black resistance. Therefore, Agent Smith represents the most repressive and reactionary elements of the white community.

In contrast to Agent Smith, Neo is developed into a figure of the more antiracist elements of the white community. One scene that provides a path into an examination of Neo's whiteness is his rebirth. In contrast to the other perspectives on his rebirth that I have already discussed, a critical whiteness studies perspective suggests that Neo's rebirth represents his new awareness of the social location of his white body. Many U.S. whites in the post-Civil Rights era believe that they are perceived by people of color as kind, nice, caring, and benevolent people (Gallagher, 1997). They imagine that their bodies are understood as signposts of positive social and moral behavior. White folks' investment in a distorted view of themselves becomes apparent when people of color (and possibly some whites) criticize whites for their lack of positive social and moral behavior. Their criticism is not just a challenge to white thought, but it is also a challenge to the meaning of the white body. In their defense of the image of a benign white body, whites dismiss and denigrate the words of people of color who contest this false image. Imagine the complexity that goes into developing a discourse that is rooted in a distorted dream rather than the real world. The result is a white discourse that continually denies the existence and importance of oppression, particularly oppression other than that based on economic class. In Neo's rebirth, he is born again, this time to understand how his membership in the white community has blinded him to the realities of oppressions that do not fit neatly into a class-dominated analysis. He learns that his commitments to his whiteness have meant dehumanization and slavery for all humankind. His horrifying white body is born visible and exposed for all to see, including himself. He looks out across the human fields to see all of those who are not yet conscious of whiteness and must be awakened. But as often happens within the white community, other whites quickly dispose of a white person who gains consciousness of white privilege; most whites will not tolerate a white person who challenges their collective unearned status. Thus, Neo is flushed into the sewer of marginality, marked as a traitor to his race.

Another scene that needs to be reexamined is Neo's fight with Agent Smith. This scene represents opposing factions within the white community, the racist and the anti-racist, fighting for control of the white image. Neo's whiteness is meaningful in that he is meant to be The Chosen One to fight the "racist whites" represented by the agents, who surveil the territory of whiteness that is the matrix. Agent Smith represents the aversive racist who does not want to allow any challenges to white supremacy to be expressed. And, he fights like hell to make sure that whiteness goes unnamed and silence is maintained. Yet, Neo, like some whites, is driven by his moral sensibilities, possibly Christian, criticalist, or both in origin, to challenge the wrongness of a hegemonic system based on a distorted and socially constructed biology that assigns differential value to bodies through the dehumanizing process of racialization (see Omi & Winant, 1994). His anti-racist struggle with the agents is superficially linked with the growing trend of critical whiteness studies. In this form of critical pedagogy, whites with a consciousness of white privilege and power are educating other whites about their obligation to end white supremacy in the world. Critical whiteness studies argue that whites need to transform other whites if white racism is to be abolished. It is possible to see Neo's opposition to the agents in this light.

However, as previously mentioned in the Black nationalist perspective, the film's potential for a powerful critique of whiteness is diminished as a result of the Wachowskis' choice to use the white savior metaphor to guide the story of Neo's transformation. By having Neo turn into a white deity with an infinite mind and body, the movie tells us that it is not only okay, but preferred that whites ignore the rules of society that construct their white bodies and minds. This is problematic for several reasons. White minds are not universal, but are instead "white" because they are part of a white body that lives within the matrix of whiteness. The reality of this matrix is that white bodies carry undue privileges as a consequence of white racism, whether whites are conscious of this fact or not (McIntosh, 1997). Also, the critiques of whiteness that have shaped the formation of the discourse on white privilege have emanated primarily from people of color, the oppressed within white racism. Critical whiteness studies is then a realm of study driven primarily by the intellectual work of people of color, even though many whites have been influential in its development. For whites to be anti-racist, they must learn to move other whites towards anti-racist and anti-whiteness ideologies (Tatum, 1997). But what we get in *The Matrix* is the message that the best way to transform whiteness is to move beyond it. In fact, there is an element of nihilism in the Wachowskis' solution to whiteness. It seems that they are suggesting that the best way to overcome an oppressive society built on oppressive rules is to simply ignore the rules. They foreshadow their conclusion in Neo's opening scene when they show us Jean Baudrillard's *Simulation and Simulacra* opened to the chapter called "On Nihilism." The film concludes with what definitely seems like a nihilistic solution. However, the problem with nihilism is that it assumes that social life is possible without rules or structures. But, such is not the case. Human relationships and communication are always rule bound, and it is not very revolutionary to imagine a world without them. A more difficult task is to imagine a world based on a more egalitarian, humanizing, and democratic set of cultural and institutional principals. I cannot understand why a movie would spend so much time on the theme of reconnecting the mind and body, only to have Neo's newly unified mind and body depart from society, as if one ever could. The idea that a white body, a white savior, can disconnect himself from the larger context of society's structures is reminiscent of the type of racial views held by those who suffer from color blindness and live in a fantasy world disconnected from the real experiences of racial oppression. Certainly, we must work towards *achieving* a color-blind world. However, it is quite problematic to suggest that any one person, especially a white person, can be an individual body and mind who by himself exists outside of the current realities of the rules of race.

It is also interesting to note that Neo is the only person in the crew who achieves this status of being able to free his body and mind from the rules of society. Within the social context of whiteness, people of color are unable to do this even if they want to because their oppression is predicated upon the construction of their open visibility as the Other. White skin privilege is one of the major problems in the culture of whiteness in that most whites do not want to recognize how their epistemological concerns are directly connected to the cultural and institutional processes that give them a particular kind of bodily experience. It is on this note that I agree with the Black nationalists that the film, in the end, reasserts white supremacy. When Neo flies off like Superman in the final scene, he becomes superhuman, which means that the category of "human" is redefined and refracted into at least two other categories, "superhuman" and "subhuman." We know that human bodies do not really fly, so why should we fantasize that they do? One explanation is that people invent superhuman qualities when they do not know how else to use their minds and bodies to change oppressive social situations. They do not know how to challenge power within actually feasible scenarios of collective social action and radical education. Some may say that the expression of superhumanism is at least a symbol of hope for an unforeseen, but liberated, future. However, I think that it can also be seen as the negation of bodily and intellectual agency. The subject does not know what it is that his body, and the mind connected to it, can do, so he transforms himself into a superhuman figure that our minds make up, which paradoxically subverts the influence of the body, and thus, the mind.

Instead of superhumans and deities, what we need are images of what real bodies and minds can do. What if Neo had been depicted as gaining more specific awareness of his white bodily privileges, as oppose to the vague allusion to whiteness that nevertheless drives the plot? What if he did not turn into a savior of the oppressed, but a savior of himself and other whites who are oblivious to the pervasiveness and persistence of white racism? What if the movie had dealt with the struggles that white anti-racists face when dealing with other whites (and the opportunity were present in the antagonism with the agents)? What if whites had been shown possible and feasible interventions that they could do with their white brothers and sisters to combat whiteness? And, what if, in the end, Neo had been transformed into an equal of all humans and not a deity? One could argue that Neo's disintegration of Agent Smith does represent the struggle for anti-racism within the white community. However, Agent Smith's body is obliterated, and, thus, nowhere, at the same time that Neo's body becomes boundless, and, thus, everywhere. Neither situation reflects the real world of humans. Whites cannot be genocidically eliminated, as suggested by Agent Smith's demise, nor can they escape their whiteness as some type of heroic individual, as suggested by Neo's superhumanism.

In summation, it is very disappointing to me to realize that a movie that initially challenges the dreamworlds of hegemony so directly and so profoundly ultimately winds up back in the land of illusion. Wake up, Neo.

## CONCLUSION: THE MATRIX OF CRITICAL PEDAGOGY

For the last three decades, critical pedagogists have struggled to extend the discourse of critical pedagogy into the United States educational system. Building on the work of Paulo Freire, they have primarily relied upon the paradigms of critical theory to guide their praxis. Although this work has been very influential in some United States contexts, it has had limited effects on a larger scale. One of the more common obstacles that critical pedagogists mention is that most of the teachers in the U.S. are members of privileged oppressor groups, and are not the oppressed. It is difficult to teach students about oppression when they are not close to the experience of oppression.

In social and historical contexts such as the United States, new conversations need to take place in order to challenge their particular oppressive realities. For example, my polyphonic exegesis of a film is an orchestrated dialogue among real identity groups that have played major roles in constructing the social hierarchies of the U.S. In our version of critical pedagogy, there is a significant tension between critical theorists and critical race theorists that can no longer be ignored. Critical pedagogy will lose any standing that it now has as a radical force if it continues to "other" critical race theorists like Black nationalists and critical whiteness studies scholars. When critical pedagogists avoid more specific and thorough examinations of real social identity relationships, opting instead for more vague and superficial treatments of the "hegemons," they are consciously or unconsciously alienating many people of color. Critical theory, in general, rarely addresses the global problem of whiteness (McLaren, Leonardo, & Allen, 2000). And, in systems of oppression such as white supremacy, acts of omission by the oppressors are also acts of collusion. Real people invest their thoughts and behaviors in what they believe to be real social identities. So, pedagogy that talks specifically about the hegemonic nature of these concretized identities, such as whiteness, is important to the psychological and political viability of critical pedagogy. In other words, this racialized challenge should be seen as opportunity to deepen and revitalize critical pedagogy and not as a move to diminish its so-called "traditions."

I would say that Paulo Freire's own words support the idea that the naming of the problem of whiteness in critical theory, and thus, in critical pedagogy, is a furthering of the critical dialogue. Those who speak from an oppressed positionality, such as African Americans, have much to teach white critical pedagogists, like myself, about the struggle for freedom for all. As Paulo Freire (1970/1993) says,

> Human existence cannot be silent, nor can it be nourished by false words, but only by true words, with which men and women transform the world. To exist humanly is to *name* the world, to change it. . . . Hence, dialogue cannot occur between those who want to name the world and those who do not wish this naming—between those who deny others the right to speak their word and those whose right to speak has been denied them. (p. 69, italics in original)

On numerous occasions, I have heard white criticalists denigrate people of color for focusing on racial critiques and not more centrally emphasizing a critique of capitalism. What white criticalists, and, for that matter, all whites, need to understand is that when you are white, it is much easier to focus on capitalism than it is on whiteness. But rather than accepting humility and undergoing an unlearning of their white identity, what I hear more often is white criticalists blaming people of color, particularly African Americans, for being "consumed by race" and "unaware of hegemony." However, Paulo Freire (1970/1993) reminds us that this is no way for members of the oppressor group to enter a dialogue:

Dialogue, as the encounter of those addressed to the common task of learning and acting, is broken if the parties (or one of them) lack humility. How can I dialogue if I always project ignorance onto others and never perceive my own? (p. 71)

Truth is not constructed outside of dialogue with the humanizing force of the oppressed. In other words, the building of solidarity and radical alliances, usually between groups with unequal power, is the only way that critical truths are formed. At times, it seems as though this basic idea is forgotten. More often, the issue of race in critical pedagogy and critical theory in the U.S. seems to bring out more "truth knowers" than "alliance builders." In other words, righteousness consumes the potential for radical love. The central question to consider is this: Is it more important to be "right" that capitalism is the totality that encompasses all other totalities or is it more important to construct movements of solidarity against all forms of dehumanization? Critical pedagogy's response to this question will determine its fate, and its membership, in the next millennium.

## References

Collins, P. H. (1990). *Black feminist thought: Knowledge, consciousness, and the politics of empowerment* (2nd ed.). New York: Routledge.

Freire, P. (1993). *Pedagogy of the oppressed* (Rev. ed.) (M. B. Ramos, Trans.). New York: Continuum. (Original work published in 1970.)

Gallagher, C. (1997). White racial formation: Into the twenty-first century. In R. Delgado & J. Stefancic (Eds.), *Critical white studies: Looking behind the mirror* (pp. 6–11). Philadelphia: Temple University Press.

Giroux, H. (1997). White squall: Resistance and the pedagogy of whiteness. *Cultural Studies, 11* (3), 376–389.

Harvey, B. (1999, April 17). Spiritualism turns *Matrix* into cult fare. *The Ottawa Citizen* [on-line]. Retrieved on December 16, 2000, from the World Wide Web: http/ottawacitizen.com/entertainment/990417/24993054.html.

Hussain, A. (2000). Apocalyptic visions. *The Journal of Religion and Film, 4* (1) [on-line]. Retrieved on October 23, 2000 from the World Wide Web: http://www.unomaha.edu/~wwwjrf/Hussain.htm.

Kuhlmann, H. (2000). Fluid realities/fluid identities: Gender in *The Matrix. Technofeminism and Cyberculture Courseweb* [on-line]. Retrieved October 23, 2000, from the World Wide Web: http://www.tc.umn.edu/~matrioo1/wost3190/kuhlmann2html.

Lloyd, P. (1999). Metaphysics of *The Matrix*. Retrieved on October 24, 2000, from the World Wide Web: http://ursasoft.com/publish/chapter1.htm.

McIntosh, P. (1997). White privilege and male privilege. In R. Delgado & J. Stefancic (Eds.), *Critical white studies: Looking behind the mirror* (pp. 291–299). Philadelphia: Temple University Press.

McLaren, P. (1994). *Life in schools: An introduction to critical pedagogy in the foundations of education* (2nd ed.). White Plains, NY: Longman Publishing Group.

McLaren, P., Leonardo, Z., & Allen, R. L. (2000). Epistemologies of whiteness: Transforming and transgressing pedagogic knowledge. In R. Mahalingham & C. McCarthy (Eds.), *Multicultural curriculum*. New York: Routledge.

Miller, E. (2000). *The Matrix* and the medium's message. *Social Policy, 30* (4) [on-line]. Retrieved October 23, 2000, from the World Wide Web: http://www.mailbase.ac.uk/lists/film ~philosophy.

Mills, C. (1997). *The racial contract.* Ithaca, NY: Cornell University Press.

Omi, M., & Winant, H. (1994). *Racial formation in the United States: From the 1960s to the 1990s* (2nd ed.). New York: Routledge.

Schuchardt, R. (n.d.). *The Matrix:* Thesis, antithesis, and synthesis. *Cleave, The Counteragency* [on-line]. Retrieved on October 21, 2000, from the World Wide Web: http://cleave.com/ Sight/The_Matrix/the_matrix.htm.

Tatum, B. D. (1997). *"Why are all the Black kids sitting together in the cafeteria?" and other conversations about race.* New York: Basic Books.

Tharps, L. (1999, May 7). *The matrix:* God is in the details. *Entertainment Weekly* [on-line]. Retrieved October 23, 2000, from the World Wide Web: http://www.ew.com/ew/ features/990514/matrix/index.html.

Thomas, S. F. (1999). The key to *The matrix. TheAfrican.Com* [on-line]. Retrieved October 23, 2000, from the World Wide Web: http://www.theafrican.com/ *Magazine/matrix.htm.*

Zizek, S. (1999). *The Matrix:* The truth of the exaggerations. *Lacan Dot Com* [on-line]. Retrieved on December 16, 2000, from the World Wide Web: http://www.lacan.com/ matrix.html.

# The Practical

*Judge a man not by what he thinks but by what he says; judge a man*

*not by what he says but by what he does.* —TALMUD

PAULO FREIRE HAS shown himself to be both a man of words and a man of action. For him the essence of dialogue itself is *the word*. But we are instructed that "the word is more than just an instrument which makes dialogue possible . . . within the word we find two dimensions, reflection and action" (Freire, 1970, p. 75).

What follows are concepts fashioned with an eye toward action. Each essay is grounded in the principles articulated by Paulo Freire and reflects actions, proposed actions and, in some cases, results, which grow from these roots. Here we see examples that give meaning to the concept of *praxis* and are reflective of the hope (Freire, 1995) of colleagues who believe in the possibility of changing the world. This commitment to the belief in the possibility of the transformative experience is both metaphysical and practical. The questions that give energy to the process are grounded in questions of social justice and the emancipation of people—questions such as this one posed by Maxine Greene when she asked, "Can freedom be authentic if it is pursued at the cost of others' freedom, others' welfare?" (1998, p. 93). The proposed responses to these problems are aimed first at the liberation of the individual for it is understood that the individual is the source of liberation.

Readers are invited to accept the challenge posed by each of the following selections. Each is a serious effort at moving from the metaphysical to the practical. But, as we read, we read in the light of Paulo Freire even as we stand in his shadow. The choice is ours as it always is. We can accept each piece and simply read it and deposit it in our bank of experience or we can accept the challenge inherent in our human potential and use each piece as an opportunity for engagement—a chance to participate in a dialogue.

*References*

Freire, P. (1970). *Pedagogy of the oppressed*. (Myra Bergman Ramos, Trans.). New York: The Seabury Press.
Freire, P. (1995). *Pedagogy of hope: revising pedagogy of the oppressed* (Robert R. Barr, Trans.). New York: Continuum.
Greene, M. (1988). *The dialectic of freedom*. New York: Teachers College Press.

*Stephen M. Fain*

# THE QUEST FOR AUTHENTIC ENGAGEMENT

## INTRODUCTION

THE WORK WE do often plays an important role in shaping our lives. That is not to say that each of us is only a product of our work. Rather, this observation is intended to underscore the fact that, although we have families, hobbies, and other interests, our work is a significant defining element in shaping, among other things, our social status and associations and our perception of ourselves. The combination of our social status, our circles of friends and colleagues, and our self-image are most significant in forming our identity. Our identity is important because it not only defines us but, in so doing, often separates us or distinguishes us from others. Through processes of association and affiliation, we gain personal strength. This strength is comparable to the strength of the collective—that group with which we identify. For example, we garner strength from the status of our respective disciplines and the institutions at which we studied and at which we work. We internalize this strength. We garner strength from our colleagues and our professional friends because we understand that we are often defined by the company we keep, and we work to keep good friends and colleagues because we are enriched by our association with them. Most of us are keenly aware that our associations and affiliations not only describe but limit and direct us. Often, they help to define ourselves and our work.

When I speak of work today, I am speaking of more than what we do. I am speaking about our work environment and our professional culture. I think it is in our best interest to strive constantly to understand not only our work but our work community—the culture in which we work. This understanding may serve as a catalyst for the improvement of both the workplace and ourselves.

There are those among us who work for the salary and the benefits—the bread and butter issues. No one can argue with these folks because we all know that survival is a basic need that must be addressed. And, there are those who are attracted to the work we do because it is liberating—that is, it frees us and lets us fly to new heights; it provides us with opportunities to soar above the day-to-day trivia of life in the common places and to become more—and even more. Work, and the workplace, has this potential. It can set our spirits free or it can stifle us. It is my belief that those of us who enter the enterprise of education in order to survive are often crushed in the workplace, but those of us who are called to education because we understand its emancipatory powers seek liberation for students, for colleagues, and for ourselves. It is my conviction that emancipation and liberation result when professionals seek out and participate in what I call authentic professional engagements, and the best people I know are constantly searching for them.

## THE POWER OF *HABITUS*

Our work forces us into a particular environment, and this milieu affects us in various ways and at various levels. We find ourselves caught up in a work culture that we often accept without examination and which often controls us beyond our awareness. Those of us who consider ourselves to be professional find that we are caught between the autonomy associated with professional practice and the conditions imposed upon us by the structures in which we practice. Our colleague Judith Slater calls this condition *habitus,* building on the work of Pierre Bourdieu. In a recent paper she offers the following observation:

> The levels of habitus in organizations are like the layers of an onion. There is the center core of traditional bureaucratic structure, and around that core are the layers of symbolic and real dispositions and behaviors that perpetuate and protect the core. The more layers there are, the more irreversible is the disposition of the organization to perpetuate the status quo; the harder it is to get the core to make fundamental structural changes in the modes of operation, and harder still to change the core beliefs. (Slater, 1999, p. 3)

Slater's observations are consistent with observations offered by others who study the culture of societies and organizations. For example, Thomas Kuhn's *The Structure of Scientific Revolutions* (1962/1996), Steven J. Gould's *The Mismeasure of Man* (1981/1996), and Steven Selden's *Inheriting Shame* (1999) provide us with concrete evidence that science, an enterprise grounded in the pursuit of understanding through objective research, falls victim to cultural forces and, as such, has made serious errors. Each of these texts "peels the onion" of science by revealing layers of facts and interpretations, demonstrating that the field of science is more of a culture than we generally acknowledge and, as such, is often less objective than we generally assume. The core value of cultural maintenance is demonstrated by the jailing of Galileo as a heretic in the 1600s, the acceptance of recapitulationist ideologies of the nineteenth-century that justified the classification of women and people of color as inferior, and the accepted practice of sterilization of the feeble-minded as scientific knowledge and race politics fused into public policy in the early twentieth century. As the layers of the culture are peeled away, we see that in the case of Galileo the core value was the Church (Kuhn, 1962/1996); in the case of the recapitulationists, the core value was the status of the privileged (Gould, 1984/1986), and, finally, in the case of the sterilization of the feebleminded, the core value was social efficiency (Selden, 1999; Callahan, 1962).

In less dramatic ways, the power of the *habitus* shapes the practices of cultures and organizations of all sorts. In the most seemingly informal ways, we see evidence of this—we observe it in fashion, be it regarding clothing or food, and we see it in "bandwagon" ideologies and what has become the "political correctness" of contemporary institutions and thought.

Slater calls our attention to the fact that the power, the "legitimacy," of the *organizational habitus* must be overcome if organizations and individuals are to transcend the traditional. This call for change, transcendence, buttressed by the challenge of overcoming the traditional is most compelling. I would venture, that for each of us this call resonates with appeal as it seems to offer us a chance to become, if not all we can be—at least more than we are.

This call for transcendence fits with the evolution of thinking related to developing organizational cultures. For instance, for the last quarter of a century, experts such as George Labovitz and Victor Rodansky (1997), Edgar Schein (1992), Peter Senge (1990), and Chris Argyris and Donald Schon (1974) have been speaking to the importance of the individual in advancing the organizational. Collectively, their work depicts a trend toward bringing the individual into the organization so as to increase organizational productivity and efficiency. The result is that little, if any, attention is paid to the individual as an entity herself; rather, she is presented as a vital part of the organization—a potential element in the matrix of the organization, rather than a unique individual. This is reminiscent of Schmidt, the little Pennsylvania Dutchman, who was the focus of Frederick Taylor's efficiency study at Bethlehem Steel from 1897–1900. He was described as a man

> who had been observed to trot back home for a mile or so after his work in the evening about as fresh as he was when he came trotting down to work in the morning . . . and that he was engaged in putting up the walls of a little house for himself in the morning before starting work and at night after leaving. (Callahan, 1962, p. 36)

You may recall the story. This man was trained using Taylor's scientific method to load ingots of pig iron onto waiting railroad cars more efficiently. As a result of scientific study and carefully supervised step-by-step training, he increased his production from 12½ tons per day to 47½ tons per day. Raymond Callahan (1962) points out that it is unfortunate that there is no report noting whether Schmidt, "the embodiment of Taylor's ideal of the first-class man and the epitome of human efficiency" (p. 39), continued to trot back and forth to work and whether he ever completed the wall he was building after the study at Bethlehem was completed. Taylor's work is important because it represents the transcendence of the industrial mind (see Gramsci, 1971/1997. pp. 277–318).

The case of Schmidt demonstrates that *transcendence,* when placed in the context of planned organizational change (human resource development—HRD) is related more to organizational advancement than the liberation of the worker. After studying quality circles, Guillermo Grenier (1988) observes that "people-building is . . . synonymous with developing a cooperative team spirit such that workers are in tune with managerial priorities" (p. 12). As one peels away the layers of the HRD onion, managerial strategies are shown to be intent on improving production rather than on the emancipation of workers. This is the *habitus* in which the worker of today generally finds herself. The core value is the advancement of the company—the worker is merely a tool of management.

Today, professionals in education find that our common places are very much like the *habitus* described by Bourdieu (1980):

> systems of durable, transposable, dispositions, structured structures predisposed to function as structuring structures, that is as principles which generate and organize practices and representations that can be objectively adapted to their outcomes without presupposing a conscious aiming at ends or an express mastery of the operations necessary in order to attain them. (p. 53)

What appears an ideal structure in which professionals could work turns out to be an oppressive paradigm. Bourdieu explains that in the practical world the *habitus* acts "as a system of cognitive and motivating structures [in] a world of already realized ends – procedures to follow, paths to take" (p. 53). Here the organization, presented as the habitus, is shown to be a tool for maintenance. It is also shown to be a trap in that *habitus* is a product of history that produces history, thus insuring control of the collective for the moment and for the future (Bourdieu, 1980, pp. 53–56). If we, professionals in education, are seeking emancipation and liberation then we must step out of our *habitus* and find authentic professional engagements to stimulate and nourish us. Or, if we stay as we are, rooted in *habitus,* our autonomy will be surrendered, our autonomy will disappear, and unknowingly we will perpetuate the *habitus*.

### *HABITUS:* OPPRESSION WITHIN A PROFESSION

In recent months I have been thinking about the state of the education profession. It seems that no matter where I go, I meet colleagues who have something to say about the external forces that are directing their work. The level does not seem to matter; classroom teachers at every level, as well as college professors and administrators are keenly aware of the fact that the reform and accountability movements are defining our work and our work places. We are told by David Berliner and Bruce Biddle (1995) that this is a manufactured crisis orchestrated by politicians and leaders of American industry. But, for me, this is a real crisis because it has affected the culture of my profession; it has shaped *habitus* of the American educational enterprise.

In the forward to Paulo Freire's *Pedagogy of the Oppressed,* Richard Shaull states that Freire operates on one basic assumption: that man's ontological vocation (as he [Freire] calls it) is to be a Subject who acts upon and transforms his world and in so doing moves toward ever new possibilities of fuller and richer life individually and collectively. (1970/1997, p. 14)

Through all of his work, Freire articulates his conviction that liberation can only come when the oppressed liberate themselves. In *Pedagogy of the Oppressed* (1970/1997), he presents this simple position by explaining the many roles that must be played and many obstacles that must be overcome if liberation is to be achieved. Oppression, he explains, is "dehumanizing," and he advises us that if oppression is to be overcome the "pedagogy of the oppressed must be animated by authentic, humanistic (not humanitarian) generosity and present itself as a pedagogy of humankind" (p. 36). I am of the belief that, of all the challenges posed by Freire, *authenticity* is the most important and most illusive requisite in the quest for liberation.

Authenticity, as I see it after my engagement with Freire's work, requires not only that one genuinely feels (as in being touched and being moved) and that one genuinely knows (as in realizing the true condition) but also that one is honest and forthright about the issue. For instance, freedom, on the surface, has universal meaning but, upon reflection, it is clear that this term has different meanings to different people. In *The Dialectic of Freedom* (1988), Maxine Greene discusses the complicated concept of freedom as a pivotal theme in the lives of Americans. She observes that the "watchword for most is indeed freedom: but the meanings vary almost infinitely" (p. 24). She then goes on to demonstrate how illusive freedom is for those populations she describes as "numbed, hungry, and compliant" (p. 25). She strengthens her point by observing that the common folk in Dostoyevsky's *The Brothers Karamazov* "would sacrifice freedom for bread and happiness at any time; they know the value of submission; they know the happiness it brings" (p. 25). Eric Fromm calls this phenomena "dynamic adaptation" (1941, p. 30). This characteristic demonstrates man's flexibility or powers of adjustment or, perhaps, willingness to accommodate—to make, or be, at peace. Some would call it more of a rationalization, or perhaps, justification, for a position that one is not sure is right but which one believes to be necessary. This process of finding a feeling of freedom where freedom really does not exist is a good example of why authenticity is often illusive.

Whereas the common citizen may feel that she understands, the professional knows. In the first case there is a belief that what one feels is genuine (authentic), and, therefore, the common citizen believes that she knows. In the second case, where the professional knows the facts but also knows that she does not feel, there is no authenticity—no humanistic generosity no hope of liberation. Antonio Gramsci explains in *Selections from the Prison Notebooks* (1997):

> The popular element "feels" but does not always know or understand; the intellectual element "knows" but does not always understand and in particular does not always feel . . . The intellectual's error consists in believing that one can know without understanding and even more without feeling and being impassioned. (p. 418)

The protocols of professional practice serve as a controlling device intended to reduce passion and increase objectivity. The humanistic generosity required to engage in the emancipation of the oppressed requires passion. And, if education is to be an emancipatory enterprise, then professional educators must find passion in their work if they are to be free to do it.

We are well aware of contemporary efforts to professionalize education. These efforts have always been cast in a positive mode. Umberto Eco (1997) tells us that to "name is always to make a hypothesis" (p. 62). What is the hypothesis attached to the term "professional educator?" The Carnegie Forum report *A Nation Prepared: Teachers for the 21st Century* (1986) saw professional teachers as those with master's degrees and national board certification. The hypothesis advanced in this case seems to be tied to content mastery and formal training. It is easy to draw the line from this training to the status of expert and then continue on to the expectation of public trust. This logic leads to a state of autonomy in practice equivalent to that traditionally afforded medicine and law: professions associated with high entrance standards at every level. The idea of education achieving this status level may be appealing to all who understand and respect what teachers do; however, this hypothesis is little more than a dream, given the facts at hand. According to the National Center of Educational Information alternative teacher certification programs are in place in forty of the fifty states; targeted sources for new teachers include military veterans, retired and released during the downsizing of the service (e.g. Troops to Teachers, a $65 million two year federal program funded for the purpose of placing downsized military personnel into careers in teaching), retirees, and liberal arts graduates. The greatest demand for alternative certification is not coming from legislatures or higher education or local school administrators but from people wanting to get licensed to teach (Bradley, 1998; National Center of Educational Information, 1998).

Across the nation, accountability testing has been accepted by governors, legislators, school boards, administrators, unions, and teachers. The profession, whatever that was, willingly walked into a Gramscian trap. We have acted as a "lazy machine" engaging in "interpretative cooperation" with our oppressors (Eco, 1997, p. 278). We have given up the hypothesis of profession; we surrendered our collective freedom to the *habitus*. We function in a *culture of silence* (Greene, 1988, p. 25; also see Freire, 1970/1979).

We are complicit in acts that prevent our emancipation when we accept the *habitus* as the source of our power and legitimacy. This condition is made clear as Michael Apple, in *Cultural Politics and Education* (1996), explains how the Right co-opts parents who seek involvement in their children's schools by accepting only two choices for involvement—either they are "responsible" parents who basically support the school or they are "irresponsible" and do not. In the end, many choose to come into the system as responsible parents rather than be out of the game. This phenomenon must be acknowledged if both parents and schools are to move to a state of liberation. If this process is not addressed, then all that follows, as the relationship between school and parent develops, will lack authenticity. The result will be an oppressive collaboration, with neither the school nor the parent experiencing emancipation.

It is not just the parents in Apple's example who find themselves in this Gramscian trap. The current popular view in America has resulted in a sea change with regard to the *habitus* in elementary and secondary schools across the nation. The school reform movement has reached levels that I think are even beyond the wildest expectations of E. D. Hirsh (1987), Chester Finn (1991), and Lynne Cheney (1995). School reform has co-opted professional educators to the point where, across the nation, school people have become public supporters of basic skills testing, teacher testing, curriculum reform, and alternative certification of teachers. As is the case with Apple's parents, either we are "responsible" professionals or we are out of the game. Trapped, many among us are now accepting the term "professional" to mean "he who delivers what the establishment demands." Autonomy is gone! True reflection is gone! And, if we consider the *habitus* in a genuinely honest, authentic way, we are not emancipated—we are immobilized; we are not liberated—we are restricted; and by accepting the conditions of "dehumanization" (Freire, 1970/1997) we are, in fact, oppressed.

Clearly, something has gone awry. The vision of professional educators, articulated by the Carnegie Forum and the programs designed to place, for example, downsized military veterans in the classrooms of America as professional educators do not share a common vision. Yet today, there is little debate regarding what separates these two views. The question of education as a profession joined by Goodlad and his colleagues (1990) a decade ago in *The Moral Dimensions of Teaching* is no longer discussed as the players are not involved in acts of compliance. We accept basic skills testing even though so many of us believe that it is not a good thing; we act as if striving to meet minimum performance standards is a way to empower both our students and ourselves in spite of the fact that we don't believe it; and we accept alternative approaches to the certification of teachers as a fait accompli, even though we realize that, in the end, this practice may completely undermine our profession. We watch as the state legislatures across the country tinker with our professional schools and colleges of education even though we know that these actions could destroy the profession, and we stand mute as these same political leaders work zealously to dismantle the public school system that has been so central to the development of our nation. We are like the peasant in *Pedagogy of the Oppressed* who responds to the oppression inflicted by the boss with the response, "What can I do? I am only a peasant" (Freire, 1970/1997, p. 43). We have become the victim of collective fatalism. We have lost our passion.

Even at the academic highest levels of our work, I see evidence of our collective subversion of our freedom in the name of the *habitus*. Meetings, such as the annual gathering of colleagues under the banner of the American Educational Research Association (AERA), have become places where processionals in education gather to mostly talk *at* each other. Vita are built, positions are sought, and cliques meet and strategize, but the meetings lack humanity. The power of the powerful is glorified, and the powerlessness of the others, the peasants, is not considered.

Status is a big thing at AERA, and those who have it work hard to sustain their positions. The nature of the engagement is evident as one moves from a symposium where a panel of highly regarded experts speak to a hall filled with eager professional aspirants to the poster sessions and roundtables where the aspirants seek the reactions of the highly regarded experts who rarely stop by. There is clearly a status that protects and defends the *habitus* at these meetings.

An example of this phenomena is found in January, 1999 *Educational Researcher*. In this AERA journal, William Wraga, then an aspiring assistant professor at the University of Georgia, presents a critique of reconceptualized curriculum theorizing. His article, "Extracting Sun-Beams out of Cucumbers: The Retreat From Practice in Reconceptualized Curriculum Studies," (1999, pp. 4–13) is a genuine effort at exploring the shift in curriculum theory from a "modern scientific view" to a "postmodern view." Its focus is William Pinar, St. Barnard Parish Alumni Endowed Professor at Louisiana State University, and a central figure in this shift. In his nine-page article Wraga calls attention to aspects of the shift in theory and asks why the postmoderns have drifted off the point of direct application to the school curriculum. (He refers to this as the "constructive legacy of the historic field" (p.12).

In his one-page response, Pinar (1999) dismisses Wraga as "reminiscent of those . . . southern preachers who resort to quoting the Old Testament to support his . . . ideas of tradition." I seek no quarrel with either author. But, I want to make the point that this debate is more indicative of the *habitus* than of the prescribed dispositions necessary to achieve the liberation of the collective advanced by Freire. Obviously intended as a dismissive slap in the face, Pinar's comments demonstrate how one works to maintain the status quo (the *habitus*) rather than how one reaches out to include and embrace. Clearly, this response was more dehumanizing than humanizing. I am compelled to ask if the invitation to join in the curriculum conversation extended to all by Pinar, Slattery, and Taubman (1995, p. 849) included Wraga. Since I believe that the invitation was a sincere one, I am forced to conclude that this example is more a result of the *habitus,* the culture of our work, than it is of any one individual.

## SEARCHING FOR AUTHENTIC ENGAGEMENTS

I believe that we have opportunities to steer a new course for ourselves and for our field. As a first step, we should consider abandoning the notion that we need to develop education as a profession, as the concept of a profession is more controlling then liberating. Second, we should begin to search for authentic engagements through which we can keep the spark of liberation glowing until we can nurture an emancipatory flame. This can be done by working to ensure that we become involved in what I think of as authentic engagements. These encounters will require that we develop our individual and collective personalities in Freirean terms. To achieve a state of authenticity, we will need to be human and generous (Freire,

1970/1997, p. 36), and we will need to focus our collective efforts on reflection and action so that in our initially small way we can begin to support a transformation of habitus (Freire, 1970/1997, p. 107).

I believe that we must accept the fact that liberation is "a task for radicals" that "cannot be carried out by sectarians" (Freire, 1970/1997, p. 21). In light of the oppressive forces of reform and the response of so many to comply, those of us who rejected the notion of "radical" are today seeking paths to liberation. First as individuals, then as small groups and even schools and associations, we have the qualities necessary to liberate ourselves. This is where the process of liberation begins. Many of us have been searching for authentic engagements where colleagues meet for the purpose of exchange and support rather than for status and power. We have sought colleagues who would challenge our ideas, not because it feeds their egos but because they understand that serious criticism is respectful and quite dispassionate acceptance is disrespectful. And finally, we have sought colleagues for friendship because we are social beings, and we understand the value of expanding our circle. We seek authentic engagements where status issues will be underplayed, insight and sincerity will be highly prized, and conversations will be begun and continued.

Peel away the layers of the onion of our field and consider the core values that drive our work. If we find that our core culture reflects the dispositions of generosity, respect, tolerance, inclusion, and mutual interest, we should celebrate. But, if, as these layers are peeled away, we realize that our culture is more oppressive than liberating, we are obligated to consider becoming active in efforts to liberate first ourselves, then our colleagues, and finally our field. If our field is healthy, then, in the core of our onion where the true flavor is found, we will find layers of the joy and passion, which ultimately provide us, individually and collectively, with a perspective energized by our imaginations and our passions, reflective of our enthusiasm, grounded in humanistic values, and focused on our quest for emancipation.

As Maxine Greene observed:

> To recognize the role of perspective and vantage point, to recognize at the same time that there are always multiple perspectives and multiple vantage points, is to recognize that no accounting, disciplinary or otherwise, can ever be finished or complete. There is always more. There is always possibility, and this is where the space opens for the pursuit of freedom. (Greene, 1988, p. 128)

*References*

Apple, M. W. (1996). *Cultural politics and education.* New York: Teachers College Press.

Argyris, C. & Schon, D. (1974). *Theory in practice: Increasing professional effectiveness.* San Francisco: Jossey-Bass Publishers.

Berliner, D. C. & Biddle, B. J. (1995). *The manufactured crisis: Myths, fraud, and the attack on America's public schools.* Reading, MA: Addison-Wesley.

Bourdieu, P. (1980). *The logic of practice*. Stanford, CA: Stanford University Press.

———. (1993). *The field of cultural production*. New York: Columbia University Press.

Bradley, A. (1998, October 14). Expiring "troops to teachers" project outfits classrooms with professionals in demand. *Education Week*.

Callahan, R. (1962). *Education and the cult of efficiency: A study of the social forces that have shaped the administration of the public schools*. Chicago: The University of Chicago Press.

Carnegie Forum on Education and the Economy (1986). *A nation prepared: Teachers for the 21st Century*. Washington: D.C.: Carnegie Forum on Education and the Economy.

Cheney, L. V. (1995). *Telling the truth: Why our culture and our country have stopped making sense—and what we can do about it*. New York: Simon & Schuster.

Eco. U. (1997). *Kant and the platypus*. New York: Harcourt Brace & Company.

Finn, C. F. Jr. (1991). *We must take charge: Our schools and our future*. New York: The Free Press.

Freire. P. (1970/1997). *Pedagogy of the oppressed*. New York: Continuum.

Goodlad, J. I., Soder, R., & Sirotnik, K. A. (Eds.). (1990). *The moral dimensions of teaching*. San Francisco, CA.: Jossey-Bass Publishing.

Gould, S. J. (1981/1986). *The mismeasure of man*. New York: W. W. Norton.

Gramsci, A. (1971/1997). *Selections from the prison notebooks of Antonio Gramsci* (Quintin Hoare & Geoffrey Nowell Smith, Eds. & Trans.). New York: International Publishers.

Greene, M. (1988). *The dialectic of freedom*. New York: Teachers College Press.

Grenier, G. J. (1988). *Inhuman relations: Quality circles and anti-unionism in American industry*. Philadelphia: Temple University Press.

Hirsh, E. D. Jr. (1987). *Cultural literacy: What every American needs to know*. Boston: Houghton Mifflin.

Kuhn, T. S. (1962/1996). *The structure of scientific revolutions*. Chicago: The University of Chicago Press.

Labovitz, L. & Rosansky, V. (1997). *The power of alignment. How great companies stay centered and accomplish extraordinary things*. New York: John Wiley & Sons.

National Center of Educational Information. (1998). *Profile of Troops to Teachers*. Washington, D.C.: National Center of Educational Information.

National Center of Educational Information. (2000, Feb. 3). News Release.

Pinar, W. F. (1999). Response: Gracious Submission. *Educational Researcher, 28* (1).

Pinar, W. F., Reynolds, W. M., Slattery, P. & Taubman, P. M. (1995). *Understanding curriculum: An introduction to the study of historical and contemporary curriculum discourses*. New York: Peter Lang Publishing.

Schein, E. H. (1992). *Organizational culture and leadership* (2nd ed.). San Francisco: Jossey-Bass Publishers.

Selden, S. (1999). *Inheriting shame: The story of eugenics and racism in America*. New York: Teachers College Press.

Senge, P. M. (1990). *The fifth discipline: The art and practice of the learning organization*. New York: Doubleday/Currency.

Slater, J. J. (1999). *The overcoming of habitus: Impediments to community through consecration of the status quo*. Presented at the Internationalization of Curriculum Studies Conference, Baton Rouge, Louisiana.

Wraga, W. G. (1999). Extracting sun-beams out of cucumbers: The retreat from practice in reconceptualized curriculum studies. *Educational Researcher, 28* (1), 4–12.

*Wendy W. Brandon*

# INTERRUPTING RACIAL PROFILING: MOVING PRE-SERVICE TEACHERS FROM WHITE IDENTITY TO EQUITY PEDAGOGY

## INTRODUCTION

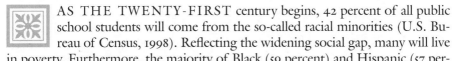 AS THE TWENTY-FIRST century begins, 42 percent of all public school students will come from the so-called racial minorities (U.S. Bureau of Census, 1998). Reflecting the widening social gap, many will live in poverty. Furthermore, the majority of Black (59 percent) and Hispanic (57 percent) young children come from families with incomes in the lowest categories (under $10,000 and $10,000–$14,999) (Chapa & Valencia, 1993). Currently employed teachers and those entering teacher education programs, whether they work in urban or suburban schools, will teach a wide array of racial, cultural, socio-economic, and language groups during their careers (Banks, 2000). Already, in some of the nation's largest cities, half or more of the public school students are low-income[1] students of color, their teachers mostly White. Demographic studies document the disparities between a student body that continues to grow more diverse while its teaching staff becomes more White (Cotton, 1993; National Education Goals Panel, 1997). With retirement and rising enrollments, two million teachers will be needed in America's schools in the next decade; almost two thirds of current teaching jobs will turn over. Teachers (composed of more than 90 percent White European American) who are products of White neighborhoods and White schools and White colleges of teacher education will be, as they have been historically, the majority of this new public school faculty (Howard, 1999; Quality Education for Minorities Project, 1990). Concerns about how White, monolingual, English-speaking teachers will meet the challenge of socially and economically complex classrooms runs through the educational literature. White teachers, it is generally believed, do not know how to address the needs of children whose language

and class and race are different from theirs, and expect these children to do poorly in their classes (Delpit, 1998; Faltis, 2001; Penfield, 1987; Noguera & Akom, 2000).

While some research has focused on the larger question of education and linking the production of inequalities to the institution of schooling itself, the failure of equal access has more often been "read outward from institutions and teachers to the children and families they served" (Connell, 1994, p. 149). The most common understanding of school failure among low-income children of color, and one deeply embedded in the individual consciousness of teachers, scholars, and policymakers "blames the victim." This understanding points to the condition of these children themselves, their homes and their communities, and their lack of social capital as the cause of their academic failure (Valencia, 1997a). Educational theorist Richard Valencia has traced the evolution of this notion and labeled it the paradigm of "deficit thinking." In deficit thinking, the perspective that students who fail "do so because of alleged internal deficiencies (such as cognitive and/or motivational limitations) or shortcomings socially linked to the youngster—such as familial deficits and dysfunctions" has, over time become a taken-for-granted belief about school failure (Valencia, 1997b, p. xi).

One particularly problematic form of contemporary deficit thinking is illustrated by the concept of "at risk." Like the 1960s educational discourse of "cultural deprivation" and "disadvantage," the at-risk concept serves to focus once again on the shortcomings of individual children and their families and ignores the strengths they bring to classrooms (Swadener, 1995). At-risk theory "turns students into burdens and trades potential for risk" (Valencia & Solorzano, 1997, p. 196), and since it is a person-centered explanation for school failure, it deflects attention away from institutionalized injustices (such as inequitable school financing, segregation, and curriculum differentiation) (Valencia, 1997b).

Attitudes and beliefs about the poor and working-class people of color that make up the paradigm of deficit thinking are "rooted in ignorance, classism, racism, sexism, pseudoscience and methodologically flawed research" (Valencia, 1997b, p. xii). Even so, deficit thinking will not go away. A national survey done in 1990 by the National Opinion Research Center at the University of Chicago found strong evidence to show that White Americans cling to racial stereotypes of a deficit nature (Valencia, 1997b). Deficit thinking continues to fit "comfortably into wider ideologies of race and class difference" (Connell, 1994, p. 150) in U. S. society and in U. S. classrooms. It operates to deflect attention away from a close examination of injustices perpetrated on low-income children of color by their teachers. A concept like "at-risk" masks the Whiteness of the problems and situations to which it is enlisted as a response and maintains the appearance that schools and teachers are exempt from pedagogical acts of racism that in the wider society would be labeled as racial profiling. So, while critiques of racial profiling focus on police as most egregious, it is really in classrooms that racial profiling has its most systematic and damaging effect. The myth of the beneficent White teacher, not unlike the myth of the beneficent neighborhood police officer, can be preserved and maintained by a paradigm of deficit thinking with roots in classism and racism.

Teachers are the significant others most strategically placed to affect the relationship between poor and working-class children of color and their schools. How they are prepared for teaching in diverse U. S. classrooms is a major concern of scholars and policy makers. One goal of the multicultural education movement in teacher preparation programs has been to provide preservice teachers with the theoretical knowledge and procedural skills to adequately serve diverse children and bring about substantive equality in U.S. schools. A growing trend in the multicultural education movement has focused on White race consciousness as a precursor to effective multicultural pedagogy (Sheets, 2000). Raising the academic performance of students of color and poverty to acceptable levels, however, remains illusive (Sheets, 2000). Rosa Hernandez Sheets (2000), in a review of the White movement in multicultural education writes: "Presently, there is no data to substantiate a causal relationship between White racial identity development and teacher competency in culturally diverse classrooms or in segregated classrooms" (p. 16). In this chapter, I will focus on class and race bias in the pedagogy of one White preservice teacher who had taken coursework in sociological foundations of education and multicultural education prior to student teaching, and I will analyze the acts of racial profiling I witnessed in her classroom. The purpose of this analysis is threefold: (1) to problematize the care and socialization of one low-status female student; (2) to propose an alternative way to think about the care and socialization of this student, drawn from current research on color-blind theories of care and the role of race and class in the formation of educational social networks; and (3) to explore some broad questions about teacher preparation that this thinking implies. My goal is to propose a pedagogy of supervision for preservice teachers that incorporates two nondominant perspectives: One, is that of Black feminist theories of care, and the second, a bicultural network-analytic model of socialization and schooling low-status students (Sheets, 2000; Thompson, 1998; Stanton-Salazar, 1997).

## STANTON-SALAZAR'S BICULTURAL NETWORK ORIENTATION

The care and nurturing of children of color for survival throughout American society is about historical intergroup relations of power (see Boykin, 1986; Boykin & Toms, 1985; Delpit, 1988; Garbarino, Dubrow, Kostelny & Pardo, 1992; Thompson, 1998). The tendency of White people generally to associate Blackness with criminality, and the tendency of Blackness to attract a disproportionate amount of attention from police and wary citizens is well documented. It causes parents of color to instruct their children to avoid disastrous encounters with police and the psychology of racial profiling (Staples, 2000). The shooting by New York City police of a new immigrant, Amadou Diallo, as he was reaching in his pocket for identification, is a nationally publicized and poignant illustration of racial and class variations in socialization to power differentials. Recent social networks research on adults has sought to explain racial and class socialization through the perspective of network analysis. Research on the role adult networks play reveals that "consistent and predictable structural variations in the interpersonal networks of people from different social classes and status groups usually translate into differential access to highly valued institutional resources, opportunities, and privileges" (Stanton-Salazar, 1997, p. 5). Interpersonal networks, however, have been demonstrated to work in seemingly contradictory ways—social networks both transmit the effects of socioeconomic background, race, and gender and permit low-status individuals to negotiate and overcome social barriers to upward mobility.

A key relationship to a "significant other" who both understands power differentials in the larger society and is willing to transmit that information is essential for low-status individuals to survive the social antagonisms and divisions that exist in the larger society (Stanton-Salazar, 1997). Variations in socialization and social networks may help explain why New York City police officers shot to kill the Black man they saw "slinking around" and "peering suspiciously" when Diallo was "merely standing" in the vestibule of his apartment building reaching for identification in his wallet (Staples, 2000, section 4, p. 14). But the importance of having a social network and a key significant other who socializes one to negotiate race and class barriers cannot be underscored enough (see Cochran et al., 1990; Hansell & Karweit, 1983; Lin, 1990; Wellman & Berkowitz, 1988; Williams & Kornblum, 1985; Wynn et al., 1987). It is illustrated best when a parent reminds a son that being a Black teenager "6 feet 2, 200 pounds, with braids and the currently fashionable baggy pants" could get him mistaken for a drug dealer and killed in New York City (Staples, 2000). In the above examples, interpersonal networks are working both to transmit the effects of race and socioeconomic class and to eradicate race and class barriers to achievement and development and survival. I believe reconceptualizing socialization as a way of teaching and learning the negotiation of the dominant culture of power within the typical school environment can be theoretically useful for moving White preservice teachers from their "White-privileged" status to an understanding of equity pedagogy in multicultural classrooms.

Social networks research counteracts notions of socialization for academic achievement that are rooted in the highly individualistic tradition of functionalist sociology. Functionalist notions are grounded in beliefs that high academic performance and upward mobility rest on "the proper development of internal motivational dynamics, geared toward a heightened sense of personal control, a myopic focus on the importance of individual effort and merit, and the internalization of individualistic and extrinsic motives" (Stanton-Salazar, 1997, p. 3). In this scenario, school personnel are only responsible for fostering the characteristic dispositions for success that the nuclear family has already developed in the student (see Wehlage, Rutter, Smith, Lesko, & Fernandez, 1989). Stanton-Salazar (1997) argues that unequal access to institutional privileges and resources in educational settings is created because low-status youth do not develop key relationships with institutional significant others who are committed to and capable of transmitting vital social capital to them. Even with generous institutional support, most low-status students who thrive in mainstream culture (that is, embrace individualism, detach from community, and go "native" in mainstream society) suffer from the psychic violence of trying to manage life in multiple worlds (see Carger, 1996; Rodriquez, 1982; Santiago, 1994; Suskind, 1999). Learning the dominant "culture of power," maintains Stanton-Salazar (1997), is not possible for most low-status students, however, because they most often have to go it alone.

Earlier notions of socialization did not acknowledge the role of key "significant others" in schools to the subsequent development and academic success of low-status students. In addition, assimilation and accommodation, whereby low-status children were socialized to internalize, identify, and conform to dominant culture, were clearly the focus of early conceptions of socialization. Contemporary scholars of socialization have moved away from assimilation and accommodation and promote a more liberal view of the process that emphasizes "the acquisition of skills and competencies needed to become psychologically resilient, problem solving, productive adults in a complex society" (Stanton-Salazar, 1997, p. 2). Neither of these orientations, notes Stanton-Salazar, has adequately addressed the developmental issues connected to growing up in a classed and raced society. Rather, they have maintained dominant group notions of individualism. With the predominating notion of individualism, several elements play an essential role in the formation of supportive ties to "significant others" in schools. Yet, the role that knowledge of, facility with, and deference to the cultural rules, communicative patterns, and network orientations play in the formation of social ties is obscured. Individualism is the general network orientation of middle-class Euro-Americans and imposes the "social character and cultural conventions as requisites for the accumulation of social and other forms of capital" (Stanton-Salazar, 1997, p. 31). Individualism is a powerful barrier to the academic development of low-status students, and it is uncontested by teachers in the typical classroom.

The network-analysis approach Stanton-Salazar (1997) uses to understand comparative race and class socialization and the mechanisms responsible for minority school failure come out of this more contemporary work in liberal sociology. Social networks research, when applied to the socialization of poor and working-class youth of color, links social ties or relationships between students and institutional agents, like teachers, to these students' acquisition of social capital and institutional support (Stanton-Salazar, 1997). Stanton-Salazar's approach utilizes an understanding of the role "significant others" play in the status attainment of low-status youth. He merges two streams of work—the systematic analysis of interpersonal relations with a comparative analysis of the way race and class operates as an exclusionary force in and across institutional domains. Out of this he constructs a network-analytic model of socialization and schooling that is anti-assimilationist and culturally democratic. He locates his orientation in the work of Darder (1991) who advocated an anti-assimilationist educational experience—a "bicultural network orientation"—for low-status students (Stanton-Salazar, 1997, p. 34).

A bicultural network orientation holds promise for educating teachers to work in diverse classrooms. It is an alternative to the deeply embedded motivational models of school success that privilege individualism and assimilation. The perspective of a bicultural network model addresses "the social and relational mechanisms by which members of oppressed groups, particularly children and youth, become successful within mainstream institutions" and requires a democratic teacher practice (Stanton-Salazar, 1997, p. 32). Stanton-Salazar's research and the research he builds on is critical, I think, to replacing acts of racial profiling with networks of social ties woven to reproduce the success of dominant groups in low-status students. To this end, I focus on two aspects of Stanton-Salazar's social capital framework that are at the core of these supportive sustaining social ties: (1) the communal, not individualistic, engagement of these students in the academic process; and (2) the learning of appropriate codes and motivation to apply in interactions with significant others. A framework for supervising preservice teachers must guide teachers toward this kind of participatory engagement with low-status students that can intervene in the reproduction of inequalities.

## THOMPSON'S BLACK FEMINIST PERSPECTIVES ON CARING

Another conceptual model critical to my focus on interrupting acts of racial profiling comes from a critique of the color-blindness found in the psychological literature on caring and in theories of caring in education. The role of "significant others" that is referenced to questions of race and class holds promise for conceptualizing a pedagogy of supervision that focuses on the creation of equity pedagogy. This pedagogy would address how low-status children can learn to overcome exclusionary forces and accumulate valuable and highly productive social capital in teaching and learning situations. Forms of caring that "significant others" enact in teaching and learning situations that are identified and referenced to race and class provide a different perspective for White teachers—a perspective based in cultures other than middle-class White culture. Such perspectives are key to the formation of social ties between White teachers and low-income students of color.

In "Not the Color Purple: Black Feminist Lessons for Educational Caring," Audrey Thompson (1998) argues that theories of care have failed to acknowledge and address the Whiteness of their political and cultural assumptions. They assume White, middle-class ideals and conceptions of caring without reference to questions of race or ethnicity. And, I would add, class. Whether "conventionally feminine relational values are invoked (as in the 'homelike' models of caring proposed by Nel Noddings, Jane Roland Martin, and others) or challenged (as in the research on female adolescents conducted by the Harvard Project on Women's Psychology and Girl's Development)" or referenced to "White, heterosexual, middle-class domestic practices" or to "White conceptions of authenticity in relationship," all these ideals for "genuine" caring result from color-blind theorizing (p. 599). If "significant others" are to be successful in democratizing the accumulation of social capital and in enhancing the social network support of low-status students to negotiate power differentials in classrooms and schools, they must forge social ties to these students. Thompson proposes that perspectives other than White, middle-class culture are central to the formation of social ties that do not alienate or do symbolic violence to low-status students. Thompson reinterprets four themes in theories of care from a Black feminist perspective. Later in this chapter, I will use these reinterpreted themes to problematize the actions of the preservice teacher I supervised.

In the first theme, which concerns the moral relevance of a situation, a Black feminist perspective removes caring from the home or private sphere that colorblind theorizing assumes and locates it in the surrounding society (Thompson, 1998). In the Black ethical tradition, Thompson explains, one does not step back from the world in an innocent stance. Loving and caring are about knowing and transforming that racist world. Caring in Black communities and families has been a shared endeavor that has focused on providing children with strategies and understandings to survive racism (Thompson, 1998). "The Black feminist tradition of caring requires helping all African Americans to survive racism;" it is an ethical tradition that emphasizes knowledge of, not blindness to a classed and raced society. So, caring in this tradition "means helping to make society just for generations yet unborn" (Thompson, 1998, p. 599).

The second theme, survival, reinterpreted in a Black feminist perspective assumes survival is primary in a hostile, racist, society. Children cannot remain innocent of the danger a classist and racist society holds for them; they must be prepared ahead of time to face with resilience the threats to their survival. In the Black feminist perspective, the third theme—the reference point for values—is quite different from those of White feminists. Thompson (1998) illustrates the nonfunctional nature of a White, middle-class ideal of femininity to the survival of Black females. Black females are taught in their communities and can see for themselves that Black women are powerful, vibrant, competent. Black females do not view one another from racist or culturally White assumptions, Thompson says; they are "not about being nice, or being a lady, or not upsetting people" (p. 536). Being female is "about being someone to reckon with" (p. 536). "From a Black standpoint, racist conflict is too obvious to be denied," Thompson explains, and Black female students are being capable and competent when confronting conflict with others in a real relationship (p. 537).

In describing the fourth theme, Thompson details the role of Black narratives as an essential element of the moral and political storytelling that has shaped Black consciousness and moral understanding. With Black narratives, attention is directed at constructing and reconstructing Black experience on Black terms and not answering White assumptions from an inferior position (Thompson, 1998). Consequently, Thompson argues, "the stories that teachers and students need are those that demythologize race relations and make it possible for us to both see ourselves and one another as we really are and to see ourselves together as we might be" (pp. 539–540). Racial-innocence narratives that are typical in classrooms do low-status children a disservice because they mythologize race relations and erase Black experience constructed on Black terms. These children, whether boys or girls, will see little of themselves and their moral and political experience in classrooms when the Black communal, historical, and political perspective is discounted.

In reinterpreting these four themes from a Black feminist perspective, Thompson raises the consciousness of White educators to the racist underpinnings of perspectives on caring. She also points to approaches that will help White teachers include in their practice perspectives on caring that are based on cultural perspectives other than middle-class White culture. I will return to these themes later and suggest what they might mean for training preservice teachers to forge social ties with low-status students and become their key "significant others."

## WHITE RACE CONSCIOUSNESS IN TEACHER PREPARATION

A White woman of European descent, I teach predominantly White female students majoring in elementary education at a highly ranked liberal arts college that is overwhelmingly White and wealthy (a majority of family incomes are $100,000 or more). The vast majority of these students make it clear that they grew up with few or no peers of color. Their Whiteness is a distant, unmarked, abstract category. Working as a critical multiculturalist (see Kincheloe & Steinberg, 1997), I have generally focused on White positionality, examining with these prospective teachers the power relationships that give rise to race, class, and gender inequalities in classrooms and schools. Many scholars concerned with school improvement point to teacher preparation as being an essential factor in changing the educational outcome for students of color (Holmes Group, 1986; King, Hollins & Hayman, 1997; Melnick & Zeichner, 1997). To this end, the exploration of Whiteness has come to occupy a predominant place in multicultural education generally and my pedagogy especially (see McIntosh, 1989; McLaren, 1997; Roediger, 1991; Sleeter, 1993, 1996). When polite educational discourse generally focuses on linking White identity development, the disease of racism, and the study of Whiteness to multicultural education, "the assumption is made that race consciousness is an essential predisposition to eradicating racist policies and practices in schooling" (Sheets, p. 16).

This assumption has informed the foundations and methods courses I teach. Interrupting the acknowledged and unacknowledged assumptions of Whiteness, heterosexuality, middle-class status, Euro-ethnicity that we Whites carry into educational settings is a primary task (see Cochran-Smith, 2000; Maher & Tetreault, 1998; Rains, 1998). Together, we interrogate the ideological formations and dominant images of schooling practices (standards, testing, textbooks, tracking, systemized models of curriculum planning, gifted education, etc.). Racism and other biases and expectations of students' achievement are investigated and linked to school organization and institutional practices. In assigned readings, students might learn how to trace the historical and cultural beliefs, hegemonic ideologies, pressure groups, and textbook markets to examine the construction of a particular knowledge. Connecting representations of schooling practices, such as ability grouping through primary and secondary sources to their roots in "race betterment" and fear of the Other, has as its focus the marking of Whiteness.

As part of their sociological foundations course, students read Richard Rodriquez's (1982) autobiography, *Hunger of Memory,* and Chris Carger's (1999) case study of a Mexican-American student named Alejandro in *Of Borders and Dreams.* Both assigned readings describe the entrée of two non-English-speaking students into the different social world of the school setting. They analyze the rules and requirements necessary for Richard's and Alejandro's effective participation within those respective worlds as well as what is takes for these students to cross a nonneutral border successfully. They analyze and compare in two papers the personal costs to these non-English-speaking students as they struggle to acquire and employ the sociocultural and school-sanctioned discourse needed to be academically successful. And they must explain the very different outcomes of their respective schooling experiences.

Education students also analyze Whiteness as a site of racialized privilege by attending to the segregated material environment of the college itself. Discourse of and about the college hides the structure of race hidden in the racial segregation in the structure of the occupations. People of color hold the majority of lowest-paid and least-secure jobs and are rarely represented in the college's classrooms. This pedagogy aims at marking Whiteness and privilege, unsettling my students, and, I hope, spurring an internal revolution as they "unmake" their experiences as being representative (hooks, 1981). Being intellectually equipped to "expose the fingerprints of Whiteness" (Kincheloe & Steinberg, 1997, p. 219) on schooling does not, however, necessarily motivate White teachers to challenge ways of seeing that justify the status quo or that sanction the suffering of low-income children of color. Once the preservice students in my institution begin their observations, fieldwork, and practice teaching in public school classrooms populated with low-income children of color, they witness (overtly and covertly), talk about (consciously and unconsciously), and engage in (knowingly and unknowingly) acts of racial profiling. Clearly, my incorporating the study of racial identity, including White racial identity, into the academic discourse has not created the cognitive dissonance they need to discover or act on alternative ways of constructing racial profiling, or to encourage them to forge agency and interrupt the course of racism in their classrooms.

## THE "RACIALNESS" OF PRESERVICE EXPERIENCE

### MARY

One story from my supervision journal of a White preservice teacher I will call Mary, illustrates the racialness of preservice experience and demonstrates the need for student teachers to study their own and others' experiences of racial profiling.

Racial profiling in the narrated moment is an instance of what Peter McLaren (1998) calls Whiteness displacing "(B)lackness and brownness—specific forms of nonwhiteness—into signifiers of deviance and criminality within social, cultural, and political contexts" (p. 67). The following story is taken from the records I kept during my second and third observations of this preservice teacher and subsequent conversations and correspondence between us during the first four weeks of her internship experience.

Mary had been placed in a second-grade classroom in an elementary school located in an outer suburban ring of Orlando, Florida, by the county school board. It was January of spring term, the final term of her last semester of undergraduate study. In her second-grade class, White children and children of color were represented in almost equal proportions. In e-mail correspondence and individual conferences during the first weeks of student teaching, Mary related to me her initial reactions to the placement the first week. Mary hated the way her supervising teacher never smiled or was personal with the class or her. She reported to me that this class had been specially assigned to this particular teacher for the purposes of raising their standardized reading test scores. These students were "at risk," she told me. At the time of this observation, Mary's supervising teacher had not left her to teach the class full time. Mary was being phased in slowly and had been assigned the planning and teaching of only one content area—reading.

Mary requested that I observe her teaching of a reading group. She was insecure about her strategies and her supervising teacher's emphasis on raising student reading test scores. When I arrived one morning, Mary was sitting in a chair, seven children scattered on the floor around her. I observed her becoming increasingly frustrated with Sherry, an African American student, who had buckled and unbuckled her shoes twice in the 10 minutes I had been observing. Mary used her body and looks to signal displeasure—shaking her head from side to side to signal "No, don't do that." Mary also corrected this behavior verbally by politely asking Sherry to keep her shoes on in the classroom. She did this by leaning down and asking the girl to look at her. "Sherry, I will not tell you again. You must keep your shoes on." Her voice was stern, and she frowned. In the middle of the lesson, the supervising teacher returned to the classroom and entered through a door behind me. As she passed by my chair, she glanced over at Mary's reading group, leaned down, and whispered into my ear: "You see that Black girl, wiggling around with her shoes off?" Her voice was irritated; I nodded without turning to look at her. "She got up this morning determined to make our lives miserable." Without another word, she rose and continued to make her way to her desk. When Mary finished the lesson, we stepped outside the room to discuss what I had seen. "This was a horrible lesson," Mary complained. "I kept getting distracted by Sherry's behavior. She just ruined what I wanted to do." I asked her to describe Sherry's reading group behavior to me and explain what she didn't like. "She kept taking her shoes on and off during the reading lesson. In fact, all morning, I've had to remind her to leave her shoes on. And yesterday and the day before it has been nothing but the same behavior."

"Did you ask her why she is taking her shoes off?" I prompted. "Can you make a guess?"

Mary looked puzzled. "She is just being uncooperative with us, wanting attention I suppose."

"Your supervising teacher told me Sherry got up this morning determined to make your life miserable. Is this how it feels to you?" Mary gave a slight shrug of her shoulders, but had no real answer to my question. Before I left, Mary agreed to ask Sherry about her shoes as soon as she had an opportunity. That evening I had Mary's answer to my question on e-mail. "Sherry's shoes were bothering her," Mary's message read, "Because her shoes are too tight."

## INTERRUPTING RACIAL PROFILING

### TOWARD A FRAMEWORK FOR SUPERVISING MARY

The suppression of color talk in schools and college teacher education courses is abating in large measure because of the multicultural education movement. "One of the predominant theoretical floors of multicultural education is its defining, marking, and deployment of the concept of identity" (Dolby, 2000, p. 899). In multicultural education, categories of race, ethnicity, and gender, for example, are focused on to help teachers learn from difference—to make the world more tolerant and respectful of difference and not to be afraid of difference in the classroom. The narrated moment from my supervision experience with Mary reveals the colortalk of a well-meaning preservice teacher and my challenge to help her reflect on racist and classist policies and practices in her classroom. While she came to this preservice experience not fully formed as a teacher, it seems to me that her teacher preparation program, and especially components and courses in multicultural education, should have given her some basic knowledge and skills to provide antiracist and anticlassist affirming educational experiences for Sherry and all the children in her care. My goal is to use this moment to highlight the racist and classist practice of this well-meaning preservice teacher. While she had previously examined White privilege through course readings, discussion, and writing in her teacher education program, she was not able to see outside of it to form a supportive relationship with Sherry. I will examine the narrated moment through the lens of Ricardo D. Stanton-Salazar's bicultural network orientation and the themes in theories of caring reconceptualized by Audrey Thompson from a Black feminist perspective. Finally, I will explore what form interrupting racial profiling might take if my pedagogy of supervision focused on moving this preservice teacher from White identity to equity pedagogy.

### PROTECTING SHERRY FROM THE EFFECTS OF RACE AND CLASS

Through a comparative analysis of race and class, Stanton-Salazar (1997) unveils the social and relational mechanisms the dominant group uses, in tacit ways, to monopolize institutional resources. From that analysis he develops a social capital framework he calls a bicultural network orientation. Were such an orientation adopted, he suggests, socialization for school success in dominant group students might be reproduced for low-status students. In his framework, social capital, conceptualized as the accumulation of key significant others—woven into a network of agents capable of and oriented toward providing and negotiating institutional support for low-status students—makes possible the learning of privileged discourse. This discourse is essential for Sherry to engage in effective social relations and problem solving in her highly politicized classroom. Successful socialization in this framework would have Sherry learning how to obtain "various forms of resources and support" from a nonfamily institutional context (Stanton-Salazar, 1997, p. 16). Six forms of institutional support—the key ingredients Mary might provide for the social integration and academic success of Sherry have been described by Stanton-Salazar (1997) as:

1) The provision of various funds of knowledge associated with ascension within the educational system. (This form of support includes implicit and explicit socialization into institutional discourses that regulate communication, interaction, and exchange within mainstream institutional spheres.)
2) Bridging, or the process of acting as a human bridge to gatekeepers, to social networks, and to opportunities for exploring other mainstream institutions (e.g., university campuses).
3) Advocacy and related forms of personalized intervention.
4) Role modeling.
5) The provision of emotional and moral support. (p. 11)

The sixth form of support is related to how the first form—funds of knowledge—is communicated and extended to low-status students. Evaluative feedback, advice, and guidance given to low-status students that is regular, personal, and soundly based determines the extent to which it is, indeed, genuine emotional and moral support as well as thoughtful institutional support (Stanton-Salazar, 1997).

While there are seven forms of knowledge that comprise the first form of institutional support, it is the accumulation of social capital—forging social ties to key "significant others"—that I will focus on as crucial to the interruption of racial profiling. Accordingly, I emphasize three kinds of knowledge that Sherry will need to learn from Mary, her key "significant other": (1) human relations knowledge (ranging from deference to diplomacy) and the accompanying skills to apply this knowledge and to forge human relationships in highly politicized contexts, and (2) "the knowledge and skills most easily associated with rational problemsolving within impersonal bureaucracies"(Stanton-Salazar, 1997, p. 16). A third kind of knowledge concerns the use of socially acceptable ways of employing language for communicative behavior. For a low-status student, this is particularly problematic.

Five reasons are given by Stanton-Salazar (1997) to account for the problems low-status children like Sherry have in learning this knowledge and thereby accumulating the social capital essential for their success. He argues that these five reasons get transformed into structural problems intrinsic to the workings of schools, and they operate to engineer the failure of students like Sherry. These powerful institutional structures must be challenged by Mary and Sherry to reproduce dominant group success in Sherry:

1) The differential value accorded children and youth in contemporary society, depending upon their social class, ethnicity, and gender;
2) The barriers and entrapments that make participation in mainstream settings a terribly uncomfortable experience for minority children and youths;
3) Evaluation and recruitment processes by which school-based agents evaluate and select minority students for sponsorship; such selection processes largely entail perceptions of the student's ability and willingness to adopt the cultural capital and standards of the dominant group;
4) What I call "the institutionalization of distrust and detachment," or the institutional engineering of conditions and prescribed roles that are antithetical to the development of social capital;
5) Ideological mechanisms that hinder help-seeking and help-giving behaviors within the school. (Stanton-Salazar, 1997, pp. 7–8)

I will call on the theories of care, reconceptualized from a Black feminist perspective, to help Mary understand the development of a sustaining and supportive relationship to Sherry and transform her into a key "significant other" willing and capable of providing Sherry institutional support.

## TRANSFORMING MARY INTO SHERRY'S KEY "SIGNIFICANT OTHER"

In her classroom, Sherry was not spared the psychology of racial profiling—her specific form of non-Whiteness seeming to signify deviance as she removed the shoes she had outgrown. To interrupt Mary and her supervising teacher's practice of assigning criminality to this behavior, a pedagogy of supervising Mary would include, among many other elements, engaging Mary in tracking the social construction process that universalizes White characteristics in her teaching practice. In this narrated moment, we see both Mary and her supervising teacher essentializing good and bad behavior from a White conception of the proper way to be. Orderliness and self-control is "good;" the breakdown of self-control "bad." Thompson's (1998) themes of care reconceptualized from a Black feminist perspective can help interrupt this process. Caring from a reconceptualized perspective would resemble the African American tradition of "othermothering" (see Collins, 1990; hooks, 1984). This tradition is oriented toward enriching the cultural bonds in the classroom, and privileges the communal bonds between Mary and Sherry, between Sherry and her classmates, between Sherry and the classroom teacher, and outward into the school at large.

In Mary's educational practice, the reconceptualized themes of caring from a Black feminist perspective would reflect the following characteristics as she goes about solving this reading group problem:

1) respect—knowing about and understanding Sherry's perspective and situation;
2) survival teaching—guiding Sherry in strategies to survive in a classist and racist classroom;
3) displacing Whiteness as an implied neutral—not regarding Sherry's actions from a position of power;
4) inquiry—a stance toward Sherry's situation and perspective that values gaining information from her, not challenging or undermining her position (Thompson, 1998).

In addition, Mary would set about reproducing dominant student success in Sherry by utilizing a bicultural network orientation to help her accumulate the social capital to survive racism without the loss of her integrity. Dominant group students are already embedded "in a network of advocates and agents" (Stanton-Salazar, 1997, p. 16) and for the five reasons described earlier (differential value, barriers and entrapments, racist and classist evaluation and recruitment processes, institutionalization of distrust and detachment, and ideological mechanisms that hinder help-seeking and help-giving), low-status students like Sherry have problems forging those kinds of relationships (Stanton-Salazar, 1997). Mary must begin to weave such a network for Sherry by becoming her key "significant other."

Guidance for Mary's transformation from a position of cultural power to that of key "significant other" comes from the six forms of institutional support (funds of knowledge; bridge to social networks; advocacy; role modeling; emotional and moral support; and feedback, advice, guidance [Stanton-Salazar, 1997]). Mary must be guided to provide Sherry with this kind of sustaining support so key to surviving racial profiling in and out of the classroom. For the purposes of this article, I will highlight only one kind of knowledge among a number of others.[2]

The first kind of institutionally based fund of knowledge in a bicultural network orientation concerns learning how to engage in effective social relations and how to solve problems in a classist and racist context. To manage life in her multiple worlds, Sherry must begin to accumulate social capital—a social network of "significant others"—in this classroom. The culturally democratic practice that Mary can set into motion is providing her with a fund of knowledge—the precise content of which is teaching Sherry to decode the appropriate codes and apply them in the social interaction occurring because she removes her too-tight shoes. Mary can create the conditions in which Sherry can flourish if she applies a theory of care that emphasizes that the experience in the reading circle is connected to color and class and their relationship is forged to protect Sherry from its consequences. Mary must teach Sherry to solve the interaction problem by seeking help and communicating her need in a socially acceptable way. Mary must be willing and capable to give it. Establishing and sustaining trusting relations between Mary and Sherry is only hinted at here and deserves to be fleshed out in another article. At the core of that relationship, however, must be a partnership that works to demythologize race and class relations in that classroom. And key to their forging a supportive and sustaining relationship is a pedagogy of supervision that guides Mary to transform herself into a key "significant other" in the nonfamily context of school.

## CONCLUSION

A pedagogy of supervision that interrupts racial profiling will guide the preservice teacher to an understanding of how the accumulation of social capital is central to reproducing the success of the dominant group in low-income students of color. I have tried to advance a framework that is beginning to shape my thinking about moving preservice teachers from White identity to equity pedagogy. This framework has implications for teacher educators because it is drawn from perspectives not based on White, middle-class culture. I have done this by building on and incorporating the work of many scholars and especially Thompson's (1998) Black feminist critique of theories of care and Stanton-Salazar's (1997) social capital framework for socializing low-status students. Two aspects of the supervision framework—protecting low-status children from the effects of race and class and transforming teachers into key "significant others"—are committed to engaging preservice teachers and their college supervisors and low-status students in the academic process communally. This commitment rejects individualism and assimilation to promote a culturally democratic pedagogy and interrupt acts of racial profiling in the typical classroom.

*Notes*

1. I use the term low-status interchangeably with low-income for students of color throughout.
2. See Stanton-Salazar (1997) for the seven principal forms of institutionally based funds of knowledge and an elaboration of the seventh—problem-solving knowledge.

*References*

Banks, J. A. (2000). The social construction of difference and the quest for educational equality. In Ronald S. Brandt (Ed.), *Education in a new era* (pp. 21–45). Alexandria, VA: Association for Supervision and Curriculum Development.

Boykin, A. W. (1986). The triple quandary and the schooling of Afro-American children. In U. Neisser (Ed.), *School achievement of minority children: New perspectives* (pp. 57–92). London: Lawrence Erlbaum.

Boykin, A.W. & Toms, F. (1985). Black child socialization: A conceptual framework. In J. McAdoo & J. McAdoo (Eds.), *Black children* (pp. 33–51). Beverly Hills, CA: Sage.

Carger, C. (1996). Of borders and dreams. New York: Teachers College Press.

Chapa, J. and Valencia, R.R. (1993). Latino population growth, demographic characteristics and educational stagnation. An examination of recent trends. *Hispanic Journal of Behavioral Sciences, 15*, 165–187.

Cochran, M., Larner, M., Riley, D., Gunnarsson, L., & Henderson, C. H., Jr. (1990). *Extending families: The social networks of parents and their children*. Cambridge, U.K.: Cambridge University Press.

Cochran-Smith, M. (2000). Blind vision: Unlearning racism in teacher education. *Harvard Educational Review, 70*, 157–187.

Collins, P. H. (1990). *Black feminist thought: Knowledge, consciousness, and the politics of empowerment*. Boston: Unwin Hyman.

Connell, R. W. (1994). Poverty and education. *Harvard Educational Review, 64* (2), 125–149.

Cotton, K. (1993, November). *Fostering intercultural harmony in schools:* Research finding [online]. Topical Synthesis #7 in the School Improvement Research Series. (Downloaded 1997, April 8). http://www.nwrel.org/scpd/sirs/8/topsyn7.html. In Dilg, Mary (1999). *Race and culture in the classroom*. New York: Teachers College Press.

Darder, A. (1991). *Culture and power in the classroom: A critical foundation for bicultural education*. New York: Bergin & Garvey.

Delpit, L. D. (1988). The silenced dialogue: Power and pedagogy in educating other people's children. *Harvard Educational Review, 58*, 280–298.

Dolby, N. (2000). Changing selves: Multicultural education and the challenge of new identities. *Teachers College Record, 102* (5), 898–912.

Faltis, C. J. (2001). *Joinfostering*. Upper Saddle River, NJ: Prentice-Hall.

Frankenberg, R. (1993). *White women, race matters: The social construction of Whiteness*. Minneapolis: University of Minnesota Press.

Garbarino, J., Dubrow, N., Kostelny, K., & Pardo, C. (1992). *Children in danger: Coping with the consequences of community violence*. San Francisco: Jossey-Bass.

Hansell, S., & Karweit, N. (1983). Curricular placement, friendship networks, and status attainment. In J. L. Epstein & N. Karweit (Eds.), *Friends in school: Patterns of selection and influence in secondary schools* (pp. 142–159). New York: Academic Press.

Holmes Group. (1986). *Tomorrow's teachers: A report of the Holmes Group*. East Lansing, MI: Michigan State University.

hooks, b. (1981). *Ain't I a woman: Black women and feminism*. Boston: South End Press.

hooks, b. (1984). *Feminist theory: From margin to center*. Boston: South End Press.

hooks, b. (1994). *Teaching to transgress: Education as the practice of freedom*. New York: Routledge.

Howard, G. R. (1999). *We can't teach what we don't know*. New York: Teachers College Press.

King, J. E., Hollins, E. R., & Hayman, W. C. (Eds.). (1997). *Preparing teachers for cultural diversity*. New York: Teachers College Press.

Kincheloe, J. L., & Steinberg, S. R. (1997). *Changing Multiculturalism*. Philadelphia: Open University Press.

Kincheloe, J. L., & Steinberg, S. R. (1998). Addressing the crisis of Whiteness: Reconfiguring White identity in a pedagogy of Whiteness. In J. L. Kincheloe, S. R. Steinberg, N. M. Rodriquez, & R. E. Chennault (Eds.), *White reign: Deploying Whiteness in America* (pp. 3–30). New York: St. Martin's Press.

Ladson-Billings, G. (1994). *The dreamkeepers: Successful teachers of African American children*. San Francisco: Jossey Bass.

Lin, N. (1990). Social resources and social mobility: A structural theory of status attainment. In R. Breiger (Ed.), *Social mobility and social structure* (pp.247–271). Cambridge, U.K.: Cambridge University Press.

Maher, F. A. & Tetreault, M.K. T. (1997). Learning in the dark: How assumptions of Whiteness shape classroom knowledge. *Harvard Educational Review, 67,* 321–349.

Martin, J. R. (1992). *The schoolhome: Rethinking schools for changing families.* Cambridge, MA: Harvard Educational Press.

McIntosh, P. (1989). White privilege and male privilege: A personal account of coming to see correspondences through the work in women's studies. In M. Andersen and P. H. Collins (Eds.), *Race, class, and gender: An anthology* (pp. 70–81). Wellesley, MA: Wellesley College Center for Research on Women.

McLaren, P. (1997). Whiteness is . . . The struggle for postcolonial hybridity. In J. Kincheloe, S. R. Steinberg, N. M. Rodriquez, & R. E. Chennault (Eds.), *White reign: Deploying Whiteness in America* (pp. 63–75). New York: St. Martin's Press.

Melnick, S. L. & Zeichner, K. M. (1997). Enhancing the capacity of teacher education institutions to address diversity issues. In J. E. King, E. R. Hollins, & W. C. Hayman (Eds.), *Preparing teachers for cultural diversity* (pp. 23–39). New York: Teachers College Press.

National Education Goals Panel. (1997). *National education goals report.* Washington, DC: Author.

Noddings, N. (1984). *Caring: A feminine approach to ethics and moral education.* Berkeley: University of California Press.

Noguera, P. A. and Akom, A. (2000, June 5). Disparities demystified. *The Nation,* 29–31.

Penfield, J. (1987). ESL: The regular classroom teacher's perspective. *TESOL Quarterly, 21,* 21–39.

Perry, T. & Fraser, J. W. (Eds.). (1993). *Freedom's plow: teaching in the multicultural classroom.* New York: Routledge.

Quality Education for Minorities Project. (1990). *Education that works: An action plan for the education of minorities.* Cambridge, MA: Author.

Rains, F. (1998). Is benign really harmless?: Deconstructing some "benign" manifestations of operationalized White privilege. In J. Kincheloe, S. R. Steinberg, N. M. Rodriquez, & R. E. Chennault (Eds.), *White reign: Deploying Whiteness in America* (pp. 77–101). New York: St. Martin's Press.

Rodriquez, R. (1982). *Hunger of memory: The education of Richard Rodriquez.* New York: Bantam Books.

Roediger, D. R. (1991). *The wages of Whiteness: Race and the making of the American working class.* London: Verso.

Santiago, E. (1994). *When I was Puerto Rican.* New York: Vintage Books.

Sheets, R. H. (2000). Advancing the field or taking center stage: The White movement in Multicultural education. *Educational Researcher, 29,* 15–21.

Sleeter, C. (1993). Advancing a white discourse: A response to Scheurich. *Educational Researcher, 22* (8), 13–15.

———(1996). *Multicultural education as social action.* Albany, NY: State University of New York Press.

Stanton-Salazar, R. D. (1997). A social capital framework for understanding the socialization of racial minority children and youths. *Harvard Educational Review, 67,* 1–40.

Staples, B. (2000, April 12). How a Blackman's wallet becomes a gun. *New York Times,* 4, p.14.

Suskind. R. (1999). *Hope in the unseen: An American odyssey from the inner city to the ivy league.* New York: Broadway Books.

Swadener, B. B. (1995). Children and families "at promise": Deconstructing the discourse "at risk." In B. B. Swadener and S. Lubeck (Eds.), *Children and families "at promise": Deconstructing the discourse of risk* (pp. 17–49). Albany, NY: State University of New York Press.

Thompson, A. (1998). Not the color purple: Black feminist lessons for educational caring. *Harvard Educational Review, 68,* 522–554.

U.S. Bureau of the Census. (1998). Questions and answers about census 2000 [Online]. Available: http://.census.gov/dmd/www/advisory.html

Valencia, R. R. (1997a). Conceptualizing the notion of deficit thinking. In R. R. Valencia (Ed.), *The evolution of deficit thinking* (pp. 1–12). London: The Falmer Press.

Valencia, R. R. (1997b). Introduction. In R. R. Valencia (Ed.), *The evolution of deficit thinking* (pp. ix–xvii). London: The Falmer Press.

Valencia, R. R. & Solorzano, D. G. (1997). Contemporary deficit thinking. In R. R. Valencia (Ed.), *The evolution of deficit thinking* (pp. 160–210). London: The Falmer Press.

Wehlage, G.G., Rutter, R. A., Smith, G. A., Lesko, N. & Fernandez, R. R. (1989). *Reducing the risk: Schools as communities of support*. London: Falmer Press.

Wellman, B. & Berkowitz, S. D. (Eds.). (1988). *Social structures: A network approach*. New York: Cambridge University Press.

Williams, T. & Kornblum, W. (1985). *Growing up poor*. New York: Lexington Books.

Wynn, J., Richman, H., Rubenstein, R. A., Little, J., with Britt, B. & Yoken, C. (1987). *Communities and adolescents: An exploration of reciprocal supports*. Unpublished report prepared for the William T. Grant Foundation Commission on Work, Family, and Citizenship: Youth and America's Future.

*Cesar A. Rossatto*

# CRITICAL PEDAGOGY APPLIED PRAXIS: A FREIREAN INTERDISCIPLINARY PROJECT AND GRASSROOT SOCIAL MOVEMENT

IN BRAZIL, THE popular or people's school, serves as alternative schooling for "street" children and illiterate adult students. Many programs are created with local sources; others are supported by nonprofit organizations, or by public, local, and international funding. Many of the children enrolled in the programs come from broken homes, or are without parents and abandoned, wandering around the large urban cities of Brazil. Ignored and living as street urchins, young children rely on begging while older children mix work with petty theft, prostitution, and drug abuse. In their struggle to survive, going to school is sometimes not the first priority. Various organizations and institutions have formed special educational centers where these children are free to attend school on a volunteer basis.

In general, Brazil has a very high percentage of student dropout rates, beginning in the early elementary grades. According to the 1980 national census, 33 percent (7.6 million) of the 23 million children aged 7 to 14 were unschooled. As many intellectuals and community leaders say, Brazil is a country where 20 percent of the population owns 80 percent of the wealth (Torres, 1994). Therefore, many scholarly debates about popular schooling in Brazil revolve around issues of equality of educational opportunity as defined by access to school, permanence, and quality. Within this context, some educational objectives were designed to provide students with basic knowledge to survive in a hostile world. Although many programs are successful, this chapter will focus on three main programs (or initiatives) that are directly or indirectly embedded in Freirean principles. The learning processes inherent in the programs utilize the daily life experiences of the children to empower them to construct their own knowledge, rather than just memorize or receive knowledge from others. In this case, the teacher uses examples of the student's real-life experiences, rather than just focusing on the mastering of a given knowledge. This approach gives students the opportunity to be agents of their own history, rather than passive and dehumanized objects. To illustrate the implementation and impact of this principle, three program initiatives will be discussed in this chapter:

1. Sao Paulo Interdisciplinary School Reform
2. Projeto Axe—A Street Children Schooling
3. City of Porto Alegre Participative Citizenship

## SAO PAULO INTERDISCIPLINARY SCHOOL REFORM

Illiterate parents experience difficulties when they assist their own children with homework. On average, 46.3 percent of Brazilians have attended school for less than two years, which represents an inadequate level of functional literacy. Seventy-five percent of Brazilians over the age of five have less than four years of formal education. Out of nearly 88 million Brazilians over the age of ten, a woeful 25.5 percent are illiterate. Tragically, parents, consumed with issues of survival within a social and economic context of poverty and inequality, face two choices: either send their children to a "demoralizing public school or keep them in total exclusion" (DOT—SME, 1989).

The children who did go to school could not see the connection between classroom activities and their daily lives. Frequently, they would forget what was learned or they would resist learning what teachers had been trying to teach.

In 1989, Paulo Freire, as head secretary of education for the municipality of Sao Paulo, addressed these obstacles by proposing an interdisciplinary approach in public school and by initiating adult education programs. The interdisciplinary concept provided a broad view of all disciplines in an interconnected way, rather than a narrow focus conducive to a single subject of expertise. This notion brought to light social empowerment opportunities for disenfranchised populations. Formerly illiterate children and adults alike became citizens who knew how to "read the word and the world" (Freire & Macedo, 1987). Consequently, these educational initiatives fostered foundational objectives that contributed to the transformation of schools into spaces ready to receive the local community's culture and knowledge to then ultimately improve social contexts. The content and process of these principles recreated democratic possibilities that allowed students to recognize that they could, indeed, effect changes at a personal and social level. It brought to light a new social consciousness where everyone could participate as a functional citizen (Freire, 1970, 1997, 2000).

Freire (1993) explains in detail how this approach works as widely implemented in Sao Paulo's Municipal School District. In short, this educational method is called "problem posing," or a problem-based approach. It invites parents, community leaders, students, administrators, and educators to brainstorm about the main issues and problems faced by the school's local community. Out of this encounter, the participants choose topics for thematic units. Educators then use the topics (themes) to develop lesson plans in an interdisciplinary system. Teachers from each discipline approach and work with the topics as viewed from their content area of specialization. From a social empowerment viewpoint, this initiative's results have been widely positive. For example, working with environmental degradation themes mobilized the community to conservation measures. Further, recyclable resources provided revenue-generating opportunities.

This interdisciplinary system works in different stages. The first is known as the "study of reality" stage. After developing generative thematic topics within the local school community's significant social context, educators analyze their relevance and assess viable circumstances in order to work according to the children's different age levels. Using a dialectic approach of applying theory into practice in a dynamic and dialogical way, a second stage takes place, encompassing the children's thought structure with the educator's conceptualization of the areas to be studied. They review the roles assumed by students, educators, and the community as a whole. Educators then construct nonfragmented knowledge with the students by approximating the daily life experiences of the students with academic content in the classroom. At this stage, the teachers serve as organizers of the curriculum and pedagogical practice. They build ongoing consciousness by reviewing their praxis. Ultimately, the program seeks improvement of educational quality, democratization of district involvement, and democratization of school access for children.

The changes implemented at the Sao Paulo School District substituted a formal curriculum for an operational one. It permeated all of the functions of the school, as the ideology of knowledge, as well as the curricular power, is constructed throughout the school. It is precisely in this area that the interdisciplinary model is justified. By utilizing local knowledge as a powerful and necessary presence, a curriculum that combines the daily operation of the school with the community's struggles is created.

Moreover, education is not politically neutral (Freire, 1970); it is intensely related to societal organization and structural reproduction. There is also the challenge to assist educators to redefine their insights. It is not expected that teachers act uncritically but rather as agents of their own oratory, of their own history, in their own time and place, on behalf of the students. The conflicts that arise out of this process must be understood as part of the learning objectives. This experience contributes to the construction of critical awareness of the complexities of the denials that surround schools. This is a collective process, not an individual one. It must expose people, through certain basic contradictions, to the existential, yet concrete and present, situation. Then, as challenging problems arise, answers are not only discovered at an intellectual level but also at an action level. This is nothing less than a call to citizenship participation. It is precisely at this point that students, parents, educators, and administrators become integral and responsible agents committed to the development of a better future.

These first steps lead to an emancipatory education that allows students and educators to understand the multiple scientific, social, cultural, political, economic, and historical aspects of their complex daily lives. The next step is to extrapolate the totality of the phenomenon contained within the reality of the community. Just as the particular reflects itself onto the general, the interpretations of local phenomenon contain broader explanations that must be studied. Therefore, the teaching and learning experience alternates between micro to macro understanding and vice-versa. In this process, memorization is discarded. What is proposed is to take the practice as the real basis of knowledge. It means to start from the local reality that generates concrete facts (language, concepts, conflicts, anxiety, aspirations) and then fosters re-creation and appropriation of these facts. Facts that are mediated by knowledge imply a positive spiral of comprehension, with each level revealing a more profound and elaborate essence and relationship to this reality. This dialectic theory-and-practice movement enables the articulation of the particular and of the general as integrated in an organized understanding of scientific, technical, and social meaning.

The students benefit from the experience of structuring their thoughts according to their comprehension of reality. As a result of working to produce selected facts, they learn to utilize new conceptual instruments. These new conceptual instruments, revealed by the teacher's orientation, facilitate a more elaborate understanding of reality. Within this context, the teacher must be careful with the construction of significant learning situations. This is achieved by relating to the student's concepts of concrete phenomenon, by encouraging the students to become active agents of their own learning, and by addressing scientific concepts in the language of the students. It is a process of guiding the students from the "common sense" orientation, obtained in empirical situations, to an organized and systematized knowledge. Therefore, it is necessary that the concepts the students work on (with the teacher's orientation), become scientific in nature (DOT—SME, 1990).

During an observation of a classroom that utilized the Freirean approach, I noticed that Mrs. Oliveria (the teacher) requested that all of the students stand when she outlined the guidelines for the activities they were about to engage in. She told the students that the left side of the classroom was for the "no" answers and the right side for the "yes" answers and that students should walk slowly to the respective side according to their beliefs about each statement to be read. The teacher then proceeded by making statements such as: "The mayor is solely responsible to keep our city clean. Do you agree or disagree?" "The community should organize itself and attempt to resolve its own problems, rather then wait for the authorities to do it. Do you agree or disagree?" It was amazing to witness the struggle of the students engaged in the decision-making process to choose between their own beliefs or to follow the choices of their peers. At times, the opinion of the students was equally divided, but most of time, the majority moved to a particular corner. After the exercise was completed, the students participated in an exciting discussion about their own choices as well as the diversity of opinions discovered in the class. In the context of this classroom's experience, the intrinsic components of the production of knowledge included critical thinking, creativity, evaluation of reality, and decision-making skills.

Ana Maria Freire explains how this pedagogical notion and consciousness raising begins. She says:

> An inner-city student from Sao Paulo was found to be incapable of doing math exercises in the classroom. On the street he applied similar concepts by selling goodies or candies, and he was able to count the money and give exact change back without any difficulty. In class he was embarrassed and was feeling disconnected because the math class was too abstract and distant from his reality. It was also found that this student was skillful, talented, and he was the chosen leader at the local grassroots samba parade.

Ana Maria Freire goes on to say that

> A child is like a plant inside a room; it turns around to face and embrace the sunlight, as the sun is crucial for its revitalization, survival, and growth. By the same token, a child may feel connected or disconnected from the learning experience, depending on the pedagogical approaches used in the classroom. (Chapman University Freirean Conference, November 16, 1999)

The questions that arise are: Whose interests are being served by the learning experience: students, educators, or dominant groups? Whose educational versions benefit the students most, and, subsequently, the local community? What aspect of Freirean educational principles present content and process for the basis of social transformative pedagogies?

Oakes (1985) says that schools reflect the culture at large, and, in this sense, to understand schools fully, one ought to understand the context in which schools are entrenched. Therefore, to interpret social context, the use of critical hermeneutics, as a rigorous methodological approach, can enable the researcher to interpret narratives (or text) and construct meaning within its cultural circumstances.

The impact of Freire's work in Brazil resonated at broad social and educational levels. The theme of the 1999 street carnival parade in Sao Paulo (as chosen by Leandro de Itaquera, a grassroots, Afro-Brazilian samba school organization) was: "For Paulo Freire, Education is a Jump to Freedom." This song represents the samba sound they prepared for the occasion; *"Wake up, my Brazil"*

> //:Wake up my Brazil
> Wake up to happiness
> I want love, I want to love
> In freedom, Today://
>
> Today, Leandro so beautiful, plays its role
> Ask permission, and shows
> Reality as it is
> Our struggle continues on the blackboard.
>
> My samba group jumps to the future
> And goes to war with pen in hand

Our colors demand education
Without prejudice or discrimination

//: Inspired by a Divine Light
We will sing with a single voice
And Paulo Freire, is present among us://

Mister
I will not let go of my rights
I too have my notion
In the universe of creation
Minds are gifted with virtue and power
All it takes is to open the door and they will flourish

The world where magic creates ideals
And knowledge is not distinguished by social class
It is time to reflect
Consciousness be in every heart

//: A gleam of light shines, change
Long live youth, children
In faith that burns
Happy future, Brazilian nation://

As a Brazilian with many years of experience working with inner city populations, I will attempt to interpret and construct meaning out of this text in close approximation to the cultural context and its narratives. At first glance, the text reveals the population's struggle and search for liberation. The *Leandro of Itaquera*'s grassroots samba school asked permission to dance in the street parade. It did so as a conscious group with an identity fully aware of its claims. The lyrics suggest that this school, through the use of dressing and a parade featuring molded allegories (fantasies and parade structures during carnival), wants to demonstrate its daily reality and struggle as it permeates to the "blackboard" of their educational settings.

It is evident that *Leandro of Itaquera*'s grassroots school discloses a level of empowered consciousness. In other words, group members have claimed the right to have their own voices and ideas in the universe of creation, rather than being fed a given curriculum or educational agenda that they don't relate to and feel disconnected from. The text shows their awareness of the source of empowerment. The people are confident of possessing minds rich with virtue and power. Their creative use of intelligence is evident in settings where educational opportunities are accessible and learning experiences enable talents to flourish. The lyrics also express an optimistic view of transforming the world into a place where "magic creates ideals." This belief, however, is not a naïve embrace of reality. *Leandro of Itaquera*'s group knows that knowledge can be constructed discriminatorily within social classes.

Therefore, the members of this community are saying it is time to reflect and take to heart their critical consciousness. This is a vivid example of a community that has learned the basic principles of Freire's transformative notions and has found creative ways to further liberate itself from existing oppression. Likewise, the

*Jornal da Cidadania* (Citizenship) newspaper (1997) reported about a community museum with an entrance sign that read: "Please touch everything." It discussed the pleasant feelings people have when they construct, embrace, and participate in the creation of their own history. This is also learned in the classroom.

In Brazil, one can observe any number of classrooms that embrace Freirean principles. For example, in the inner city of Rio de Janeiro, a teacher was observed asking the students to write about their life histories. The teacher, together with the students, made books out of cardboard material. Then, the students drew and wrote their personal stories in it. The students felt so proud of their books that many carried them everywhere they went because that work meant a great deal to them. As a result, they were not only reading other people's books, but their own as well, which proved to be a valuable and empowering experience for all of them.

## PROJETO AXE — A STREET CHILDREN SCHOOLING

Another school model of popular education has been used in northeastern Brazil. A nonprofit organization (Projeto Axe) has already taken thousands of children out of the streets through emancipatory education. The program is located in the city of Salvador in the state of Bahia. Axe, a Yoruba word as defined by the popular Afro-Brazilian religion of Candomble, refers to the awakening of inner sources of power and positive energy (Foster, 1994).

Terra Nuova, an Italian nongovernmental organization, and the National Movement Agency initially provided the funding for Projeto Axe. The program gained national and international attention. Many other cities started using a similar approach, either in Brazil or in other parts of the world. Educational leaders in cities such as New York and Los Angeles are implementing the same philosophy while working with gang members. It is proving to be effective in assisting children to vent and extrapolate their anger, fears, and frustrations into positive energy and to discover new inner meaning in their lives. The Axe' Bahia program reinvents a curriculum that incorporates a variety of activities closely related to the customs and traditions of local life and culture.

For example, in this part of Brazil, the local community participates in a dance that is known in Portuguese as Capoeira. It is considered to be a folkloric martial art. The origins of the Capoeira can be traced to colonial times. The first African habitants of this region were brought there as slaves by the Portuguese colonizers. The slaves, then, invented the Capoeira to liberate themselves from slavery. The colonizers thought the slaves were just dancing as part of their religious rituals, but in reality, they were practicing and adjusting the "ritual" as a means to kick the colonizer slavemaster down from his horse. Capoeira, developed initially as a self-defense instrument for liberation, became a historical, regional symbol of emancipation.

Today, the Capoeira is enriched with a folkloric quality innate to the Brazilian culture, particularly in the region of Bahia, where the majority of the citizens are

Afro-Brazilian. It is common to see Capoeira matches and practices in public places and on the streets. Therefore, the Axe' Bahia project used Capoeira as an integral component of its curriculum, together with other educational content and processes. The Capoeira is a positive instrument for the development of concentration, focus, and physical and emotional growth. Together with other core activities, the positive results gained by incorporating Capoeira into the curriculum is obvious as program participants are reintegrated into society as functional and dignified citizens.

This project has been in existence for about ten years. The program content is based on self-motivation, creativity, critical thinking, and dialogue about real street-life issues and experiences, identity, social rights, and moral values. The curriculum includes ample opportunity for the flexible discovery of knowledge constructed according to unexpected needs and student performance. Through this process, the children learn to connect their classroom activities with real-life experiences. They establish their learning pace by producing knowledge through collective engagement activities, utilizing percussion, dance, art, culture, entertainment, and literacy classes. This lively schooling has great significance for children, who are part of an emergent process. Here they learn to transform their personal life-stories into an evolving educational experience that contains new life possibilities. They develop hope, self-esteem, and new notions of citizenship. The classroom discipline is constructed democratically between the students and the educators. This enables them to create a workable environment, characterized by the respect they share for each other's differences. Above all, they learn to trust their newly discovered potential to change their own lives.

The project also includes vocational education. Environmental awareness, together with practical recycling, provides resources for the program's self-support. This aspect of the project enhances the children's abilities to become collaborative authors of ideas that provide them with real, practical ways to make a living. According to the (London) *Financial Times* (1994), the project is working with three thousand out of sixteen thousand "street" children in the city of Salvador, Brazil. The majority of those who succeed with the program's support either find jobs or are reunited with their families. Although this success is notable, the reality is that an unacceptable number of children remain on the streets of Brazil. The private sector is becoming more involved by assisting with the vocational aspect of the program and by employing many of the students.

The program is growing and receiving worldwide recognition. *Projeto Axe,* in collaboration with the municipality of Salvador, has recently opened a public school. Other private, professional, governmental, and institutional organizations, such as UNICEF Brazil, the Brazilian government, the U.S. State Department, and prominent personalities are endorsing and supporting this program's success. The *Los Angeles Times* (1994), *Washington Post* (1995), and *Financial Times* (1994), among other newspapers, have documented aspects of the project's outstanding performance and results.

The success of this program is not a magical performance with mystical attributes; it requires a gradual course of action. As a staff member, Marcos Carvalho, explains, "We can only do that [successfully move children out of streets] if the children are offered real alternatives that they can freely accept. It is a delicate, and complex process." According to Carvalho, the street educators play an important role, requiring constant pedagogical accompaniment to reflect, inquire, and revise practices during the reinvention of daily experiences. Initially, educators reflect on their own lives to understand how their personal educational experiences affected them. Then, they are able to better understand the children and transmit a sense of security to them. Also, educators learn to understand the process of social marginalization that reproduces itself on the streets with its psycho-affective side effects. By being aware of street practices, and by accompanying the children's struggles, educators can develop pedagogical alternatives. Therefore, according to Carvalho, the first phase of the work is observation. He recommends that street educators exercise consistency by revisiting the same location at the same time each day. During this phase, educators immerse themselves in a casual, yet anthropological, discovery of the children's daily behaviors and life experiences. The children eventually approach the adults and ask, "Who are you?" and the educator(s) answer, "Who would you like me (or us) to be?" From this point on, a dialogue begins by uncovering the children's desires and stories. Educators are also discouraged from taking a paternalistic approach and providing loans to children who are accustomed to survive by begging. Instead, the program fosters the beginning of what is called the pedagogy of desire.

The pedagogy of desire, inspired by Lacan (1978), avoids the development of resistance in the students by understanding the relationship between the symbolic and the real. The establishment of a symbolic form of consciousness that is freely and independently able to adopt its own social construction and realize its essence is preferred to an apparatus that produces the criminal, the insane, and the destitute. This symbolic form of consciousness comes as no surprise in connection with a language of possibility and non-oppressive space, even within hegemonic social conditions. For example, the symbolic word *Exu,* culturally present in local religious rituals, has been historically interpreted by many as the manifestation of evil. In the Axe's pedagogical context, this expression can be a welcoming and inclusive anthropological demonstration, which allows children to express their rebellious feelings toward a system that is not working for them, and, on the contrary, is working "against" them or unable to understand their struggles and needs. Through the construction of a pedagogy of desire and schoolwork enjoyment, the next step is to attempt to enter into children's world without homilies or any authoritarian conversation. As is common in any relationship, mutual discovery takes time and trust. At this stage, the children express great interest in playing, and so, the implemented curriculum is designed for outdoor field trips. The children leisurely play games while educators continue to talk to each child about his or her family, survival efforts, sex, and other issues. The majority of the children of Salvador, Bahia, are not orphans; they have families, as is true elsewhere in Brazil. But many of them, for a number of reasons, are forced on the street with broken family ties. If they do have parents, some cannot, or will not, feed them. Others are born out of prostitution, exploited by international tourists who visit Brazil for that purpose, or even by locals who also take advantage of uneducated young women. According to Carvalho, the children's fragmented stories are a mosaic to be recomposed. After this initial introductory period, Axe's staff members begin to introduce some pedagogic instruments, such as a theatrical game or other indoor educational entertainment. For street children who are accustomed to plentiful outdoor space, a structured classroom can be reminiscent of feelings once experienced at repressive institutions. Usually in closed spaces, the children feel they have to restrain their behavior in the presence of other people and participate within social rules. The children gradually imagine future possibilities outside of street life if they remain in communication with the educators. Many visualize the home bitterness they were familiar with, and, as a consequence, foresee an unhappy future. During personal interviews with children found in similar settings throughout Brazil, social, circumstantial struggles, and projection of future possibilities are shared. One child said, "Future! Who knows? I could be dead tomorrow." Another one said, "Growing up, watching this [slums, drug dealing, and crime] on a regular basis, the future seems bleak. The drug dealers have a lot of money and women, but they die early. They don't make much of their lives. But we cannot even trust the police either." A third child stated, "In the future I will most likely be in jail." These are just a few examples of many similar fatalistic statements.

The projections of better possibilities are accompanied by the feelings of trust and hope learned at Projeto Axe. One child from Axe, [as videotaped] said, "Many kids on the street are in need of support and love. I didn't know what love was until I came to Axe." As documented on the same video, many of Axe's students participate in a parade funded by public and private sponsors. One student said, "People think that the parade is for rich people, but they are wrong." The students make their own costumes and participate in the parade. It helps them develop self-esteem. All of the different cultures, music, and histories are represented in the parade. Through it, the children learn to celebrate life as a whole. They learn that what is simple and humble is also beautiful. They learn to develop a sense of pride and to transform their lives without repression. Through artwork, they find that, in the world of creativity and imagination, there is no right and wrong, all colors are beautiful, all shapes and mixes are gorgeous. As educators and children develop their association with trust, aspirations for different lifestyles emerge. The search for housing and employment is another inviting challenge. As real world expectations may differ from their own, they must learn how to face life in life's terms using instruments of hope. They become skilled at caring for themselves in a healthier way, rather than relying upon paternalistic assistance. Through this experience, they discover their rights, as citizens, while engaged in the struggle to secure dignified human conditions. For "street" children, emotional and physical growth is harder than it is for children in better conditions. They have to know different ways to respond to situations encountered on the streets; they have to learn to claim rights and at the same time ward off disrespect and intrusion in their lives.

It takes time and experience before the students are able to discern their own rights—as well as the rights of others—and to develop the assertiveness necessary to properly defend themselves. To address their survival-level reality, the project uses pedagogical approaches with a political aim. It initiates open dialogue with public authorities in order to build basic support services at the community level that will provide transformative opportunities in the children's lives. According to Axe's director, Cesare Della Rocca, the program must be in a state of continual critical assessment to ensure that its actions, aims, and mission are aligned with the social demands and reality in which it operates. Its institutional mission is based on the principles. of fundamental human rights, construction of scientific knowledge, and active respect for the student's values and cultural practices. The project also offers networking possibilities to address the needs of those in extreme poverty. These individuals often are deprived of public protection, and denied the opportunity to develop their human, biological, psychological, social, cultural, and spiritual potential. The project is actively involved with both municipal and state governments to influence public policies as advocates for children's human rights and health care concerns. Ultimately, the lessons of this positive educational experience expose issues of community organization for resource distribution and question the effectiveness of certain programs to provide democratic upward mobility for those most in need. In addressing this particular social situation, the Porto Alegre experience is subsequently brought into focus.

## CITY OF PORTO ALEGRE PARTICIPATIVE CITIZENSHIP

In Porto Alegre, as in the majority of other southern Brazilian cities, it is customary to drink a hot tea known as *chimarao*. Traditionally, the people gather in small groups early in the morning or late in the afternoon to drink chimarao. This caffeine drink is passed around in a dried calabash shell container with a fancy gold suction pump. A person drinks, and after finishing, the pot is filled again and passed on to the next person. During this gathering, the participants have an opportunity to have casual conversations. Many anthropologists have analyzed this tradition and have determined that its cultural context is a major contributing factor to the local strong citizenship development and positive politicization.

In Porto Alegre, one of the largest cities in southern Brazil, the opportunity for social and economic upward mobility is proportional to new and democratic citizenship participation. The most internationally noted project is known as "Participatory Budget." In this exercise of their citizenship, the members of each community gather at local meetings and decide as a group how the community will allocate its financial resources. They decide how the financial resources designated for that particular community should be distributed among community objectives including education, health care, or others. The community also decides how the budget should be prioritized according to public safety and related needs. Customarily, in other parts of Brazil, the mayor or governmental authorities have absolute control over the budget and its distribution. Frequently, many authority figures are not challenged in their decisions, which often leads to corruption and misappropriation of funds. Since citizens are not educated to participate, and have been instructed to blindly follow orders, many people have difficulty imagining themselves as citizens with rights. In contrast, the democratic leadership of the Labor Party in Porto Alegre provided the opportunity to local citizens for participation in many other important decisions for the betterment of their lives. In other words, the population became active agents of their own history.

After winning the election, the local members of the Labor Party, who had for years worked on the construction of critical consciousness in the community, had an opportunity to initiate this collective democratic system. They started a democratic popular citizenship participation program to assist the people found most in need. This initiative was heavily intertwined with popular educational programs reinforcing the ideal that schools need not exist merely to produce skillful future labor, but rather to focus on the enhancement of democratic citizenship. This ideal is possible when indeed there is equity, critical engagement, and democratic participation (Fraser, 1997).

According to the Prefeitura Municipal de Porto Alegre's (1993) *A Paixao de Aprender: Aprender participando, aprendendo a participar* (The Passion to Learn: Learn by Participating, Learning to Participate), education is the process of humanization of human beings. In other words, it is a collective and individual construction of knowledge, values, attitudes, and sentiments in the direction of conscientization (critical awareness and action). With this mindset, education involves the development of autonomous, critical, and creative agents who comprehend reality in its multiplicity and in its conflictive interests. Interfering in this reality often means opposing exploitative, dominant groups. Thus, education calls for proactive positions to build a more just society, less unequal, and authentically democratic.

A report by the Prefeitura Municipal de Porto Alegre (1994), *Escola Cidada, Aprender e ensinar participando* (The Citizenship School, Learning and Teaching by Participating), argued that the popular public administration should have an educational commitment to the collective public interest. Popular schooling must integrate the whole community, including its civil and social movements, into its mission statement and curriculum elaboration.

An education that incorporates the popular culture has empowering attributes and qualities that start with early childhood education. Along this line of thought, Freire's (1970) position is that "There is no teaching without learning, no learning without teaching." Educators are open to embracing the student's cultural and local identity as dialectical sources for content and academic process. It is a validating, and ultimately a humanizing, experience when students are not considered to be blank slates to merely receive knowledge—and teachers are not considered mere transmitters of knowledge either. Both teachers and students are open to learn from each other and to produce (or construct) knowledge together. For teachers, constant reflection on daily practices in order to gauge effectiveness eventually leads to revision of content and process based on emergent discoveries. It becomes hands-on, or participatory, research, applied to the teaching and learning of the classroom praxis. By the same token, students also need to use participatory research while engaged in the search for their passion. Then, their curiosity for the "new" and rediscovery of the "old" still useful to present life circumstances, makes itself "new" again. By applying hands-on experiences during the discovery process, students learn to contribute to self- and collective enlightenment. According to Freire (2000), what students discover by themselves is usually retained for life. This is an empowering, popular education model, based on transformative pedagogies, that contributes to personal and social emancipation.

Educators are challenged to be creative and to deconstruct existing pedagogical methodologies of memorization and other authoritarian practices of education. As the latter dictates repetition and replication of preexisting knowledge, which students don't identify with, or even find practical, applications to real-life situations invariably fail as students soon forget what they had memorized. The problem is often that traditional methodologies represent an "easy" pedagogical alternative, which customarily locates educators in positions of privilege and authority. Although to some, this may represent a pragmatic initiative in search of a magical recipe, in reality, it may prove to offer only short-term positive effects with a net experience of disempowerment overall.

Additionally, popular and democratic education may contain other important theoretical implications. The questions that can arise are: Should the pedagogical approach be centered on the students or on the teachers? What should be the teacher's role?

According to Giroux (1998), teachers should not be the center of knowledge and power if the knowledge they advocate reproduces the hegemonic social order. Teachers must become transformative intellectuals who practice a pedagogy in which both teachers and students become agents committed to the study of daily life, as opposed to memorization. Students have difficulty doing this process alone; they need a teacher who can help them identify hegemonic structures and create a critical language (Aronowitz & Giroux, 1985). Consequently, the teacher has a leadership role and knowledge that is potentially liberating and important or limiting for students.

Critical pedagogical approaches can help students construct an engaging knowledge based on their realities and also help them to use their background experiences as a self-empowerment tool (Freire & Macedo, 1987). This means building schools as sites for cultural contestation, as they must be places for historical, critical, and transformative action (McLaren & Leonard, 1993). In this process, critical educators emphasize how social identities are constructed within unequal relations of power in the schools (Weiler, 1988). The interdisciplinary approaches to learning and cultural differences address the dialectical and multifaceted experiences of everyday life. One particular example illustrated by Freire (1970), says that if the agents (teachers and students), are dichotomized, the knowledge, which ought to be constructed between and among both, will be very limited.

The educational role that contributes to the transformation of schools into spaces ready to receive the culture and knowledge of the local community is very important as it has implications as to how students engage in schooling. In order to achieve this "readiness," educators are called on to identify and deconstruct hegemonic structures to recreate democratic possibilities. Thus, Giroux's (1985) version of the educational practices of teachers as transformative intellectuals, is one where teachers constantly reflect upon their position in the social order. Also, the students are acknowledged as having a role as transformative intellectuals. Yet, it represents a challenge that promotes an increased awareness of this understanding and conveys a sense of urgency for change. Such changes are based on the development of a discourse that unites a critical language with the language of possibility for both teachers and students, enabling them to recognize that they can indeed effect transformations in their schools, communities, and lives.

## Note

A shorter version of this paper was published in *Childhood Education,* Vol. 77, pp. 367–374 in 2001; with their permission the longer version is published in this book.

## References

Aronowitz, S. & Giroux, H. (1985). *Education under siege: The conservative, liberal, and radical debate over schooling*. South Hadley, MA: Bergin and Garvey.

Chapoval, T. (1994, April 10). Project rescues Brazil's street children. *Los Angeles Times*.

Devroy, A. (1995, October 16). First lady advocates investing in people: GOP social cuts apparent aim of remarks. *Washington Post*.

DOT—SME (1990). Estudo Preliminary da Realidade Local. *Prefeitura de Sao Paulo*.

Foster, A. (1994, January 11). Glimmer of hope for Brazil's street children: Angus Foster visits a pioneering project to rehabilitate and educate a deprived generation. *Financial Times*.

Fraser, J. (1997). *Reading, writing and justice: School reform as if democracy matters*. New York: State University of New York Press.

Freire, P. (2000). *Pedagogia da indignacao*. Sao Paulo: Unesp.

Freire, P. (1997). *Pedagogy of the heart*. New York: Continuum.

Freire, P. (1996). Pedagogia da autonomia: Saberes necessarios a pratica educative. Sao Paulo: Paz e Terra.

Freire. P. (1993). *Pedagogy of the city*. New York: Continuum.

Freire, P. (1970). *Pedagogy of the oppressed*. Sao Paulo: Paz e Terra.

Giroux, H. (1998). *Paulo Freire and the discourse of politics*. American Educational Research Association Conference, San Diego.

Giroux, H. (1985). Critical pedagogy, cultural politics and the discourse of experience. *Journal of Education, 167* (2), 22–41.

Lacan, J. (1978). The four fundamental concepts of psychoanalysis (Alan Sheridan, Trans.). New York: Norton, 112. [Translations are occasionally modified; see *Le Seminaire,* Livre

XI: *Les quatres concepts fondamentaux de la psychanalyse,* ed. Jacques-Alain Miller (Paris: Seuil, 1973).]

McLaren, P. & Leonard, P. (1993). *Paulo Freire: A critical encounter.* London: Routledge.

Oakes, J. (1985). *Keeping track: How schools structure inequalities.* New Haven, CT: Yale University Press.

Prefeitura Municipal de Porto Alegre. (1993). *A Paixao de aprender: Aprender participando, aprendendo a participar.* Porto Alegre: Author.

Prefeitura Municipal de Porto Alegre. (1994). *Escola Cidada, Aprender e ensinar participando.* Porto Alegre: Author.

Torres, C. (1994, May). Paulo Freire as secretary of education in the municipality of Sao Paulo. *Comparative Education Review.*

Weiler, K. (1988). *Women teaching for change.* New York: Bergin & Garvey.

*Laureen A. Fregeau and Robert D. Leier*

# PRAXIS AND TEACHER VISIONS OF SOCIALLY JUST SCHOOL REFORM

> *The essential thing, I maintain later on, is this: hope, as an ontological need, demands an anchoring in practice. As an ontological need, hope needs practice in order to become historical concreteness.*

> —PAULO FREIRE (1995)

## INTRODUCTION

THERE IS HOPE in grassroots reform, in teachers, parents, students, and community members knowing they have the power to transform their reality—even if just a little. The TERRA[1] process described in this chapter is designed with this goal of hope in mind. The goal is that teachers, with the help of parents, students, and community members, can envision, research, design, and implement bottom-up educational reforms that promote a more socially just future.

Some critical theorists, such as Paulo Freire (1973) and Henry Giroux (1988), conclude that, for critical social reform to occur, teachers must become grassroots educational activists who recognize their capacity and potential as both intellectuals and leaders in reform that follows a social transformational model. We agree. Two basic education reform models are adapted from socioeconomic development paradigms originally focused on economic development and development education programs in developing countries. These models, referred to as "top-down" and "bottom-up" reform approaches to development, have been applied to a political framework of educational reform in industrialized countries such as the United States. Top-down reform[2] is designed, developed, and implemented by outsiders and power holders for those deemed as needing assistance, with no design input from the recipient. Bottom-up, also called "grassroots," refers to reform[3] in which the target population takes part in designing programs they deem appropriate for their goals, not the goals of outsiders.

Applied to education, top-down reforms are designed at the state, federal, or district levels to be implemented by teachers on the target student population. Top-down education reforms are generic, assumed to fit all students and communities. Bottom-up education reform is initiated at the school, community, or classroom level. It is specific to the target population. Two assumptions are made in this paradigm: one, that to be successful and lasting, reform design must be specific to the school or community; and two, the target population (teachers, students, parents, community) must have ownership of the design and, therefore, must have voice in the design of the reform. It must be grounded in the reality and self-identified needs of the target population, using the "educands local context as the point of departure for a prolongation of their understanding of the world" (Freire, 1994, p. 86).

The authors' model described in this chapter focuses on reform designed by teachers with the assistance of colleagues, parents, students, and community members, for the designers' classrooms, schools, and communities. It is thus positioned within the bottom-up paradigm of education reform. The model introduces K-12 teachers and adult educators in graduate level social foundations courses to the process of becoming education activists prepared to promote bottom-up social transformational education reform. The model was named the Teacher Envisioned Research and Reform Approach, or TERRA. The fundamental objective of the semester-long TERRA process is to help educators realize that their desire to help all children achieve can begin to be fulfilled through the realization that they have the power to facilitate and initiate socially just school reform. The TERRA model continues to evolve through an ongoing development process as more practitioners' experiences with the TERRA process are examined.

The research presented here examines how TERRA, implemented in graduate level multicultural and social foundations courses, prepared K-12 teachers and adult educators as transformative intellectuals through a praxis model experience (Freire, 1970; Aronowitz & Giroux, 1985; Shor, 1986). TERRA consists of a reflective process, as described by Maxine Greene (1986), and an action component, whereby participants (students in the graduate classes) identify structural inequalities (Nieto, 2000) and social inequities in their school systems, research possible solutions, and then propose and implement reform plans to reduce these inequalities. The authors examined if, after experiencing this transformative process, the teachers have

1) gained critical awareness by experiencing and understanding critical social realization, reflection, and action (praxis model) through the course activities and while researching and formulating reform plans for their classrooms, schools or communities;

2) perceived themselves as transformative intellectuals, as empowered (either via viewing power as relational or via self-developed power) or as critical participants in a democratic society, able to help transform inequalities and inequities in their school or community at a grassroots level;

3) envisioned reform that can be categorized as promoting social justice;
4) implemented planned reforms in their classrooms, schools or communities;
5) encountered obstacles to reform and, if so, have reflected on this and created courses of action to overcome the obstacles.

## THEORETICAL FRAMEWORK

Education professionals are often asked to examine the theoretical sociological contexts of schooling in multicultural and social foundations graduate courses. In summative course evaluations, Jackson (1994) found that these students categorize sociological theory as inapplicable to their school practice and environment and therefore useless. Social inequalities and injustices in their educational systems may be discussed and acknowledged; however, the concept of praxis is often ignored and an opportunity for the active reconstruction of society through education is lost (Jackson, 1994). The reproduction of the inequities in society is reinforced through some of the very individuals (teachers) being oppressed (Bourdieu & Passeron, 1990). TERRA provides the opportunity for the concept of praxis, as defined by Paulo Freire (1970, 1973), to be understood and the process to be experienced.

Relating the theory to the process, the basic components of the process involve empowering oneself by

1) understanding one's social reality,
2) reflecting on that reality and experience,
3) realizing that it can be changed and imagining how (Ryan, 1994),
4) deciding one has the power to make change, and
5) taking action to make changes in that reality.

The "understanding of one's social reality" occurs when the student relates course content (on structural inequalities in school and society as related to race, religion, gender, class, politics of education, sexual orientation, diverse family structures, worldview) and field and literature research to self through dialogue journals,[4] class discussions, and experiential cross-cultural activities. "Reflecting on reality" occurs through oral, silent, and written meta-analysis of all these activities. The "realization that reality can be changed" and "deciding they have the power to make change" comes through the process of knowing others have had the power to change realities and again later while implementing reform plans. "Imagining how" occurs in the process of creating the reform plan and gathering others' ideas for reform. "Taking action" is the implementation of the created plan.

John Dewey (1916) wrote extensively about the importance of finding solutions to common societal problems through education. He believed schools to be places where problem-solving skills should be developed and nurtured. Teaching should be a function of social change which, according to McLaren (1992), should "be an effective tool in developing critical and unbiased understanding and, thereby, greater educational, political, economic and cultural justice" (p. 7). According to Ashendon, Connell, Dowsett and Kessler (1987), teachers' interest and understanding of educational reform is an important strategic issue and needs to be encouraged and developed.

Giroux (1992) sees the integration of community, school, students, and teachers as a collective power force in addressing social injustices within the school community. TERRA provides the opportunity to develop problem-solving skills and practice them by addressing the problems of social injustice facing schools and communities. Participants (students in our graduate courses) are encouraged to integrate other teachers, students, administrators, parents, and community members in the research and planning of their reform plan. Freire and Shor (1987) observe that teachers may be stuck in the old paradigm of authority (top-down). The TERRA process requires that teachers incorporate the worldviews of parents, colleagues, students, and community members into their understanding of the problem and into the design of the reform plan.

Just as Dewey viewed democracy as a "way of life," Lappé and DuBois propose the importance of "living democracy" rather than merely living in a democracy (1994). "Doing democracy," as defined by Lappé and Dubois (1994), and integrated into the Research and Reform Plan approach, provides the opportunity and experiential foundation for teachers to become transformative intellectuals who have the understanding to empower themselves, and to help colleagues, students, parents, and community members recognize their power. Understanding relational power enables participants (in collaboration with their colleagues, students, parents, and community members) to reconstruct society through and in association with public and private schools and education (Britzman, 1986; Giroux & McLaren, 1989).

TERRA differs with other teacher-as-researcher models in that it questions (Dolbec & Savoie-Zajc, 1995) whether teacher-research, especially top-down models where students collaborate with university faculty, prepare graduate students to understand a bottom-up approach to education reform. TERRA does not encourage research collaboration between university faculty and teacher (graduate student) researchers. Rather, TERRA, a process model, intends for the university faculty to be a guide in the process and never a designer or implementer of the research. Ownership of the research by the teacher-researcher (student in our graduate classes) is key to the TERRA process and, we feel, to the development of bottom-up teacher-(and student-, parent-, community-) envisioned school reform.

## BACKGROUND OF THE STUDY

Participants in this study were education professionals and graduate students who had completed the TERRA process while in graduate level semester-long social foundations courses taught by the authors at the University of South Alabama. They were primarily K-12 public school educators or counselors employed in southern Alabama, northwestern Florida, and southeastern Mississippi. All participants were candidates for graduate degrees (masters degree and education specialist certificate). Due to teacher demographics in these regions, more than 90 percent of participants were female. Teachers who chose to participate did so voluntarily because they had identified a need for social reform in their school or community.

Very few participants had ever heard of Paulo Freire before taking our classes. Even fewer had ever participated in grassroots reform in schools or at any level. Most were familiar with top-down philosophical, pedagogical, and reform models that are politically popular in the participants' states.

## METHODOLOGY

Data were collected through structured and unstructured interviews with teacher-researchers, class discussions, observations, and document reviews. Interviews were conducted with current and past participants. In-class observations were made of participants' discussions during the TERRA process. Documents examined included student reflections on their participation in "public life," project proposals, Reform Plan reports, reflective dialogue journals, open-ended summative course evaluations solicited participant reviews of the process, school documents reflective of reform plan implementation, follow-up interviews, and researcher observational records.

## THE PRAXIS PROCESS

The process through which the students created and eventually implemented their reform plans is important to the context of the data presentation and interpretation. The process began with the participants' search for self-understanding of their worldview and place in society. Self-understanding of the participants' social reality was facilitated through a series of exercises, simulations, readings, experiences and discussions in which students identified themselves within the social, political, ideological, and historical framework of society. The process continued with reflection. Through in-class discussions, readings, and dialogue journals, participants identified and reflected upon sociocultural issues and social injustice in schools and society and then related experiences and problems facing their schools. Reflection was followed by informal field investigations into the feasibility of addressing reform issues through discussion with school administrators, colleagues, students, parents and community members, examination of classroom materials and practices, and review of school documents. Participants followed preliminary investigations with formal investigations into various perspectives of the problem through a review of the literature and through their selected field research method(s). The inclusion of parent, students, colleague, and community member's input was required during the participant's field research. These investigative stages were followed by analysis of the field data, design of the reform plan, and reflection on the Reform Plan Approach process. The Reform Plan design stage was a reflexive process where students reviewed their visions for reform with individuals who participated in their preliminary investigation, classmates, and others. Participants used knowledge of their relational power to design implementable plans for reforms.

RESULTS

Reform plans created by participants varied, with three major reform categories emerging: curricular reform, sociology of schools reform, and community related school.

Reform Plan Categories:

1) *Curricular reform plans* included: reforms of available school resources and materials or individual classroom curriculum and materials reforms. These reforms aimed at decreasing injustices rooted in historical bias, gender bias, race bias, dysconscious racism (King, 1991), ability grouping, monocultural content, class bias, family structure bias, homophobia, and other biases.

2) *Sociology of school reform plans* included: improving teacher understanding of student home culture, reducing home-school cultural discontinuity by recognizing and including home culture in the classroom or school; addressing culturally associated learning, communication and discipline styles; reenvisioning how dialectal differences should be viewed and addressed by teachers, antigender-bias task forces, prejudice reduction programs to combat racial conflict, and information dissemination designed to increase participation of marginalized students in leadership programs.

3) *Community related school reform plans* included: outreach to improve school and teacher-parent relationships and parental involvement in schools; adhoc committees to inform the community about gender bias issues in schools and enlist community participation in reducing gender bias and intercultural violence; and development of a collaborative community center for home-culture-based adult learning and child enrichment.

Reform plans varied according to the participant's employment status, experience as an educator, and ability to implement school and community based reform. Participants who were currently employed teachers generally focused on reforms tied to their places of employment. Alternative master's candidates (not yet teaching) often focused on issues relevant to their children, community, and future employment as an educator. The most extensive and successful reform efforts included school, parents, and community in planning. Below, we include participant reflections and feedback and a reform plan case study to illustrate the results of the TERRA research objectives.

The authors' first research objective was to examine how participants (students in our graduate classes) experienced and understood critical social realization, reflection, and action, while researching and formulating reform plans for their classrooms, schools or communities.

Most participants exhibited an understanding of critical social realization, reflection, and action. A variety of participant reflections and feedback (from journals, evaluations, discussions, interviews, and self-analysis) illustrates this. Some examples include a participant who had viewed Standard English as "correct school language" but found that "Ebonics is a real language and that the students at the elementary school are definitely fluent speakers of this language." Another participant, examining teacher expectations of marginalized students, was "surprised by attitudes and opinions of teachers who I thought were more 'open minded.'" A participant who had previously accepted students' derogatory remarks about homosexuals was "approached by one of my secondary students who confided in me that she thought she was a Lesbian." And, a participant having understood "the need for religious tolerance and understanding while taking the course," after the course, discovered "the need for sexual harassment policy in schools."

The authors' second research objective was to examine how participants perceived themselves as transformative intellectuals, as empowered (either via viewing power as relational or via self-developed power) or as critical participants in a democratic society. Despite some obstacles to implementing participants' plans, most felt they had (or could obtain) the power to make reforms pertaining to social injustices in their schools and communities. Again, a variety of participant reflections and feedback (from journals, evaluations, discussions, interviews, and self-analysis) illustrates this. Although responses are too numerous to list in their entirety, some examples include the collaborative group of participants who stated that their research "was a strong element in convincing us that our idea was very much needed." And, the participant who, upon completion of the course, perceives herself as "capable of implementing reforms and have an idea for another reform plan. I intend to transfer to a school where implementation of such plans is acceptable." Another participant reported that the process "has given me the knowledge so that my opinions will be valued." A participant, who thought change had to happen on a "big scale" and therefore in a top-down paradigm, concluded that she "can make a difference—even if it is in baby steps . . . can make changes in my classroom that will help all students succeed."

The authors' third research objective was to examine how the participants successfully implemented their reform plans in their classrooms, schools, or communities and, if not, a description of the obstacles they encountered. As for the previous objectives, a variety of participant reflections and feedback (from journals, evaluations, discussions, interviews, and self-analysis) illustrates this. Examples of successful implementation included a participant who started her reform at the classroom level and "continues to successfully use curriculum reform design in the classroom, with colleagues using it successfully as well."

Responses concerning obstacles and how they were overcome came from the participant whose "principal is resisting implementation of [her] reform plan so [she] intend[s] to implement it when principal leaves or retires." A team of participants "despite time limits which keeps the reform plan team from implementing the plan through in-services, have implemented the reform plan through informal instruction of colleagues and in their practice." A participant discovered she had the power to successfully implement the plan if it was presented to the administration in stages, so she will "continue to propose changes in the plan to administration [as long as] they are pleased with the latest suggestions."

CASE STUDY

The following case study illustrates how the combined planning efforts of teacher-researcher, parent, colleague, and community led to the successful bottom-up reform of social injustices.

Victoria M. teaches in Pickens Elementary School. Located in a small rural community in the southeast, this K-3 school primarily serves a mostly poor, mostly African American student body. Students at Pickens achieve high scores in ability; however, their performance in reading and language arts is low. Students from Pickens are usually placed in low-ability groups when they enter fourth grade and transfer to Level Pines Elementary nearby. Level Pines serves mostly white students from poor and working-class families.

Victoria's initial data indicated that Pickens' teachers felt their students might have "serial memory deficits." This conclusion was based on teachers' observations that students had severe problems decoding certain sounds, learning rhymes, identifying nouns, and using correct subject-verb agreement. This problem occurred despite the use of "appropriate instruction," low teacher/student ratios, extra instruction time, guided practice and re-teaching. Teachers at Pickens felt that the students lacked the language base, skills, and motivation needed to learn. They felt the problem was due to poor parenting during the students' early years. Parents had a different view of the problem. They felt the school did not value their culture and that, in the teachers' eyes, their children were "second-class citizens."

After learning this parent perspective, Victoria focused her research on the language and culture of the parents and children the school was serving. With the parents' cooperation and a search of literature on the problem, she discovered that the language, culture, and learning styles of Pickens' students varied greatly from the mainstream. What Pickens' teachers defined as deficits were cultural differences. Victoria reflected on the information she had gathered from teachers, parents, and literature. Her conclusion was that the teachers were mislabeling and misteaching the students. She envisioned reforming teacher attitudes and instructional strategies that respected the parents' and students' home language and culture while preparing the students to operate successfully within the power structure of schools and society.

Victoria created a plan that began in her classroom. It included discussion of the value of home language and Standard English, comparisons between the two, and efforts to include parents. As she discovered the reasons for lack of parent participation (conflicting work hours, illiteracy, and lack of trust in schools), Victoria envisioned expanding her Plan. She met with her colleagues for a brainstorming session during which they created a "wish list" of objectives. These included use of an on-campus community center, enlisting teachers, high school and college students as tutors, enlisting members of the community as student mentors, and establishing community activities for children and adults. As the reflection-action process continued, the group discovered underlying class and race hostilities between groups in the community. These hostilities contributed to the parent mistrust of the school. The group is currently working on bringing the groups together to work out their differences. They hope the new community center they established will be neutral ground for all community members to meet and know each other[5].

## CONCLUSIONS

*One of the tasks of the progressive educator . . . is to unveil opportunities for hope, no matter what the obstacles may be.*

— PAULO FREIRE (1995)

TERRA facilitated participants' discovery of their ability to identify social injustices within their schools and communities, broadened their world view, encouraged the envisioning of bottom-up educational reform, and, enabled participants to discover the power they had to:

1) create implementable grassroots-level plans to reform education in their classrooms, schools, and communities (such as acculturating colleagues to community and student cultures, developing discrimination reduction strategies, exposing disproportionate placements of low-income students, minorities, and boys into special education, resolving intergroup community conflicts through school-sponsored conflict resolution programs, and increasing parent and community involvement in school reform);
2) understand and participate in a democratic process involving relational power in school and community, which leads to school reforms promoting social justice; and,
3) via the research process, view themselves as intellectuals able to transform their classrooms, schools, and communities toward a more positive, socially just, and democratic reality.

Individual participants created reform plans, researcher observations, and interviews to support each of the above results. Participants expressed newfound confidence in their abilities to participate in the processes of research and school policy making. Through first-hand observation and participation, these educational professionals clearly saw the need for reforms that promoted a more socially just and participatory democratic society. Conversely, numerous teachers realized, through the barriers they encountered in researching the problem or implementing their reform plans, their subordinate position in the educational structure and felt unempowered to make these needed changes. This resulted in a variety of reactions: retreat, anger, and frustration. The most common reaction was a new determination to somehow overcome the barriers and implement their reforms at some future time. Participant suggestions to address future obstacles to implementation included: support from university faculty when presenting reform plans to school administrators; collaboration with other teachers or school personnel; mentoring from those who have successfully implemented plans; and advice from those who have encountered barriers.

The authors conclude that participants bring a sense of social justice to the TERRA process. This sense of justice must be clarified and focused through many worldviews, including worldviews of all those affected by possible reforms. The authors realize the importance of course activities designed to help participants identify their social reality and place within the social context of this nation, and to expand their worldview. Awareness of one's social reality is key to expanding that awareness to include others' realities. It is also key to participants' awareness of how their place in the social structure delimits their visions for reforms and thus the need to seek out others' worldviews in order to design socially just and effective reforms. Participants were invited to expand their worldviews by experiencing others' social and cultural contexts through various course activities. Without experiencing others' contexts and worldviews, participant reforms would have been limited to their own worldviews.

External observers conditioned to expect "big picture" reforms might find the participant-designed reforms and visions of small significance. However, bottom-up reform is, by definition, not the big picture. Large-scale reform is usually top-down and is generalized from a central idea that is disseminated and applied to many schools and communities. It cannot be specific to the needs of the specific school or community, nor does the school or community "own" such reforms. Bottom-up reform designs must be specific and appropriate to the classroom, school, or community where they will be implemented. Schools and communities must sense ownership of the reforms. We conclude that small-scale, bottom-up reforms will be more effective locally, and meet with less resistance than reforms within a top-down paradigm.

Reform from the bottom up does meet with resistance from power holders who are designers and implementers of top-down reform. There is evidence of this both within this study (resistance from administrators) and in Paulo Freire's experiences in his literacy campaign in Brazil (1973). Designers and implementers of bottom-up reforms must be aware of this potential resistance and plan how it will be overcome.

Most importantly, participants in TERRA found hope for a more socially just educational future in their visions of school reform and in the realization of their power to be active participants in reforming schools. This hope must be nurtured and must generate further reforms that promote social justice in education and society. There should be ongoing research to reenvision and improve TERRA that would illustrate the contributions it can offer to the development of a new approach to teacher education that integrates theoretical perspectives into a practical application. TERRA combines the concepts of Freirean praxis, Dewey's education for democracy, and Lappé and DuBois' relational power and "doing democracy" to reform teacher preparation into a critical and experiential process by which the participants move toward becoming critical citizens of a democratic society.

## Notes

1. Terra is "earth" in Portuguese and Creolo. We think it is an appropriate acronym for a process promoting grassroots reform.

2. Examples of the top-down paradigm can be found in the work of major development agencies such as U.S.A.I.D. and World Bank. For more on this see Gutek (1997) and Lappé, Collins, and Kinley (1980).

3. Examples of bottom-up development education can be found in the classic works of Paulo Freire and Ivan Illich. (See Freire, 1974; Illich, 1971).

4. The idea for dialogue journals for critical reflection on course materials and self was introduced to us by Vivian Zamel at the University of Massachusetts at Boston.

5. The case study is adapted with permission from the unpublished participant final project report of S. Mims (1999).

## References

Aronowitz, S. & Giroux, H. (1985). *Education under siege*. South Hadley, MA: Bergin & Garvey.

Ashendon, D., Connell, B., Dowsett, G., & Kessler, S. (1987). Teachers and working class schooling. In D.W. Livingstone and contributors, *Critical pedagogy and cultural power*. South Hadley, MA: Bergin & Garvey.

Bourdieu, P. & Passeron, J-C. (1990). *Reproduction in education, society and culture*. California: Sage Publications.

Britzman, D. P. (1986). Cultural myths in the making of a teacher: Biography and social structure in teacher education. *Harvard Educational Review*, 56 (4).

Dewey, J. (1916). *Democracy and education: Introduction to the philosophy of education*. New York: MacMillan.

Dolbec, A. & Savoie-Zajc, L. (1995). Problems emerging from the practicing of action research in graduate programs in education. Paper presented at the annual meeting of the International Conference on Teacher Research, Davis, CA.

Evans, T. & Winograd, K. (1992). The quality of experience of preservice teachers as they engage in an ill-defined action research task. Paper presented at the annual meeting of the American Educational Research Association, San Francisco, CA.

Fregeau, L. & Leier, R. (1997). Teacher Envisioned Research and Reform Plan Approach (TERRA): Preparing teachers as transformative intellectuals. In L. Fregeau & R. Leier, (Eds.) *SEAES Conference Proceedings*, 1995–1997, 34–46. Mobile: University of South Alabama.

Freire, P. (1970). *Pedagogy of the oppressed*. New York: Herder & Herder.

Freire, P. (1973). *Education for critical consciousness*. New York: Continuum.

Freire, P. (1994). *Pedagogy of hope: Reliving pedagogy of the oppressed*. New York: Continuum.

Freire, P. & Shor, I. (1987). *A pedagogy for liberation; dialogues on transforming education*. South Hadley, MA: Bergin & Garvey.

Giroux, H. (1988). *Teachers as intellectuals: Toward a critical pedagogy of learning*. South Hadley, MA: Bergin & Garvey.

Giroux, H. (1992, December). Curriculum, multiculturalism, and the politics of identity. *NASSP Bulletin, 76* (548), 1–11.

Giroux, H. & McLaren, P. (1986). Teacher education and the politics of engagement: The case for democratic schooling. *Harvard Educational Review, 56* (3).

Giroux, H. & McLaren, P. (1989). *Critical pedagogy, the state, and cultural struggle*. Albany, NY: State University of New York.

Greene, M. (1986). In search of a critical pedagogy. *Harvard Educational Review, 56* (4).

Gutek, G. (1997). *American education in a global society: Internationalizing teacher education*. Prospect Heights, IN: Waveland.

Illich, I. (1971). *Deschooling society*. New York: Harper & Row.

Jackson, F. R. (1993–1994). Seven strategies to support a culturally responsive pedagogy. *Journal of Reading, 37* (4).

King, J. (1991). Dysconscious racism: Ideology, identity, and miseducation of teachers. *Journal of Negro Education, 80* (2), 133–146.

Knoblauch, C. H. & Brannon, L. (1993). *Critical teaching and the idea of literacy*. Portsmouth, NH: Boynton/Cook.

Lappé, F. M. & DuBois, P. M. (1994). *The quickening of America*. San Francisco: Jossey-Bass.

Lappé, F. M., Collins, J., & Kinley, D. (1980). *Aid as obstacle: Twenty questions about our foreign aid and the hungry*. San Francisco Institute for Food and Development Policy.

McLaren, P. (1992). Writing from the margins: Geographics of identity, pedagogy, and power. *Journal of Education, 174* (1), 7–24.

Neisser, U. (1976). *Cognition and reality: Principles and implications of cognitive psychology*. New York: Longman Publishing Group.

Nieto, S. (2000). *Affirming diversity: The sociopolitical context of multicultural education* (3rd ed.). New York: Longman Publishing Group.

Ryan, F. X. (1994). Primary experience as settled meaning: Dewey's conception of experience. *Philosophy Today, 38* (1).

Shor, I. (1986). Equality is excellence: transforming teacher education and the learning process. *Harvard Educational Review, 56* (4).

Wink, J. (2000). *Critical pedagogy: Notes from the real world*. New York: Addison Wesley Longman.

*Dawn Emerson Addy*

---

# COMMUNITY DIALOGUE: A TOOL FOR SOCIAL ENGAGEMENT AND CLASS AWARENESS

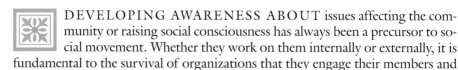 DEVELOPING AWARENESS ABOUT issues affecting the community or raising social consciousness has always been a precursor to social movement. Whether they work on them internally or externally, it is fundamental to the survival of organizations that they engage their members and reach out to the broader community on these issues.

South Florida has long been a racially and ethnically diverse community. Seemingly continuous waves of immigrants, other newcomers, and longtime residents alike have contributed to our unique culture and history. Neighborhoods, churches, workplaces, and labor organizations have often been and, for the most part continue to be, segregated across these differences. These same cultural and racial differences have also divided us on issues ranging from educational and economic opportunity to language differences and from immigration laws and policies to inter-ethnic relations. Ethnic and racial tensions have become an accepted part of daily life. The only constant appears to be continuous change.

What do these population shifts mean for the future of our democratic and economic systems? What challenges and opportunities will these changes in our communities present to workers and their organizations? What does it mean to arrive in this country as an immigrant and suddenly become part of a marginalized identity group or to come from a majority community in one's home culture into one where you are perceived as part of a minority? What does it mean for generations who have grown up in South Florida to have their children move away because they cannot find a job in their field even though it does not require Spanish/English skills? These are some of the questions residents of the South Florida area grapple with in our study circle dialogue sessions.

When the idea of study circle dialogues was first proposed in South Florida, the dialogues were designed to focus on race and immigration. We soon discovered that it is impossible to talk about racism in Miami without also addressing issues of ethnicity, economics, and language. With help from the Study Circle Resource Center, a project of the Topsfield Foundation, Inc., we developed our own discussion guide, "Changing Faces, Changing Communities: Immigration & Race, Jobs, Schools, and Language Differences."

Over the past five years, we have been building a broad-based coalition of community leaders across racial, ethnic, economic, religious, and political identities.[1] Realizing the need for open, public communication, they embraced the study circle discussion process. Our initial funding came from community-based, private foundation grants. In 1996 Many Voices: One Community (MV:OC) had been formed. In November 1997, MV:OC held its first kick-off event for a community-wide study circle program on immigration and community change. More than seven hundred people participated in forty-five study circles throughout Miami using our newly developed study circle discussion guide. Since that first event, numerous study circle sessions have been organized throughout South Florida followed by Action Forums and Congressional Exchanges. Many Voices: One Community remains fixed on reaching the goal of inclusiveness inherent in the name of the organization. Today, the executive board reflects the broader Miami-Dade population. MV:OC has developed over two hundred facilitators (from diverse groups across race, ethnicity, age, ability, sexual orientation, gender, religion) and relies on them to facilitate study circle dialogues for day-long community study circle sessions.

The study circle concept has been used widely in Sweden as an adult education technique. Study circles are based on the premise that everyone has experiences and knowledge to share and bring to the circle with the purpose of gaining understanding among the group. Study circle techniques vary, but in general they: facilitate understanding and openness; are convenient, inexpensive and informal; utilize adult education learning principles; are collaborative, not competitive, with participants learning from the process of dialogue as well as from the content.

Study circle dialogue techniques have been used for well over one hundred years. Lecture-teaching models of study circles were quite popular in the United States and Sweden during the late 1800s and into the 1900s, with the development of new social movements: trade unions, the temperance movement, the Social Democratic Party, and cooperatives (Oliver, 1992). More recently, the International Union of Bricklayers and Allied Crafts adopted the study circle format for member education and the growth of member democracy (McMahon, 2000). Webster defines "dialogue" as an interchange and discussion of ideas, especially when open and frank, to seek mutual understanding or harmony.

There are many variations of study circle structure that may lead one to believe that any form of group discussion could be considered a type of dialogue. That is why it is equally important to explore what study circles are not about. Study circle dialogue is not about debate. A debate expects a "winner" or a "loser," and one tries to win over the opposition. In dialogue, the goal is not for one party to impose ideas on the other; rather, it is to enable participants to see an issue or position in a new light so that they can react to their own thoughts and come to their own conclusions on the topic. Debate is divisive, in that everyone feels obligated to defend his or her own point of view.

However, if my point of view comes from my experiences as an exile; a dark-skinned Bahamian who has moved into a system of U.S. racism and disenfranchisement; an Hispanic who has been denied entrance into an apprenticeship program and believes it is due to his accent and ethnicity; an Anglo who perceives he or she did not get a job because he or she is not bi-lingual (meaning English/Spanish); a direct descendant of holocaust survivors; a direct descendant of slaves; a direct descendant of slave owners; how can I ever be "won over" if I do not perceive the "other point of view?" Or, how can I be "won over" if I perceive the "other point of view" to come from my oppressor? Can I fully understand the point of view in others if I, myself, have not experienced their oppression? Therefore, consensus cannot be a goal in the study circle process. A dialogue is not an argument. Although logical thinking and reflective reasoning are important, there are times when people's positions are formed less by reason than by historical circumstances, emotions, and experiences.

Study circle dialogue is not a lecture. The purpose of a lecture is for someone to give, and someone to receive, information in what is generally a one-way communication process. Even if a discussion follows, the purpose of the lecture is for an expert to impart information to the audience. One of the direct functions of a study circle facilitator is to ensure that lecture does not occur. Participants must have equal opportunities to share their experiences and perspectives. It avoids authoritarianism of a typical teacher/student environment and promotes a "problem-posing" humanistic educational experience. If the dialogue is allowed to be dominated by one or several individuals, the process loses the richness gained from the variety of perspectives within the entire group. It is therefore fundamentally important that each group is composed of a diversity of people.

Dialogue gives voice to a "deepened consciousness" (Freire, 1999) of the individual's situation. Freire described the outcome as an "historical reality susceptible of transformation." He contends that humans cannot attain full humanity as individuals in isolation. Study circle dialogues lay the groundwork for fellowship and solidarity. Through a process of understanding, relationships of trust are built. Participants broaden their humanity to think and make decisions beyond themselves and their own experiential base. This ultimately results in self-empowerment toward broader civic investment, transforming into civic action. The participation of organized labor is a voice for economic concerns within the community. We cannot deny the relationship between "voice" and "power." Providing a safe place for participants to voice their concerns, and then channeling those voices into community action, is a powerful tool for change.

Dialogue is not like focus group discussions where participants are often paid to attend. Study circles are comprised of volunteers who are concerned citizens who participate out of their own sense of community investment. Study circles typically comprise twelve to twenty participants, unlike town hall meetings or public hearings. Participants are often placed into dyads or triads to facilitate individual participation. The study circle process fosters civic investment and responsibility. Study circle dialogues are a powerful tool for building trust relationships and strong community coalitions.

A study circle dialogue is not an informal conversation. In spite of the seemingly relaxed atmosphere of the small groups, these dialogue sessions have specific goals, tasks, and structure. There are assumptions made about group processing, and preparations made before the group convenes. These dialogues have action components structured into their format. They explore ideas for political, economic, and social change. MV:OC provides several opportunities each year for former participants to engage in action planning (Action Forum) or to engage in dialogue with politicians (Congressional Exchange).

As one participant put it:

> The end of a dialogue session does not necessarily provide the "right" or "proper" answers, the completion of tasks or an end to the dialogue. A closure may involve raising questions with no easy answers or challenging group members to consider different options which they may not have heard before. At times, the closing of one dialogue is the beginning of future endeavors or a new process in forging positive relationships. (Jim Howe, Director of Miami National Conference for Community and Justice)

The MV:OC mission is to promote community building, in-depth conversation, and civic investment by concerned residents who call South Florida their home. These discussions lead to concrete actions, ranging from neighborhood crime watches, monitoring legislation, involvement with schools, involvement with economic issues, health issues, homeless issues and more.

### MOSAIC 2000

In January 2000, Miami-Dade County Mayor Alex Penelas launched the community-based Mosaic 2000 initiative. MV:OC was invited to the drawing board of this initiative, along with other community group leaders. Shortly after the formation of the initiative, the Elian Gonzalez refugee case began to heat up within the Cuban-American community. Statements and actions taken by Cuban-American leaders heightened racial tensions and economic disparities, creating a volatile environment. Cuban-Americans could not understand why other ethnic groups did not understand and support their viewpoint. They believed that, since they were being oppressed, other oppressed groups should have understood their pain and have been more supportive. They even tried to portray their situation as being similar to slavery and the holocaust. Why didn't African Americans or the Jewish groups understand their plight?

The "other" community groups were outraged that Cuban-Americans would try to equate the Cuban experience with their oppressions. The backlash from the variety of South Florida diverse communities was swift and shocking. Two counter-Cuban parades took place, with strange images of Blacks and Whites marching together, American flags flying next to Confederate flags. African Americans felt they were not supported by Cuban-American leaders in their efforts to save affirmative action in Florida. Haitian and other immigrant communities felt the Cuban-Americans had not heard or supported their needs for equitable opportunity for all immigrants in immigration laws and procedures. Fresh wounds were gaping open in every sector of the South Florida community. The only common ground was the pain felt throughout the area. All community groups believed themselves to be dehumanized and victimized in their struggles.

Workplaces and labor groups were paralyzed in the harsh glare of these issues. Many were afraid to speak for fear they might lose a friend. Many were afraid to speak for fear of retaliation and retribution by powerful anti-Castro supporters. The silence and rage across ethnic, racial, and economic lines was deafening. At a time when we all needed desperately to talk to one another, we could not speak the words. The need for community intergroup dialogue was immense.

The Mosaic 2000 Initiative embraces a series of ongoing events: artistic projects; song and concerts; a white ribbon campaign for community peace and unity; an interfaith healing event; and, at the center, the core, the crown jewel, of this initiative is the community dialogue process. Dialogues may be structured to have a particular focus, such as immigration, economics, racism, or leadership. Whatever the focus for the dialogue, broader issues within the community are raised throughout the dialogue.

### SAMPLE CASE: DIALOGUE ON ECONOMIC STATUS

One such dialogue, held in fall of 2000, focused on economic status and equitable opportunity. Subject matter experts briefly described the current economic picture for residents and newly arrived immigrants. In a simple four-hour discussion format, economic issues in Miami-Dade County were explored by some of its citizens.

Each session was carefully structured to stimulate diverse perspectives and initiate honest and heartfelt discussion. The first session opened with this statement:

> Some people say that immigration issues and race relations as they impact the workplace have been getting better over the years and that we have made significant progress toward equal access to jobs, economic opportunity and positions within business. Some feel that equity schemes such as Affirmative Action are no longer necessary and in some cases, highly inappropriate as a means of "leveling the playing field."
>
> However, there are others who seem less hopeful about relations among racial and ethnic groups. They have observed and been distressed by the rise in hate crimes over the past decade and tension not only between Blacks and Whites, but among other groups as well. In the Miami-Dade community, we saw how the Elian Gonzalez situation drove wedges between various ethnic communities and within places of

work across the county. The purpose of this session is to examine common phenomena about economic status as it impacts neighborhood groups and how race and immigration issues affect the workplace and the economy. Through a structured "Study Circle" dialogue process we will explore some of the beliefs that underlie the characteristics of those relationships.

Participants were placed in pairs that changed to a new partner with each question asked. They were instructed:

Let's think about our neighborhoods, places of work, and the large events that made the news last year.

1. Introduce yourself and describe the neighborhood you currently live in. What is its economic status for the most part? Who lives there (racial and ethnic composition)? How do your family and others in your neighborhood relate to other neighborhoods and community groups that are different from yourselves? (Racially, ethnically, economically?)
2. What is the community atmosphere in your neighborhood? Are there issues or events that have pulled the neighborhood together (or apart)? What have those been? Describe.

Many participants expressed experiences of "lack of community." Others said, "It is easy to complain but difficult to offer help or find solutions." First-generation immigrant communities are often too busy working to survive to be concerned with "others" in the broader community. Many bedroom communities have "no contact with the community we live in," especially in areas of unincorporated Dade where there is no apparent neighborhood structure. Those with children gain a sense of community through school and interactions with other parents. Ethnic enclaves seem to offer the best sense of community, however, for some neighborhoods. "Common adversities (such as hurricanes) have brought us together to help each other, rally, talk, and give us a sense of security." When neighborhoods are segregated across economic status the broader community issues tend to become "low income versus high income."

3. In your opinion and observations, has discrimination been eliminated or lessened over the past ten years? (In your neighborhood, within business practices?) Have attitudes on immigration and race relations in employment improved or disintegrated due to laws supporting minority groups? (What have you heard? What is your opinion from your experiences?)
4. How would you characterize attitudes about immigration policies and race relations in your workplace? Is it merely a Black/white color issue or do "immigration" and "race relations" encompass a broader view of global awareness and caring for the "human race?"
5. Racism is a potent and destructive force in any society or organization. How do we reach out to people across our ethnicities and break out of a defensive mode of thinking? How do we engage people at all levels of the workplace in listening

and participating in a continuing dialogue on immigration issues and race relations? How can we promote and support better attitudes about immigration and race relations at work?

Since this dialogue was "post-Elian," it is not surprising that the participants responded to these questions within the purview of the Elian Gonzalez experience. One elder Cuban-American woman stated, "We stopped listening. No one recognized the human element of difficulty in this situation. Cubans were resentful of the response from other ethnic groups. If only I'd heard a simple, 'I know it's a difficult time for you.' People wanted to speak rationally but it was too emotional."

Between counties there was a vast difference in media coverage and public perceptions: One Hispanic (non-Cuban) Miami-Dade resident pointed out, "In Broward County it was treated like foreign politics; in Dade County it was treated like local politics." There was an opportunity for dialogue to understand other points of view but many were fearful of openly expressing their personal viewpoint. Friendships broke down and an "us versus them" environment often developed.

"A lot depended on the ethnic makeup of the workplace; the Black/Hispanic workplaces became hostile." An African American woman described that she felt betrayed by the Cuban community in their struggles to preserve Affirmative Action earlier in the year. African Americans perceived the Cuban pleas for understanding to be arrogant and insensitive to the African American experience and the experiences of other non-Cuban immigrant groups like the Haitians. The Elian situation highlighted the disparities in immigration law and was described by a young man from Haiti as "different treatment for different groups." That is why it was framed as a "narrow Cuban issue" for most of the United States.

"Elian was too much of an emotional issue, especially for Hispanics from other countries with issues, like Nicaragua with Sandanistas," said a Nicaraguan immigrant. People from non-Cuban Hispanic groups were often fearful of any public show of nonsupport, fearful of reprisal and punishment by Cuban nationalistic factions. Not all Cuban-Americans agreed with the Cuban-Nationals. One Cuban-American man stated that, "People cling and retreat to their ethnicity, but this was a time when we needed people to become involved."

Multi-cultural/racial/ethnic involvement does not come easily in Florida. "Bigotry is big in Florida," said one Anglo-American participant. "Lest we forget, we need only to look at a map to see that Florida is part of the Deep South." People with personal remembrances of "colored" schools, drinking fountains, beaches and bathrooms are still a lively part of the community. One Bahamian woman recalled, "Black children have very recently been called 'little monkeys' by public officials who remain insensitive to issues and history of the Black community." Affirmative Action has not been perceived as helping all of society since it is viewed as primarily promoting Blacks. Dialogue participants agreed that the narrow perception needs to be changed and the way Affirmative Action functions systemically may "need to be fixed," but not done away with: "Barriers in employment practices and hiring are real," said an African American county worker. Some studies have indicated that county workers are Anglo-and Black-dominated. However, hiring policies have failed to blend all units of county workers in a multiethnic manner." An Anglo woman added, "Those who did not feel personally engaged in the debate did not want to get involved. People tend to lack a sense of interdependence and co-determination across the county."

As the first session was debriefed, participants expressed their appreciation of the tight structure with time limits strictly adhered to, because "it forces us to listen," one person commented. Another added, "We have found that our different backgrounds may not be a topic we typically want to discuss openly with others." In the dialogue process they were forced into such discussions. However, they learned that, through the structured dialogue process, they could tackle these difficult issues in a respectful and responsible manner. "We need to learn to synthesize and process our experiences as a community," one participant said.

In the next session, the participants worked in small groups of three or four and then were expected to report back to the entire group. Each group was given a case to read and discuss (using the same dialogue-process ground rules.) They were instructed to ask themselves the following questions:

- What is your first response to this case? Does it affect you or your community?
- What experiences have helped to shape your opinions? Do you have any similar cases to share?
- Give examples of something that happened to you or a member of your family.
- Why is it an important issue for you? Or is it?
- Is it an example of a common experience in your community?
- Given the situation in the case described, what, if anything, should or can be done?
- What, if anything, do you think businesses, government, churches, unions, and neighborhood groups or individuals should do?

Given the shortage of time, only two groups reported back to the general session. The first case examined was:

> A man who has lived in this country all his life wants to start up his own business. He hears a radio advertisement announcing a new small business start up program. He calls for information and finds out the program is dedicated to funding loans for recent immigrants.

This scenario seemed all too familiar to participants. Many had personal stories with similar issues: "This will create justifiable resentment because one group is picked over another," one man said. "The government 'sets us up against each other' instead of encouraging us to work together," agreed another. Several participants expressed anger about government systems and practices that supply "ammunition for discrimination practices going on."

They could identify with the man's pain. "He wants to be economically independent and established. And if he wanted to hire others, they will not be hired, a loss for the community as well," one Haitian man remarked. He continued,

"Blacks have trouble getting bank loans that will make them successful. The typical minority business loan averages two or three thousand which is not enough to really help." "Special funding is meant to put people at the same starting point, like a handicap in golf," remarked another. Anger and resentment are often shared by longtime residents, regardless of color. From a White/Anglo perspective, "part of 'White privilege' is that when something is not available to us we become indignant and we believe we are suffering," stated an Anglo businesswoman.

The participants agreed that, although many immigrants come to this country with an entrepreneurial spirit that benefits communities on the whole, much ethnocentric anxiety gives rise to urban legends about minority loans and immigrant "give-away" programs. "In Detroit there were stories about free loans to Middle-Eastern immigrants to start small businesses; in L.A., it was all about the Koreans getting free loans," said an Hispanic woman. "It sets up a community for mistrust," said another. "The ripple effect is enormous—my dad can't get his loan. . . . It advances stereotypes," she concluded.

And it would certainly be a mistake to assume that newer immigrant groups share the same experiences. As one Haitian participant noted, "What radio station is he listening to? Haitians can't get loans, yet they are newer immigrants." Forces such as race, gender, and immigrant status all impact this situation differently and there is no equal starting point for all.

Although it was the responsibility of one group to report on this case, in the general session, all were encouraged to join the discussion and respond to the issues raised. The next case discussed was:

> An undocumented immigrant takes a job as a domestic. After several weeks of work, her employer refuses to pay her. She is afraid to go to the police because she doesn't want to be deported.

The group sympathized with her plight. Typical responses included: "She won't be able to eat or feed her kids. She is scared especially if she doesn't know how to access shelters or know what kind of relief may be available." "There can be an impact on support systems, she may be afraid to access services, and this may result in domestic violence, eviction, homelessness. Often she will not seek medical services. She could have even been raped or abused by her employer." The participants identified the ethnic reinforcement of prejudice and the importance of the internalization of such prejudice to enable its success: "Powerless, she gets the constant sense of, 'I can't do anything,'" they agreed. "Blame goes onto the victims." This internalized oppression extends and is even supported by members of the very group being oppressed: "At Krome [federal immigration detention center], immigrants are often intimidated by their own people. Prisoners become depressed and may give up caring about themselves. This is a huge mental health problem," stated a Haitian-American.

Other major aspects identified in this case were: "This employer wants to get someone to work for free. That is slave labor." Another participant agreed, "Society is not enhanced by such practices." One participant observed, "The worker could be male or female—homeless is defined as being without a permanent place to live." An elderly White male stated, "There is an assumption that there is a support network 'out there' somewhere; but churches are not social workers and don't provide clear support systems; they also have limited resources." Unethical employment practices affect more than just the individual: "This forces children into the job market," said a Mexican-American woman. "Then you need to have as many hands picking as we can to support the family." Unethical employment practices affect our families, our schools, our systems, and our communities.

Realizing our interdependence is an important aspect of community building. In another case, the ability for community members to communicate and be open to understanding was explored.

> An ethnic community feels isolated. "No one is listening to our issues." "No-one understands our issues." They believe they need to educate others on their issues but they are not certain how this can be done. It is frustrating for all but has also aroused feelings of anger and fear for many.

One of the participants told the story of "a community off Route I-95 that was promised that a wall would be built to protect them from the traffic sound. All they got was a chain link fence, 15 feet from the highway. The community is made up of Whites, Blacks, Hispanics, and Caribbeans. It was not until they organized and worked together that they were able to get the attention of the mayor and the commissioners to be heard." Responses included: "It takes going door to door". . . "A common problem is a good way to organize a community."

The group was asked, "Do you think it is necessary for a common problem to arise before people will come together?" A participant responded, "It took ten years to talk to my neighbors"; . . ."They speak three languages"; . . ."They are planning the next event"; . . ."They have found the power of joining with other people, Human Services, PACT [a church affiliated group] and ACORN"; . . ."Our community has been mobilizing around health care and the living wage." The group observed that living in isolation means you never get to know each other's feelings or needs.

The group was then asked: "What are the individual 'human costs' of these situations? As a community, what are the consequences of allowing this disparity to 'trickle down' to us as individuals or at the neighborhood level in terms of crime rates or demand on social and educational systems?" The participants agreed that by allowing disparities to continue, our ongoing socioeconomic problems could only get worse: "Nothing has trickled down. We [the African American community] have remained at the same levels of unemployment"; . . ."People don't get treatment from social services. Thirty to forty percent of the schools that failed were Black." The end result is: "People stop caring, stop trusting"; . . ."We end up with low voter turnout"; . . ."People in Overtown have talked about the need for business development, but economic development has not made a difference in the poorer communities"; . . ."We need to create public places where people can talk and build trust."

Back in the large group again, participants worked together to develop specific strategies to be used to address those concerns at four levels of involvement:

1. Individual.
2. Organizations: neighborhoods, churches, unions.
3. Workplace.
4. Political, government.

All were instructed to use the planning guidelines (provided) and to select a reporter to record main themes and action ideas.

## INDIVIDUAL ACTION STRATEGIES

### PROMOTE INVOLVEMENT

- Get involved with others who are different from ourselves is difficult because we are often segregated, even at work.
- We need to keep trying to be part of the solution.
- I only started getting involved over the last year.
- If we leave the community and don't do anything, we don't change anything.
- We are the "us" that takes it away from "others."
- Educate ourselves.
- Agree we have some racism.
- Being part of a dialogue is important. . . .We have met. . . .It is important this event occurred.
- Make a commitment to speak out and educate others on the issues.
- Let people know where you stand; fight for social justice.
- More can be done, don't go back into isolation.

### PROMOTE RESPONSIBILITY

- Hold people at the top accountable.
- The point is trying to find action at all levels.
- We need to politicize the environment—as individuals we will not be able to solve the world's problems.
- It takes a community that knows "what is right" and how to access, support, and voice concerns.
- Everything isn't O.K.
- Becoming involved is the first step; accepting some personal responsibility is the next step.

### PROMOTE UNDERSTANDING

- Realize cultures are always surprising.
- When we talk, we find we are not that different; we are all entitled to a slice of the pie.

- Poverty and despair are not news, but expressions of racism and inequality are desensitizing our culture.
- We need to recognize diversity within groups, such as Anglos or Asians.
- We are the object of bigotry and prejudice . . . We are happy we are all here to talk about these things, sharing what is going on. It makes me think of the abolition movement when others helped in the fight for freedom.
- Ethnic and racial discrimination are the same thing. To think otherwise complicates our lives.

## ACTION STRATEGIES IN THE WORKPLACE, THE POLITICAL ARENA, AND OTHER ORGANIZATIONS

### PROMOTE INVOLVEMENT

- There are many resources available, but people don't always know how to access them or use them . . . no linkages between communities.
- Organizations often compete and are not linked. We need to take advantage of connecting forces.
- All people need access to services.
- It takes power, voice, and influence to make a difference.
- We need to continue to communicate.
- Schedule follow-up conferences.
- Design more structured and specific promotional information to get people to attend.
- Make the dialogue ongoing through newsletters and e-mail.
- Form a support group for confronting injustice.
- Have one or two main goals that will fit multiple organizations.

### PROMOTE RESPONSIBILITY

- Organizations need to be accountable for being part of the solution.
- Political decisions need to be for all.
- Persons in power need to be held to higher standards.
- Politicians need to be visibly representative of *all* the citizens of Miami-Dade County.
- If it's a boom time for the nation, then we need our share.
- Provide better opportunities for leadership development.
- Provide better methods for support of leaders. They become stagnated and lose momentum.

### PROMOTE UNDERSTANDING

- So much could be, but is not. How can we get our organizations to listen to each other?

- Organizations need to promote and produce the "right kind of dialogue."
- Attitudes occur when some are denied the ability to support their families.
- Use facilitators more to push us toward forming networks.
- Meetings promote wearing our organizational hats, not the rich dialogue that is needed to build trust.
- Take study circles into the communities.
- Look at what is being done in other communities around the world for examples of community building.
- We need to follow-up on the dynamics of this conference by reaching more young people (chat rooms?) and helping them to develop community building skills.

Freire (1999, p. 106) described humankind as "beings of praxis, differing from animals, which are beings of pure activity." We, as humans, have the means to critically objectify the world and our experiences within it. By engaging in processes of reflection and analysis, we can gain understanding and transform that understanding into strategies for change. Therefore, this dialogue process is revolutionary in its inherent call to action.

"To impede communication is to reduce men to the status of 'things'" (Freire, 1999, p. 109). One of the great myths of our time is that the media is communication. Media produces a well-organized documentation of events, all too often from the perspective of the power elite. This is not the whole story. This is not the only story. In study circles, we gather to tell our stories and create a more humanistic community reality.

When a group experiences a period of chaos but cannot understand what is going wrong, there is a window of opportunity when individuals reach out and actually listen to others and try to engage others to help find solutions. I believe that window is currently open in the South Florida community. Through ongoing dialogue sessions, we are committed to "co-intentionally educating"[2] each other on our communal interests and issues. Only through group struggle and recognizing our interlinked dependency on the success of each other, can we liberate our South Florida community to become a civil society.

*Notes*

1. Members of Many Voices: One Community (MV:OC) coalition include: American Friends Service Committee, Catholic Charities, Chinese Federation, Church World Service, Florida International University-Center for Labor Research and Studies and FIU Diversity Initiative, Ginn, Scroggens & Assoc., Government Supervisors Association-South Florida, Haitian Support, Inc., KIDS Voting Dade County, League of Women Voters, Lutheran Ministries, Miami-Dade Community College, Miami-Dade Equal Opportunity Board, National Conference for Community and Justice, Office of Latin Affairs, SGI International, Spanish American League Against Discrimination, South Florida AFL-CIO, University of Miami, United Way of Miami, World Relief Corps and the affiliations continue to grow. These are the organizations represented by MV:OC executive board members.

2. A revolutionary leadership must accordingly practice co-intentional education. Teachers and students (leadership and people), content on reality; both are subjects, not only in the task of unveiling that reality, and thereby coming to know it critically, but in the task of re-creating that knowledge. As they attain this knowledge of reality through common reflection and action, they discover themselves as its permanent re-creators. In this way, the presence of the oppressed in the struggle for their liberation will be what it should be: not pseudo-participation, but committed involvement. (Freire, 1999, p. 51)

## *References*

Freire, P. (1970, 1993, 1999). *Pedagogy of the oppressed*. New York: Continuum.

Gozdz, K. (1993). Building Community As A Leadership Discipline. In *The new paradigm in business* (pp. 107–114). New York: Putnam and Sons.

McMahon, J. (2000, Winter). The birth of SCOTT: A study circle on teaching techniques. *Labor Studies Journal,* 24 (4), 84–87.

Oliver, L. P. (1995, March/April). Is the United States ready for a study circle movement? *Adult Learning,* 37–52.

Oliver, L. P. (1992, Spring). Study circles: Individual growth through collaborative learning. *New Directions for Adult and Continuing Education 1992 (53).*

Study Circles Resource Center. (1993). *The study circle handbook; A manual for study circle discussion leaders, organizers and participants.* Topsfield Foundation, Inc.

Study Circles Resource Center. (1998). *The study circle handbook; A guide for training study circle facilitators.* Topsfield Foundation, Inc.

*Charles Reitz*

# ELEMENTS OF EDUCATION: CRITICAL PEDAGOGY AND THE COMMUNITY COLLEGE[1]

THE FALSE PROMISES of community colleges in the United States have been repeatedly discussed over the past decades by critical educationists like Fred Pincus (1974, 1980), Jerome Karabel (1972), Kevin Dougherty (1994), L. Steven Zwerling (1976), and Burton Clark (1960). They have convincingly argued that the publicly stated functions (enhanced opportunity, mobility, personal growth, and advancement) tend to be overshadowed by the community colleges' unstated functions (screening, tracking, cooling out). They have established that the hidden curriculum has a social control function that primarily assists the societal process of capital accumulation. The schools maintain illusions of equal opportunity and unimpeded mobility even while they program students for differential roles in an unequal society: sorting, selecting, and channeling them in ways that preserve the current class system. In addition, community colleges (at times sooner, at times later) actively convince or passively discourage certain types of students to opt out of postsecondary education altogether. By treating the social system(s), and subsystems, of domination and oppression as if they were generally valid and fair, community colleges tend to legitimate and stabilize these systems of unjust power relations in the economy, culture, and society. The overall result is the production of a labor force that overwhelmingly accepts wage-labor and capitalism as normal, and whose individual members will thus tend to view themselves subjectively in ways that replicate the unequal social division of labor and wealth.

Today, the scholarship of Pincus, Karabel, Dougherty, Zwerling, Clark, and others like Bowles and Gintis (1976), continues to present a significant challenge to those of us working within the nation's community colleges who believe in the progressive nature of our work here. Because we stand in solidarity with our students and because we endeavor toward mutual empowerment and social transformation, we must continue to ask: How do we put critical pedagogy into practice in the community colleges in ways that can actually make this a productive/emancipatory/transformative experience for students and for ourselves? How shall we theorize our common circumstances, both with regard to our shared problems and even more importantly to our shared prospects? What is it exactly that makes our pedagogy critical?

The following examples are intended to show just what can be done to adapt a pedagogy of the oppressed to community colleges in the United States. In recent publications (Reitz, 2000a, 2000b), especially in an article titled "Liberating the Critical in Critical Theory" (Reitz, 1996), I have tried to respond to many of the theoretical issues raised here. But practically speaking, the problem is to figure out just how a pedagogy of the oppressed ought to impact our subject matter, our classroom dynamics, and our mission to community if it is to negate the negation represented by the dynamics of capital accumulation in the United States. Many of the ideas I am noting here emerged when several campus colleagues[2] and I discussed Paulo Freire's work and critical pedagogy as problems. The perspective we developed is something I call *EduAction;* innovative teaching strategies grounded in radical social analysis that can bridge the gap between the classroom and the community, theory, and practice.

Even Ernest Boyer (1988, p. 1) has recognized that "Community is a climate to be created, not a region to be served," and has recommended community building as the key future task of the community colleges. Likewise, many of our colleagues are developing initiatives with much transformative power along the lines of service learning, multicultural education, civic literacy, civic action, and critical thinking. What follows is a synthesis of suggestions that I believe are consistent with a critical educational philosophical response to the challenges posed above. I hope they can serve as a basis for continuing discussion of this problematic.

## ELEMENTS OF *EDUACTION*

1. Above all else teacher attitude and tone must establish an active rapport and solidarity with students. This involves real teacher commitment to developing the talents of students and to facilitating student success.
2. Each section of each course should start off in a participatory way with the teacher posing thematic questions, such as: What makes higher education "higher?" What makes critical thinking "critical?" These questions introduce students to a transformed subject matter when the teacher and the students both view disciplinary content as a set of problems, not principles. Philosophy, for example, involves problems of knowledge and logic, problems of ethics. We all may make many choices about what to believe and what to do, but what makes a choice a moral choice, a logical choice? Discussion of these problems invites participation in a thought process that single-dimensional moralizing or arid deductivism would choke off.

3. By starting, in addition, a directed dialogue with students on social problems and prospects, basic student-generated themes emerge that require ongoing investigation. Freire (1993) focuses this process on three areas. Students identify: (1) the most serious and disturbing limit situations (obstacles, contradictions, negations) that they (and by extension, all of us) need to know more about as challenges to their (and our) fulfillment and humanization; (2) student action(s) in response to these limit situations, both actual and possible; and (3) structures of society and institutional realities that require transformation in order to obviate these limit situations in the future. Students also need to be invited to evaluate whether and how the themes generated can become the axes of the course's academic content. The American Friends Service Committee (AFSC) has developed a very useful technique for operationalizing Freire's problem-posing and dialogical suggestions. Called the "Listening Project," this AFSC strategy involves teachers working together with students on a survey project concerning community problems, values, patterns of interconnectedness, and discussion of actual and possible civic actions. The survey gets students to interact as they compare their own assessments with those of others in class and is designed to build a context for reflection on points of view that can simultaneously generate discourse. It does this particularly well where the questionnaire probes into causality in a highly sophisticated way, stressing multiple and complex factors that lead to deeper inquiry and deeper understanding. (American Friends Service Committee, 1997)

4. Course content also needs to be reconstructed in accordance with multicultural and interdisciplinary interests, and emancipatory prospects. EduAction needs critical thinking, discussion of comparative and opposing viewpoints, directed discussion into the roots of oppression—class, race, and gender inequalities, the dynamics of capital accumulation, etc. Part of the teacher's responsibility is to empower (and overcome fatalism) through dialogue directed toward real political prospects embedded within the current social situation. Space does not permit further detail here, but the reader is advised to consult Lloyd Daniel's (1995) *Liberation Education: A Strategy for the 21st Century;* also the "Doing the Possible" and "Agenda for Change" sections of David Korten's (1996) book, *When Corporations Rule the World;* as well as Mark Zepezauer and Arthur Naiman's (1996) *Take the Rich Off Welfare.*

5. The teacher must become "the guide on the side, not sage on the stage" (Karre, 1993, p. 18). Guidance consists in providing study questions for reading assignments and for small group work and discussion opportunities that will facilitate collaborative learning. Sometimes small groups can be supplied with transparencies and felt-tip pens to summarize group responses to study questions. When these responses are displayed via the overhead projector, the entire class can participate in discussion. When different groups work on different dimensions of a problem or related, yet separate, study questions, their responses may be pieced together jigsaw fashion in group discussion. During the discussions within student teams or small groups, the teacher should feel comfortable

enough actually to walk away from the classroom. On the other hand, the teacher's presence during general group discussion with the entire class is absolutely necessary to bring the theoretical analysis deftly and appropriately to bear. Critical thinking questions can be posed methodically, and I have devised a work sheet[3] to guide student interrogation of texts. The identification and evaluation of six philosophical criteria (author's definition of problem, suggested solution(s), cause(s), values, line of reasoning, and evidence) constitute an intelligent heuristic for information processing.

6. Term assignments should take the form of study/action projects or study/service projects, which aim at getting students to assess the prospects of engaging in effective civic work for the public good. These projects are started very early in the semester and hinge upon students choosing a scholarly article from a wide-ranging anthology (assigned as a textbook in each course) that addresses a social or philosophical problem of significance to the student. The project combines a critical interrogation of the selected article with a student search for local, regional, or national organizations that are also attempting to address this or similar problems. Students must identify an action-oriented group (or groups) within their communities from whom they could learn more about the nature of the problem and assess possible solutions. Using as much ingenuity as possible, teachers ask students to devise a plan by which they could be of service to one of these groups on a relatively short-term volunteer basis. Utilizing the categories and guidelines for critical thinking on the work sheet described above, students make short presentations to small groups about the ideas of the author they chose. They also report on what they have learned from their volunteer activities. Toward the end of the semester they formally write up their analyses of the essay they chose and couch this within an evaluation of their community action or service experience. On our campus, a Service Learning Office arranges definite larger-scale service learning opportunities (in local schools and at the juvenile detention center) that are of particular interest to many students. The point here is that we must be promoting community impact education: the service learning experience is intended to lead to both community-building and to civic action daring to reconstruct the social order.

7. As instructors, there are definite institutionalized changes we are able to make that allow us to accomplish Freirean goals. For example, some faculty at various colleges have been able to include the study of oppression and student/faculty involvement in community action and community development in their divisional (or college-wide) objectives for curriculum, educational activities, and future assessment purposes. We can successfully resist defining outcomes in terms of replication of oppressive social division of labor and wealth. Some social science faculty have worked with students and their college's office of student activities to establish a recognized student group that has as its purpose campus wide discussions of contemporary social problems and issues. In one instance this is called *Campus Forum,* and it has brought the following

critics of U.S. politics and culture to campus to make presentations and interact with students and faculty: Philip Agee (opposing the Gulf War and the C.I.A.), Kwame Ture (Stokely Carmichael, on Pan-African socialism), Michael Parenti (on imperialism), Lisa Faruolo (spokesperson for Leonard Peltier), Henrietta Mann (Lakota spokesperson), Mark Lane (on J.F.K. assassination), Jerry Mander (on electronic media and control of knowledge), Ronnie Dugger (on the Alliance for Democracy and the resurgent populism aiming at taking back the economy and politics from corporate control), and Hiber Conteris (on human rights abuse in Latin America). Student reporters for the campus newspaper get involved, and videotapes are also made for subsequent classroom use.

8. The community college must become an engine for community development and transformation. Economics instructor Steve Spartan has made several concrete proposals in this direction that are intended to be institutionalized in the near future. First, the establishment of a Center for Analysis of Local Issues. This umbrella organization would bridge the gap between campus and community by tapping the talent of faculty as resource persons analyzing community problems, questions, and needs, as well as helping to formulate appropriate community responses. Students can be involved as co-investigators into community issues. For example, a sociologist, working with a local church group and local government representatives, has already dedicated entire sections of a certain course to designing and carrying out student-driven research on "latch-key kids" in Kansas City, Kansas. Another institutional proposal involves the development of CONTAC (Community Organizations Network and Training Assistance Center) to encourage and coordinate civic activism, and GAIN (Government Agencies Information Network) to access and exchange community data. Course work has also been proposed in this vein that could be educative for the educator: an "Introduction to Local Development" course could enroll some members of our own social science faculty as well as local government and business personnel. Faculty involved here will learn from, and network with, practitioners in the field, as all share experiences and debate points of view. This will even generate revenue to the college in the form of state aid at the same time as participants could be afforded tuition remission.

9. Finally, and perhaps most importantly, comes the necessity of building coalitions—locally, regionally, and nationally—with progressive organizations and individuals. As community college instructors here, we have quite naturally also developed friendships with progressive faculty at other local colleges and universities. Attempting to formalize this somewhat, we have established a loosely knit Kansas City Progressive Network. We hold monthly potluck dinners on Sunday afternoons at our members' homes. Students are invited as well as others not working in higher education. Members of the Green Party, the Labor Party, and the Alliance for Democracy are actively involved in this network. Our common goal is ending corporate control of our economy and

government. We have been meeting now for just about three years. We have organized local conferences, brought in speakers, run candidates locally, and overcome much of the isolation that is, from time to time, quite debilitating to serious critics of our culture. One significant accomplishment has been a lengthy discussion of the political shape we would like to see this country take in the future. This is crystallized in the Kansas City Progressive Network's discussion document, *Charter 2000: A Comprehensive Political Platform* (Reitz, 2000). The *Charter* presents a positive vision of desirable social outcomes and is already being circulated widely to stimulate discussion of its contents. Addressing the problems and prospects of justice, peace, abundance, ecology, human rights, democracy, education, health and childcare, etc., it attempts to be a comprehensive political program around which progressive individuals can unite. David and Patricia Brodsky deserve special thanks as primary drafters of this revised and expanded discussion document. The *Charter* is available for review on the web at http://www.wmc.edu/academics/library/pub/jcp/issueI2/reitz.html.

In conclusion, let me acknowledge that today the larger tendencies of social change world wide are generally regressive. Economic and political globalization is leading not towards multiculturalism and mutuality, but to the politics of polarization and privatization. A reactionary racialization in politics is also occurring (the mobilization of bias against immigrants and ethnic minorities through mainstream political parties as well as through the militias and the corporate media). Reactionary politics also involves the rationalization of the irrational within culture (from resurgent religious fundamentalism and new age millennialism, to philosophy without foundations and the several nihilistic versions of postmodernism).

Yet in this period of destabilization, new forces are also emerging in the United States bringing previously isolated groups of progressives together in working coalitions and alliances: the New Party www.newparty.org, the Labor Party www.igc.apc.org/lpa/, the Greens www.greens.org/index.html#newmexico, the Alliance for Democracy www.world.std.com/ÿ7Eolchaptr, etc. Within this nation's community colleges in the 1990s, there was also positioned a greater concentration of first-generation academics than anywhere else in academe. Among these is also a greater proportion of Ph.D.'s and union activists than ever before. Fewer of them have the inherited elitist worldviews of the sons or daughters of earlier generations of U.S. academics, who also tend to teach in the more prestigious strata of the postsecondary system. Catalyst groups within the community colleges and other higher education institutions have quite remarkably moved educational theory and practice forward in recent decades, especially through the antiracist and antisexist multicultural education reform movement. Additionally, voices like that of Ira Shor advise the reconsideration of a class-based politics and educational philosophy, given the intensity of recent economic polarization and the obsolescence of the ideology of the Soviet threat. Rebellion is once again afoot, and the support for it more widespread. Witness the August 1997 UPS strike; the militant resistance to union-busting in Decatur and in Detroit; the one-hundred-plus teach-ins on U.S. campuses during October and November 1996 against corporate control of the economy, culture, and politics; the uprisings in Chiapas, in Peru, in India. The culture wars waged by the reactionary right against progressive policies in education, the arts, and social-needs oriented programs testify to the latent power of contemporary social movements, which (though now in many ways subdued) is still greatly feared in establishment circles. The dialectic of social and educational change is not without emancipatory potential.

EduAction flows from the basic conclusion of Frederick Douglass: no struggle, no progress. EduAction can build a movement sense of solidarity and community among these emergent forces and furnish the future with the philosophical foundation it requires. Plato's *Republic* asked to what extent we are enlightened or unenlightened about our being. Hegel's *Phenomenology* asked (in its sections on the mind alienated from itself and the mind assured of itself) whether our being is our own. Reason appeared to him as an acquisition of mind, won through struggle, not only against error, illusion, deception, and self-deception, but also against oppressive social forces. Consistent with his teaching, the civilizing forces of our age, the organized popular struggles against racism, sexism, poverty, war, and imperialism have educated this nation about oppression, alienation, power, and empowerment. Nowhere did the professoriat lead in this effort, although many individual college teachers played important roles. In our epoch, humanity may come into possession of itself only by struggling to learn in spite of and outside of institutions of domination. The theory of our alienation must analyze, as did Marx in the *1844 Manuscripts,* the dynamics of capital accumulation involving the seizure of surplus value during the social production process that separates productive individuals from the product of their labor, from control of the labor process, from solidarity with other members of the work force, and from the political potential of the human species itself. Only the political restoration of this product, the democratic reallocation of control, the egalitarian restoration of community, and a cultivated sense of the common good as society's highest power, will permit us to attain education's most venerable goal: to know ourselves and to be ourselves. The purpose of EduAction is to grasp intellectually and to grasp politically the being that is our own.

*Notes*

1. An earlier version of this paper appeared in the electronic *Journal of Critical Pedagogy,* Vol. I, No. 2. April 1998. My thanks to colleagues Mark Krank at Western Montana College and Aeron Haynie at University of Wisconsin Green Bay, and especially to Steve Spartan at Kansas City Kansas Community College, for formulating certain of the points raised in this article during many discussions about our practice.

2. I offer Steve Spartan, Morteza Ardebili, Barbara Morrison, Elizabeth Budd, Tamara

Agha-Jaffar, Ken Clark, Steve Collins, Mary Grunke, and Roena Haynie my immense gratitude for their stimulating insights (and for the generative power of their criticism and disagreements). By the same token, the perspective I have synthesized here as "EduAction" is intended to speak for no one but myself. I assume sole responsibility for these notes, and any criticism of the viewpoint or framework expressed here should be directed at me alone.

    3. This worksheet is drawn largely from P. J. Baker and Louis E. Anderson (1987), *Social Problems: A Critical Thinking Approach*. Belmont, CA: Wadsworth Publishing; also from E. Vedung (1982), *Political Reasoning*. Beverly Hills, CA: Sage Publishing; and N. Rescher (1977), *Dialectics: A Controversy-Oriented Approach to the Theory of Knowledge*. Albany, NY: State University of New York Press.

    4. For Winter 1997 Listening Project Questions see www.lib.wmc.edu/-pub/jcp/issueI-2/reitz.html.

    5. CHARTER 2000. A COMPREHENSIVE POLITICAL PLATFORM. Document contained in full in Charles Reitz (2000), *Art, Alienation and the Humanities: A Critical Engagement with Herbert Marcuse*. Albany, NY: State University of New York Press, pp. 267–84. Available on the web at http://www.wmc.edu/academics/library/pub/jcp/-issueI-2/reitz.html.

## References

American Friends Service Committee. (1997). Unpublished survey constructed by its Kansas City office.

Boyer, E. L., et al. (1988). *Building communities*. Washington, DC: American Association of Community and Junior Colleges.

Bowles. S. & Gintis, H. (1976). *Schooling in capitalist America*. New York: Basic Books.

Clark, B. R. (1960). *The open door college: A case study*. New York: McGraw-Hill.

Daniel, L. (1995). *Liberation education: A strategy for the 21st century*. Kansas City, MO: New Democracy Press.

Dougherty, K. J. (1994). *The contradictory college*. Albany, NY: State University of New York Press.

Freire, P. (1993). *Pedagogy of the oppressed*. New York: Continuum.

Karabel, J. (1972). Community colleges and social stratification. *Harvard Educational Review*, 42 (4), 521–562.

Karre, I. (1993). *Busy, noisy, and powerfully effective: Cooperative learning in the classroom*. Stillwater, OK: New Forums.

Korton, D. (1996). *When corporations rule the world*. West Hartford, CT: Kumarian Press.

Pincus, F. (1980). The false promises of community colleges. *Harvard Educational Review*, 50 (3), 332–361.

Pincus, F. (1974). Tracking and the community colleges. *The Insurgent Sociologist IV* (3), 17–35.

Reitz, C. (1996). Liberating *the critical* in critical theory: Marcuse, Marx and the pedagogy of the oppressed—Art, alienation and the humanities. *Researcher, 11* (2), 40–50.

Reitz, C. (2000a). *Art, Alienation, and the Humanities: A Critical Engagement with Herbert Marcuse*. Albany, NY: State University of New York Press.

Reitz, C. (2000b). Liberating *the critical* in critical theory: Marcuse, Marx and the pedagogy of the oppressed—Art, alienation and the humanities. In S. Steiner, H. M. Krank,

P. McLaren, & R. E. Bahruth (Eds.), *Freirean pedagogy, praxis, and possibilities: Projects for the new millennium*. New York: Falmer Press.

Zepezauer, M., & Naiman, A. (1996). *Take the rich off welfare*. Tucson, AZ: Odonian Press.

Zwerling, L. S. (1976). *Second best: The crisis of the community college*. New York: McGraw-Hill.

*Arisve Esquivel, Karla Lewis, Dalia Rodriguez,*
*David Stovall, and Tyrone Williams*

---

# WE KNOW WHAT'S BEST FOR YOU:
# SILENCING OF PEOPLE OF COLOR

> *Our silence has been long and deep . . . we have always been spoken*
> *for. Or we have been spoken to. Or we have appeared as jokes or flat*
> *figures suggesting sensuality. Today we are taking back our narra-*
> *tive telling our story.*                    —TONI MORRISON

THE CURRENT FACADE presented throughout the world es-
pouses a color-blind, race-neutral democracy. In reality, people of color
continually confront systemic educational policies resulting in the silencing of community voice. Presently, policies utilize race-neutral and color-blind
rhetoric to pacify communities of color, while maintaining the status quo (i.e.,
White privilege). This document demonstrates the pervasiveness of mainstream
ideology in the implementation of educational policies. Through the documentation of five distinct educational policy cases, this analysis seeks to place the voices
of people of color at the forefront of emancipatory ideology. It is our position that
Paulo Freire's vision has yet to be realized, particularly in communities of color.
Freire notes there are two stages in the pedagogy of the oppressed; however, it
seems that we cannot get beyond the first stage of awakening. Thus, the second
stage of teaching the oppressors has yet to be fulfilled. Consequently, we contend
that, in order to develop pedagogies for oppressed populations, we must first recognize the racist systems in which we operate (Freire, 1996).

The concept of racism as endemic to everyday life is viewed as an assumption
without merit. Color-blind or race-neutral policies are interpreted as a necessity
for the creation of a meritorious society. Antidiscrimination law is considered by
the courts as the only measure by which to determine racism. Narrative, as an attempt to provide contextual analysis for instances of race and racism, is considered

presumptive. Democrats and Republicans engage in liberal discourse to address issues of fairness. The behavior of Whites is argued as a de facto standard that guarantees willing participants a more viable chance at the improvement of their human condition. The law as neutral policy should have as its only concern the rights of the individual. Group dynamics are the exception. Racism by and large is a figment of our imagination beyond the isolated incidents prompted by the few ignorant members of society. In the eyes of the mainstream, we all get along, as long as we do not question White privilege.

The following five snapshots will reveal that, regardless of space and time, racist educational systems have systematically oppressed communities of color. These examples at first might seem disjointed; they have been chosen to demonstrate that the discourse at the macro level does not correspond with the realities at the micro level. These stories reveal that, throughout time and across the Americas, people of color are not a priority. Their educational needs have rarely been addressed, and, in many instances, they have been shut out of the educational system. Our aim is to analyze these five cases and begin to address the problems that communities of color face.

## THEORETICAL FRAMEWORK AND METHODOLOGY

The theoretical framework for this analysis interweaves Paulo Freire, Critical Race Theory (CRT), Latina/o Critical Race Theory (LatCrit), and Black Feminist Thought. This multilayered theoretical framework situates oppressed communities' voices at the center of the analysis.

CRT (Crenshaw, Gotanda, Peller, & Thomas, 1995; Parker, 1999) allows us to understand that law produces and is the product of social power by placing race and racism at the core of legal and policy analysis. CRT also seeks to "de-cloak" the seemingly race-neutral and color-blind ways in which law and policy are conceptualized, discussed, and formulated, with respect to their impact on poor people and persons of color, and proposes alternative solutions in an effort to achieve social justice. By utilizing CRT as methodology and theory, this document brings forth a central issue of not only the issue of diversity but also the importance of people of color speaking with their experiential knowledge in order to reconstruct and deconstruct the discourse that often serves to perpetuate structural inequality.

Any discussion of silencing the voices of people of color must be included within the rubric of racism. CRT focuses on race but also describes the importance of the use of narrative. Narrative is important within the snapshots presented because they focus on the voices of disenfranchised groups. Moreover, in the discussion of racism as a systemic process endemic to daily life, CRT is crucial in the analysis of policy formation and results. The goal is not to identify the creators of the policy as racist but to identify their contribution to de facto racialized practices in relation to educational policy. With the use of color-blind language, the original tenets of civil rights legislation for some thirty-six years have been reversed to support a system advocating the return to a segregated system of education.

We place CRT in the span of such critique for several reasons. First, the deconstruction of color-blind policy is crucial to the identification of new discourses that continue to limit the capacity of people of color. Second, CRT, as oppositional scholarship, does not make the attempt at inclusion. From its inception, the belief has been that CRT will be met with harsh opposition. In that understanding, it is substantiated and valued by scholars in various disciplines who embrace the idea that CRT is a call to work. Third, CRT is new. Its realms have not been fully developed in the deconstruction of color-blind rhetoric and in the creation of praxis-oriented work. Although the attempts to do so have been identified, there is considerable work needed. CRT needs to situate itself firmly in the context of historical developments in the contestation of racism. Where contemporary accounts are effective in courts of law as testimony, CRT in the larger sense has not embraced a historical foundation. Although far from being devoid of history, inclusions in the mode of the Harris (1995) account provide necessary contexts in which to situate the development of Whiteness and White privilege.

Latina/o Critical Race Theory (LatCrit) confronts the Black/White paradigm that exists within CRT. Within this paradigm the experiences of Latinas/os are rendered invisible. Thus, LatCrit is an offshoot of CRT and speaks to the gaps that exist within the theory. LatCrit places Latinas/os at the center of the theoretical framework and teases out the multiple histories and experiences of Latinas/os within the U.S. As with CRT, LatCrit also uses and values narratives and storytelling to document Latinas/os' experiences (Valdes, 1996).

Black Feminist Thought, which arose because of the lack of attention to Black women within the feminist movement, is important because it deals with the intersectionality of race, class, and gender. Collins (1990) suggests that sharing lived experiences, and how they inform us, is a form of knowledge building about the world. Black Feminist Thought allows us to have a deeper understanding of marginalized groups and is empowering. There is power in the telling and reading the authentic stories of others (Willis & Lewis, 1999). These snapshots do that.

The use of narratives dominates the literature in Black Feminist Thought because, through the act of telling one's story, the reader can begin to see connections to African American intellectualism and empowerment (Etter–Lewis, 1993; Gates, 1989; Ladson-Billings, 1996; Morrison, 1994; St. Jean & Feagin, 1998). Narratives illustrate the issues of race, class, and gender domination and oppression in the United States (Morrison, 1994). The use of these theories allows one to tease out, when necessary, race, class and gender and talk about multiple positioned people. The following snapshots take up the notion of narratives exemplified in the works of Paulo Freire, Critical Race Theory, LatCrit, and Black Feminist Thought.

The interweaving of these theoretical methodologies highlights the information gleamed from archival sources, social justice literature, and interviews. The time period for this analysis takes the reader from nineteenth-century Jamaica to contemporary U.S. society. The following five snapshots document the experiences of communities of color and their actions to address systematic inequalities.

## SNAPSHOTS AS ENTRY WAYS

*The authors caution the reader that the limited scope of these particular interpretations is due to the space constraints of this undertaking. Bear in mind, the subsequent paragraphs of this section touch briefly upon the attitudes, values, beliefs, and actions of communities of color whose stories are yet to be told in their entirety. These brief snapshots are intended to highlight specific moments in time and hear communities of color speak for themselves.*

### SNAPSHOT #1: NINETEENTH CENTURY JAMAICA: "THEY SEND THEIR CHILDREN TO LEARN SOMETHING"

The commitment to education in the Afro-Jamaican community was evident in the early decades of the nineteenth century. In fact, slaves began the process of educating themselves and their children prior to Emancipation and the establishment of government schools in the 1830s. Gordon (1998) points out that ex-slaves were observed by missionary societies to be acquiring alphabets, primers, bibles, spelling books, and prayer books. These were not isolated incidents, as missionary societies island-wide reported similar scenarios. In many instances, adults were reported to receive instruction on reading from children attending day schools. In a report on the Jamaica Union Society, the findings spoke of the itinerant instructors who went from house to house among the peasant class to improve literacy. The report concluded

> that the older children who attended regular day schools were very well known, in many instances, to employ a portion of their leisure hours in instructing adults and others who have no time and opportunity to profit by the regular schools. It was said that children thus employed, earned from 3d. to 1s. currency per week for each pupil, and were enabled, from this source, to clothe themselves and assist their respective families. (Latrobe, 1838)

There is no questioning the level of commitment to acquiring literacy skills on behalf of the people from this evidence, but more importantly this evidence gives us a lens with which to view community involvement in education alongside the efforts of missionary societies and colonial authorities. What transpired in a few instances in this early era of Jamaican educational history were Afro-Jamaican children and adults alike coming together to "impart mutual instruction" when time permitted (Gordon, 1998). These interactions were more than transfer of knowledge; they demonstrate a collective reinforcement of their commitment to the struggle for independence in nineteenth-Century Jamaica. Studies of post-emancipated societies in the Americas have shown that this struggle had its base in self-determination, irrespective of White ruling authority (Anderson, 1988; Butler, 1998; Gaspar, 1985).

If any thought unified the ex-slave community following Emancipation, it was the refusal to remain laborers under the similar circumstances of slavery. Given their concern for a literary education, Afro-Jamaican parents objected to the proposed industrial/agricultural curriculum being advanced by the authorities both in

Jamaica and England (first in the 1840s and again in the 1880s). Bear in mind that the members of the Jamaican Legislature were plantation owners or had ties to the plantations. Lyndon Howard Evelyn, a planter from Savannala–Mar, suggested that instruction based on classical education had no place in a country where the majority of the population had been recently enslaved:

> The mental, therefore, must never in these establishments be suffered to usurp the pre-eminence, or paramount; whether of principle or conduct of word or act. The in-structions, the periods of employment, the direction, discipline, examinations, re-wards, should all have reference to or be guided by that which is of practical industry or that of Agricultural advancement; in the first instance! (Evelyn, 1845)

Without question, Evelyn echoed the common sentiments of the ruling class. With no concrete legal method of holding peasants to plantations, manual educa-tion was viewed as one way to keep Blacks close to crop cultivation. As a commu-nity, Blacks refused to see their children indoctrinated in this manner, not because they did not see any merits in agricultural/industrial teaching but because they ob-jected to it, given that the society continued to exploit and abuse Black labor. The Rev. P. Williams, a Baptist Minister on the island, explained:

> [Black] parents do not consider that schoolmasters can teach agriculture better than they can themselves. They have objected to it in the past . . . when attempts were made to establish industrial schools. Teachers in a few instances got the children to work a ground for them, and the parents objected. [Black Parents] said they send their children to learn something, and not to work grounds for the teacher. (House of Commons British Sessional Papers, 1900)

Even in a society created on their labor and subordination Afro-Jamaican peo-ple still found ways to make their presence known through active resistance to ed-ucational policies incompatible with community needs. Mothers and fathers re-fused to see their children educated in a manner resembling their lives on plantations that entailed backbreaking labor under the watchful eye of the over-seer. As such, Afro-Jamaicans struggled and carved out a niche for themselves within the parameters of colonial society. Boycotting schools, along with other measures, provided outlets for Afro-Jamaicans to articulate community needs.

SNAPSHOT #2: WHY WE KNOW WHAT'S BEST FOR YOU: THE END OF
AFFIRMATIVE ACTION IN CALIFORNIA

To identify and give voice to the silenced voices of people of color in higher educa-tion, the creation of Proposition 209[1] in California serves as a relevant example. As intent is argued, the attempt is not to identify proponents of Prop. 209 as mali-cious conspirators. However, as fewer African American and Latino students are admitted to the University of California system, the voices of these students re-main absent. Prop. 209 should be viewed as an intentional silencing due to the de-cision of the University of California Board of Regents and the legislature to fol-low the policy. The rationale supporting the termination of affirmative action is found in its literal interpretation. Although the language may appear impartial, the effects reveal a disparate reality from the policy's color-blind intent. Citing institutional racism, political pressures, and denial as primary culprits in the creation of Prop. 209, this section teases out the underpinnings of policy threatening the admission of students of color to the University of California (UC) system. Hence, the further silencing of voices.

Historically higher education remained a "white old boys club until the 1960s" (Platt 1997, p. 7). African Americans and Latinas/os, not admitted to traditionally White institutions (TWI's) in California until the mid-60s, functioned as beneficiaries of programs that

> made it possible for previously excluded populations to make it through high school and into higher education and/or better paid working-class jobs. . . .(It) provided opportunity and support for previously excluded groups to apply to and move into formerly hostile institutions. In higher education, this took the form of aggressive outreach and recruitment, "Bridge" and remedial programs that provided psychological, cultural and technical encouragement. (p. 11)

Affirmative action at its height placed enormous pressure on exclusive institutions to "diversify" business contracts, admissions, and promotions. Inclusion of people of color would not have been possible without such programs. Between 1970 and 1990, the number of African American college graduates doubled. In the same time period, the number of female Ph.D.'s increased more than tenfold. When the Center for Individual Rights (CIR) and other organizations began to attack these programs, the Supreme Court supported their critique and backed away from support of programs assuming the "existence of institutionalized inequality" (*University of California Regents v. Bakke*, 1978). Consequently, the burden of proof was placed on the institution to demonstrate how they were moving towards inclusion. Affirmative Action, according to its current interpretation, must be "narrowly tailored, serve a compelling interest, and be subject to strict scrutiny" (Platt, 1997, p. 13).

In terms of silencing, the actions of the state of California have served to limit the access of people of color to higher education. As the policy has been implemented, the silencing is manifested in the decrease in the number of Blacks and Latinas/os attending colleges and universities within the UC system.

SNAPSHOT #3: DIVERSITY AS THE SILENCER: THE UNIVERSITY OF MICHIGAN AFFIRMATIVE ACTION CASE

In most affirmative action cases, minority students are not included and most universities take the position that minority students' voices are unnecessary in court cases. As a result, minority students are not involved in the actual judicial process, resulting in the failure to take part in introducing evidence, present their own witnesses and arguments, or make arguments that universities themselves are unwilling to admit (Shaw, 1998).[2] As a result, the voices of students of color are silenced. By analyzing the University of Michigan's diversity argument, as well as events leading up to the affirmative action case, through a Freirian lens, we can shed light on the dialogue created at the University of Michigan campus. Through Freire's (1970) concepts of dialogue and *conscientização* we can come to a deeper understanding between issues of power and education.[3]

The plaintiff, Jennifer Gratz, a White applicant, was denied admission to the College of Literature, Arts and Sciences, at the University of Michigan (*Gratz v. Bollinger,* 1997). She alleged that the admissions policy violated the equal protection clause of the Fourteenth Amendment. Drawing on expert witnesses from across the country in a variety of disciplines, scholars presented evidence on how diversity should be the basis for affirmative action policy in higher education (Anderson, 2000; Bowen & Bok, 1998; Foner, 2000; Gurin, 2000; Sugrue, 2000). Scholars documented historical discrimination and current segregation in the state of Michigan and at the University of Michigan. However, due to the precedent of *University of California Regents v. Bakke* (1978), the crux of Michigan's argument was based on the issue of diversity. As precedented by *Texas v. Hopwood* (1996), the University of Michigan's advocates realized that they could no longer simply rely on the argument of diversity for the sake of diversity, nor could they solely rely on the argument of historical discrimination. Thus, Michigan's goal was to prove the benefits of diversity as well as that of affirmative action policy in higher education. Empirical analysis was gathered for the case to demonstrate how students learn better in diverse settings by increasing engagement in active thinking processes in informal interactions. This, in turn, causes growth in intellectual engagement, motivation, and intellectual and academic skills. Students also acquire a better appreciation for the ideas of others as well as making them better equipped to understand, consider, and deal with conflicts from different perspectives.

The university initially claimed to adequately represent students of color. Several statements of support were publicly announced to demonstrate support for students of color, and several panels to discuss issues of diversity as well as the affirmative action case were created.[4] However, we have to ask ourselves what "diversity" represents as a legal argument versus what "diversity" means for students of color. As the crux of the legal argument, diversity seems to cloud the real issue at hand; that is, the argument avoids the issue of everyday racism that students of color continue to experience in predominantly White universities (Feagin & Sikes: 1994; Hurtado, 1992; Dublin, 1996). In the initial stages of the Michigan case students' voices were not heard and the legal issue of diversity created a distorted perception that Michigan's goal was to represent students of color, ignoring the everyday reality of racism. Without the testimonies of students of color, voices were once again silenced.

Left out of the judicial process, students at Michigan sought representation through protests, organizing to demonstrate their support for affirmative action policy. Prospective students also created a dialogue through a variety of strategies. Students pursued a dialogue with the courts by petitioning to be heard. African American and Latina/o individuals who applied or intended to apply to the university made a motion to intervene. After the motion was denied, student voices appealed the motion, and the Sixth District Court determined that student voices would be heard.

As Freire (1970) states, a liberating praxis must entail a dialogue between leaders and the oppressed; in this particular case the oppressed were students of color. Students' voices were eventually heard, but only through the pressure of university students and community organizations that intervened, fighting for a voice and creating a dialogue with university leaders and the judicial system. The court's final ruling was that diversity is a compelling state interest, ruling in favor of the University of Michigan. Students continue to experience subtle-to-overt racism and discrimination on predominantly White campuses. The call for hearing students' voices in affirmative action cases, such as the Michigan case, is a call to bring the experiences of students of color to the forefront in an effort to enlighten the court system on the reality of racism on our college campuses.

### SNAPSHOT #4: LATINA/O STUDENTS AT THE UNIVERSITY OF ILLINOIS AT URBANA-CHAMPAIGN

Silenced voices emerge at moments in a continuous line of struggle from the late 1960s push for La Casa Cultural Latina, to a 1992 Cinco de Mayo sit-in, to the development of the Latina Latino Studies Program. The historical relationship between Latina/o students and university officials at the University of Illinois at Urbana-Champaign (UIUC) has been tumultuous. Latina/o students in the late sixties began an initiative to redefine who a university student was and, in the process, redefined the university itself. Along the way they encountered obstacles put forth by university administrators who did not look favorably upon this newly included segment of the student population. UIUC archival sources reveal the efforts of Latina/o students to improve conditions on campus. Students actively fought for a cultural center, La Casa Cultural Latina (La Casa), in order to address the low recruitment and retention rates of Latina/o students and faculty.

The public discourse maintained that they were supportive of Latina/o students. Furthermore, they saw the need for a cultural center and established it in 1974. However, a private discourse of confidential memos and letters from one administrator to another expressed no need for the cultural center. Although university administrators established La Casa, they set it up to fail. For example, from its inception, the cultural center was not given the adequate funds to be successfully managed. The heavy burden of managing the center was placed on graduate students who served as directors, and undergraduate students who were the support staff. Moreover, in their memos, university officials perceived Latina/o students as deficient and problematic. Finally, Latina/o students were seen as being unable to speak English or Spanish. Thus, university administrators believed Latina/o students would never be fully integrated into the "normal" flow of campus activities.

We document this failure through competing narratives and counterstories. There is a war between stories (Delgado, 1989). The dominant group's story is seen as real, neutral, and justifying the status quo, while the outgroup's story is seen as extreme or implausible. For example, UIUC administrators have the power to disclose certain facts as neutral truth in which race is never a factor. Latina/o students' counterstories reject the university's good intentions and document how the university works against Latina/o students.

Daniel Solorzano and Octavio Villalpando (1998) explain that students of color are in marginal positions. This can be oppressive, but it can also be a site of resistance, empowerment and transformation. This is why Latina/o students must understand their histories at UIUC and other campuses. Conversely, university administrators must come to terms with the history of Latina/o students. The numerous ways Latina/o students have been and continue to be marginalized need to be addressed. UIUC needs to recognize and solve the problems Latina/o students confront if it truly believes in all segments of the student population. Thus, the struggles from the late sixties are still present today. Silenced voices emerge on moments of a continuous line of struggle from the late sixties' push for La Casa, to a 1992 Cinco de Mayo sit-in, to the development of the Latina Latino Studies Program, and to the current situation of La Casa. Latina/o students today echo Latina/o students from the late sixties:

> I think that they need to listen to the problems that we see so that we can change things. The university just wants us to fit into their little mold so that they can show that we have diversity here. I don't think that they care if we graduate or not as long as they have Brown and Black faces walking around campus. There has to be a joint effort to help students of color to graduate and not just be admitted into the university. I think that if students felt that they had a relationship with the university more students would have a better view of the administration. They need to stop seeing and treating us as "a bunch of radicals who keep complaining" and instead they should start seeing us as active and concerned students. (Latina UIUC senior student)

SNAPSHOT #5: THE MISSING VOICE IN SCHOOL REFORM

> I am very, very, very close with my kids . . . they're my babies. . . .I make it a point to really get to know my kids, to let them know how much I care, so when it gets in a situation that I need to be firm and that I need to be rough and tough on 'em they understand why. It's not just . . . that it's just a job to me. Because it's not. I really do . . . I care about my kids. I care about all the kids in the building.[5]

African American women know that their position as instructional aides requires more than the job description. Their role is to continue "uplifting" youth by providing assistance by any means necessary (Perkins, 1983). However, the role of instructional aide has no power and therefore cannot be a legitimate agent for change. As we discuss school reform and improving education for minority children, our vision of what schooling is and who is involved needs to be widened. Through listening to the voices of instructional aides, we can get to Freire's second stage of "teaching the oppressors."

Instructional aides are an important part of the educational process. As a society, we claim that education is important, yet we do not provide training for all the staff. When we think of schools, we think of children, teachers, and principals, but we often overlook a support staff that assists the children, teachers, and principals. Their duties can include: working one-on-one with students, working with students in small groups, lunch room supervision, playground supervision, and assisting the teacher in any other areas they deem necessary. Due to various factors, including the Individuals with Disabilities Education Act (IDEA), PL 94–142 (1974), many children spend more time with an instructional aide than a classroom teacher. Some instructional aides claim that they know the students better than the teacher. Moreover, other instructional aides believe they do the teacher's job, but without the pay. One aide, Olinthia, says

> but when you think about our kids . . . they're hungry, they're behind . . . you've got to think of their needs. It's just like they're all your babies and you know . . . if your kids, your own personal kids needed something to eat and you wanted a new pair of shoes, what are you gonna do? You're gonna have to wait on those shoes and feed your kids. And I think it's the same way with the kids here. You have to make those exceptions. You've got to be firm with them, but they also need to know you care and if you're not willing to do those things you're making it hard on yourself.

As a researcher, it took me a while to understand what Olinthia meant about the students being her babies. Darlene Clark Hine and Kathleen Thompson (1998) state, "Black women's history teaches us that, unless we fulfill our duty to family and community, there is no satisfaction and no possibility of peace" (p. 308). Olinthia is not only committed to her family in the sense of being a positive role model for her children, but also to her community which includes the children at school. She sees herself as their only hope in the midst of rejection. Her comparison of her students to her own children means that there is no difference. However, the teachers at Olinthia's school saw difference steeped in race and class and acted negatively towards the children defined by those differences. The school in which Olinthia works has a high percentage of low-income children, evidenced by the number of those eligible to receive a free lunch. The school district where Olinthia works has more Black instructional aides than Black teachers. Race, class, and gender have to be addressed within school reform discussions if the goal is "education for all." Education is always seen as the hope for the hopeless, the gateway to equality of opportunity, but C.W. Mills (1956) reminds us that things are not always what they seem. We espouse one ideology, but act upon another. America is a democracy that does not always grant everyone a voice. The status quo ensures this.

## POLICY IMPLICATIONS AND CONCLUSIONS

The previous five snapshots speak to the theoretical and methodological characteristics of Paulo Freire, Critical Race Theory (CRT), Latina/o Critical Race Theory (LatCrit), and Black Feminist Thought. The snapshots reveal six common aspects irrespective of their specific locations in place and time. First, they deal with the social construction of race in the Americas. Second, some discuss, at multiple levels, the impact that class has on the lives of people of color. Third, a discussion of gender is relevant within each snapshot, even though in some it is embedded. Fourth, the power of narratives reveals silenced voices in marginalized communities. Fifth, each snapshot recognizes the power of telling one's own story in one's own words. Finally, the snapshots portray systemic institutional racism and its impact on communities of color on a daily basis.

In closing, our combined studies document the voices of oppressed communities and their efforts to name and combat the systemic racism in educational policies. Our snapshots capture moments in the complexities of oppression at both the macro and micro levels. Moreover, these cases emerge at specific points of space and time to form a bridge from nineteenth-century Jamaica to present day Champaign, Illinois. In an era of race-neutral discourse that legitimizes the current racially bound power structure, it becomes even more imperative for the emergence of unheard voices. Although Paulo Freire is credited with documenting the lives of oppressed people, his work is part of a continuum of work, including the works of CRT, LatCrit, and Black Feminist Thought, that attempt to document the efforts of people of color in the struggle against oppression. As educational practitioners, it is our responsibility to continue our foremothers' and forefathers' visions of liberation.

*Notes*

1. Proposition 209: The Amendment to the California Constitution (Article 1, Section 31) interpreted as the termination of affirmative action in the state.

2. In cases such as *Texas v. Hopwood* (1996), the district court and the U.S. Court of Appeals for the Fifth Circuit thrice denied motions of Black and Mexican-American students who had applied or intended to apply to the University.

3. Paulo Freire (1970, 1996) defines *conscientização* as learning to perceive social, political, and economic contradictions, and taking action against the oppressive elements of reality.

4. The diversity argument held that experiences during college have significant effects on the extent to which graduates are living racially and ethnically integrated lives.

5. Olinthia is an African American woman in her mid-thirties, married with three children. She is currently working on her degree in Early Childhood Education at a local community college and hopes to transfer to receive her bachelor's degree and teacher certification. When she was interviewed she was in her third year as a behavioral disorder instructional aide, but was titled inclusion aide and worked in an after school program with University of Illinois students and other instructional aides. Her narrative is one of seventeen instructional aide's stories about their role and professional development.

*References*

Anderson, J. D. (1998). *The education of blacks in the South, 1860–1935*. Durham: University of North Carolina Press.

Anderson, J. D. (2000, February). Expert report of James Anderson. Gratz v. Bollinger, 1997. http://www.umich.edu/~urel/admissions/legal/expert/foner.html.

Bacchus, M. K. (1994). *Education as and for legitimacy developments in West Indian education between 1846 and 1895.* Ontario: Wilford Laurier University Press 1994.

Bell, D. (1984). *And we are not saved: The elusive quest for social justice.* New York: Basic Books.

Bowen, W. G. & Bok, D. (1998). *The shape of the river: Long-term consequences of considering race in college and university admissions.* Princeton: Princeton University Press.

Butler, K.D. (1998). *Freedoms Given Freedoms Won Afro-Brazilians in Post-Abolition Sao Paulo and Salvador.* New Brunswick, NJ: Rutgers University Press.

Collins, P. H. (1990). *Black feminist thought: Knowledge, consciousness, and the politics of empowerment.* New York: Routledge, Chapman & Hall.

Crenshaw, K., Gotanda, N., Peller, N. & Thomas, K. (Eds.). (1995). *Critical race theory: The key writings that formed the movement.* New York: New York Press.

Delgado, R. (1989) Legal Storytelling: Storytelling for Oppositionists and Others: A Plea for Narrative. *Michigan Law Review, 87,* 2411–2441.

Delgado, R. (Ed.). (1995). *Critical race theory: The cutting edge.* Philadelphia: Temple University Press.

Delgado, R. & Stefancic, J. (1993). Critical race theory: An annotated bibliography. *Virginia Law Review, 79,* 2411–2441.

Dublin, T. (1996). *Becoming American, becoming ethnic: College students explore their roots.* Philadelphia: Temple University Press.

Etter-Lewis, G. (1993). *My soul is my own: Oral narratives of African American women in the professions.* New York: Routledge.

Evelyn, L. H. (1845). *Six Essays on the best mode of establishing and conducting industrial schools: Adapted to the wants and circumstances of an agricultural population, written for a prize of one hundred pounds.* London: unknown.

Feagin J. & Feagin, C. (1995). *White racism: The basics.* New York: Routledge.

Feagin, J. & Sikes, M. (1994). *Living with racism: The black middle-class experience.* Boston: Beacon Press.

Foner, E. (2000, February). Expert report of Eric Foner. Gratz v. Bollinger (1997) http://www.umich.edu/~urel/admissions/legal/expert/foner.html.

Freire, P. (1970). *Pedagogy of the oppressed.* New York: Continuum Press.

Freire, P. (1996). *Pedagogy of the oppressed* (Rev. ed.). New York: Continuum.

Gardner, W. J. (1873). *A history of Jamaica.* London: Elliot Stock.

Gaspar, B. D. (1985). *Bondmen and rebels: A study of master-slave relations in Antigua with implication for Colonial British America.* Baltimore: Johns Hopkins University.

Gates, H. L. (1986). *"Race," writing, and difference.* Chicago: University of Chicago Press.

Gordon, S. (1998). Schools of the free. In Moore and Wilmot (Eds.). *Before and after 1865: Education politics and regionalism in the Caribbean.* Kingston: Ian Randle.

Gratz v. Bollinger, 135 F. Supp. 2d 790 (1997).

Gurin, P. (2000, February). Expert report of Patricia Gurin. Gratz v. Bollinger (1997) http://www.umich.edu/~urel/admissions/legal/expert/foner.html.

Harris, C. Whiteness as property. In Crenshaw (Ed.). *Critical race theory: The key writings that formed the movement.* New York: New Press.

Hine, D., & Thompson, K. (1998). *A shining thread of hope: The history of Black women in America.* New York: Broadway Books.

House of Commons British Sessional Papers (1900). *Extracts From the Evidence Given Before the Jamaican Education Commission,* I, xxi.

Hurtado, S. (1992). The campus racial climate: Context of conflict. *Journal of Higher Education, 63* (5), 539–569.

Johnson, K. & Martinez, G. A. (1999, July). Cross over dreams: The roots of LatCrit theory in Chicana/o studies activism and scholarship. *University of Miami Law Review, 3,* 342–401.

Ladson-Billings, G. (1996). Silences as weapons: Challenges of a black professor teaching white students. *Theory Into Practice, 35* (2), 79–85.

Latrobe, C. J. (1838). *Return to an address of the Honourable House of Commons dated 5th February 1838.* London: House of Commons.

Levinson, B. A., Douglas, E. F. & Hollard, D. C. (Eds.). (1996). *The cultural production of the educated person: critical ethnographies of schooling and local practice.* Albany: SUNY Press.

Mills, C. W. (1956). *The power elite.* New York: Oxford University Press.

Morrison, T. (1994). *Lecture and speech of acceptance, upon the award of the Nobel prize for literature, delivered in Stockholm on the seventh of December, nineteen hundred and ninety-three.* New York : A. A. Knopf.

Parker, L. (1998). Guest editors' introduction: Critical race theory and qualitative studies in education. *Qualitative Studies in Education, 11* (1), 5–6.

Perkins, L. (1983). The impact of the cult of true womanhood on the education of Black women. *Journal of Social Issues, 39* (3), 17–28.

Platt, A. M. (1997). End game: The rise and fall of affirmative action in higher education. *Social Justice, 24* (2), 103–144.

Shaw, T. M. (2000, February). The debate over race needs minority students' voices. *Chronicle of Higher Education,* p. 72.

Smith, L. T. (1999). *Decolonizing methodologies: research and indigenous peoples.* London & New York: University of Otago Press.

Solorzano, D. G. and Villalpando, O. (1998) Critical race theory, marginality, and the experiences of students of color in higher education. In C. Torres & T. R. Mitchell (Eds.). *Sociology of Education.* Albany, NY: State University of New York Press.

St. Jean, Y. & Feagin, J. R. (1998). *Double burden: Black women and everyday racism.* Armonk, NY: M. E. Sharpe.

Sugrue, T. (2000, February). Expert report of Thomas J. Sugrue. Gratz v. Bollinger (1997) http://www.umich.edu/~urel/admissions/legal/expert/foner.html.

Texas v. Hopwood, 518 U.S. 1033 (1997).

University of California Regents v. Bakke, 438 U.S. 265 (1978).

Valdes, F. (1996). Foreword. Latina/o ethnicities, critical race theory, and post-identity politics in postmodern legal culture: From practices to possibilities. *La Raza Law Journal, 9* (1), 1–31.

Willis, A. I. & Lewis, K. C. (1999). Our known everydayness: Beyond a response to White privilege. *Urban Education, 34* (2), 245–262.

# CONTRIBUTORS

DAWN EMERSON ADDY is a faculty member at the Center for Labor Research and Studies at Florida International University. She earned her doctorate in Work, Community and Family Education at the University of Minnesota. Her research interests are primarily labor, community and issues of diversity.

RICKY LEE ALLEN is an instructor in the Department of Language, Literacy, and Sociocultural Studies at the University of New Mexico. His research and publications focus on whiteness, critical spatial theory, critical social theory, and critical pedagogy.

MICHAEL W. APPLE is John Bascom Professor of Curriculum and Instruction and Educational Policy Studies at the University of Wisconsin, Madison. A former elementary and secondary school teacher and past president of a teachers union, he has worked with educators, unions, dissident groups, and governments throughout the world to democratize educational policy and practice. Among his many books are *Official Knowledge* (Routledge), *Cultural Politics and Education* (Teachers College), and *Educating the "Right" Way: Markets, Standards, God, and Inequality* (Routledge Falmer).

WENDY W. BRANDON is an associate professor of education at Rollins College. She has directed reading enhancement programs, writing, and service-learning programs. Her research interests are antiracist scholarship and teacher education.

ARISVE ESQUIVEL is a doctoral student at the University of Illinois Urbana-Champaign in the Department of Educational Policy Studies. Her research interests include Latinas/os in higher education, Latina/o Studies, and student movements.

STEPHEN M. FAIN is a professor of curriculum history and theory at Florida International University. Prior to joining the faculty at Brooklyn College, Professor

Fain taught at both the elementary and secondary levels and served as an elementary school principal. He was one of the founding faculty at Florida International University. He is currently working with colleagues on a project on schooling and public space and is a past president of the American Association for Teaching and Curriculum.

RAMIN FARAHMANDPUR is a doctoral student at the Graduate School of Education and Information Studies at the University of California, Los Angeles. He is also a lecturer at the Charter School of Education at California State University, Los Angeles. His current areas of interest include globalization, critical pedagogy, and Marxist social theory.

ANA MARIA ARAÚJO FREIRE, the wife of Paulo Freire, holds a Ph.D. in education from São Paulo Catholic University (PUC-SP). She is co-editor of *The Paulo Freire Reader* (1998) with Donaldo Macedo and the author of *Literacy in Brazil*. She has presented internationally at conferences and as guest speaker on such themes as educational reform, social justice, and emancipation.

LAUREEN A. FREGEAU was first introduced to the work of Paolo Freire in 1980 as a Peace Corps volunteer in Guatemala. She studied at the University of Massachusetts with Donaldo Macedo and received her Ph.D. in educational theory and policy from the Pennsylvania State University. She is associate professor of educational leadership and foundations at the University of South Alabama, where she prepares educators to appreciate diversity, promote equity in education, and realize their potential as teacher-researchers and social change agents.

VERONICA GESSER is a former graduate student of Paulo Freire. She received her doctoral degree from Florida International University in Miami in the Curriculum and Instructional: Instructional Leadership program. In 1996 she received her master's degree in curriculum and supervision at Pontífícia Universidade Católica-PUC in São Paulo, Brazil.

JILL L. HAUNOLD is a writer and a doctoral candidate in education at Boise State University. A former middle school teacher, her research focus is on the social reconstruction of childhood. She has co-owned an outdoor store for the past 13 years with her husband and sons, Bill, Connor, and Duncan.

GERARD HUISKAMP received his Ph.D. from the University of North Carolina at Chapel Hill and is currently an assistant professor of political science and Latin American Studies at Wheaton College. He has authored or co-authored articles on Marxism and religion, rural women's organizing and identity formation, and democratization and social movement theory. He is currently completing *The Privatization of Politics and Movement: Enacting Citizenship in Rural Mexico*.

JOE L. KINCHELOE is a professor at CUNY Graduate Center—Brooklyn College. His new works include *Contextualizing Teaching* (Longman) with Patrick Slattery and Shirley Steinberg, *Measured Lies, the Bell Curve Examined* (St. Martin's Press), and *White Reign, Deploying Whiteness in America* (St. Martin's Press) with Shirley Steinberg.

ROBERT D. LEIER teaches cultural foundations of education at the University of South Alabama-Mobile and has been a research associate with the Harvard University School of Education in rural education reform. He studied with Donaldo Macedo, Vivian Zamel, and Elsa Auerbach at the University of Massachusetts-Boston, and did his doctoral work in international development education at Pennsylvania State University in the Department of Education Theory and Policy. His research and teaching advocate issues of social equity with educational reform.

KARLA LEWIS is a doctoral candidate at the University of Illinois Urbana-Champaign in the Department of Educational Policy Studies. Her research interests include African American women in higher education and colonial education.

PETER McLAREN teaches in the Urban Schooling Division at the Graduate School of Education and Information Studies, University of California, Los Angeles. His works have appeared in 15 languages. His most recent books include *Critical Pedagogy and Predatory Culture* (Routledge), *Revolutionary Multiculturalism* (Westview Press), *Schooling as a Ritual Performance* (3rd edition, Rowman and Littlefield), *Life in Schools* (3rd edition, Longman), *Red Chalk* (with Mike Cole, Dave Hill, and Glenn Rikowski published by the Hillcole Group, England, Tufnell Press), and *Che Guevara, Paulo Freire, and the Pedagogy of Revolution* (Rowman and Littlefield).

CHARLES REITZ teaches philosophy, labor studies, and multicultural education. His recent book is *Art, Alienation and the Humanities: A Critical Engagement with Herbert Marcuse* (SUNY). He has written "Liberating the Critical in Critical Theory," in *Freirean Pedagogy, Praxis, and Possibilities* (Falmer Press) edited by Stanley F. Steiner, H. Mark Krank, and Peter McClaren.

DALIA RODRIGUEZ is a doctoral student at the University of Illinois Urbana-Champaign in the Department of Educational Policy Studies. Her research is in sociology of education and includes issues on affirmative action policy, racism/discrimination in higher education and the formation of racial/ethnic identity in the classroom.

CESAR A. ROSSATTO graduated from UCLA and is now a social studies assistant professor at the College of Education, Florida International University. He has worked extensively in the inner cities of Sao Paulo, Brazil and Los Angeles. He is multilingual (English, Spanish, Portuguese, and Italian) and is committed to social justice, activism, and dialectic/dialogical education and praxis.

JUDITH J. SLATER is an associate professor at Florida International University in Miami where she is involved with curriculum theory, evaluation, organizational analysis, and women in higher education. Her books include *Anatomy of a Collaboration* (Garland), *Acts of Alignment* (Peter Lang) with Ana Pasztor. She has co-edited *Schooling and Public Spaces* (Houghton Mifflin) with Stephen M. Fain and David Callejo and *Teen Life in Asia* (Greenwood).

SHIRLEY R. STEINBERG is at Montclair State University and is co-author of *Contextualizing Teaching, Measured Lies, and White Reign* (Longman), and *Multi/Intercultural Conversations: A Reader* (Peter Lang). She has established herself as a leading editor of educational texts dealing with such questions as multiculturalism and social justice.

DAVID STOVALL is an assistant professor at the University of Illinois Chicago in educational policy. His most recent research focuses on Proposition 209 and Critical Race Theory.

TYRONE WILLIAMS is a doctoral student at the University of Illinois Urbana-Champaign in the Department of Educational Policy Studies. His research interests include the history of education in the nineteenth century Caribbean and the southern United States.

# INDEX